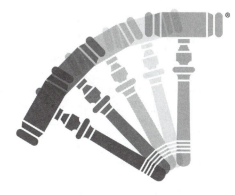

Casenote® Legal Briefs

CRIMINAL LAW

Keyed to Courses Using

Dressler and Garvey's
Cases and Materials on Criminal Law

Sixth Edition

Wolters Kluwer
Law & Business

Copyright © 2013 CCH Incorporated. All Rights Reserved.

Published by Wolters Kluwer Law & Business in New York.

Wolters Kluwer Law & Business serves customers worldwide with CCH, Aspen Publishers, and Kluwer Law International products. (www.wolterskluwerlb.com)

No part of this publication may be reproduced or transmitted in any form or by any means, electronic or mechanical, including photocopy, recording, or utilized by any information storage and retrieval system, without written permission from the publisher. For information about permissions or to request permission online, visit us at wolterskluwerlb.com or a written request may be faxed to our permissions department at 212-771-0803.

To contact Customer Service, e-mail customer.service@wolterskluwer.com, call 1-800-234-1660, fax 1-800-901-9075, or mail correspondence to:

Wolters Kluwer Law & Business
Attn: Order Department
P.O. Box 990
Frederick, MD 21705

Printed in the United States of America.

1 2 3 4 5 6 7 8 9 0

ISBN 978-1-4548-3282-9

About Wolters Kluwer Law & Business

Wolters Kluwer Law & Business is a leading global provider of intelligent information and digital solutions for legal and business professionals in key specialty areas, and respected educational resources for professors and law students. Wolters Kluwer Law & Business connects legal and business professionals as well as those in the education market with timely, specialized authoritative content and information-enabled solutions to support success through productivity, accuracy and mobility.

Serving customers worldwide, Wolters Kluwer Law & Business products include those under the Aspen Publishers, CCH, Kluwer Law International, Loislaw, Best Case, ftwilliam.com and MediRegs family of products.

CCH products have been a trusted resource since 1913, and are highly regarded resources for legal, securities, antitrust and trade regulation, government contracting, banking, pension, payroll, employment and labor, and healthcare reimbursement and compliance professionals.

Aspen Publishers products provide essential information to attorneys, business professionals and law students. Written by preeminent authorities, the product line offers analytical and practical information in a range of specialty practice areas from securities law and intellectual property to mergers and acquisitions and pension/benefits. Aspen's trusted legal education resources provide professors and students with high-quality, up-to-date and effective resources for successful instruction and study in all areas of the law.

Kluwer Law International products provide the global business community with reliable international legal information in English. Legal practitioners, corporate counsel and business executives around the world rely on Kluwer Law journals, looseleafs, books, and electronic products for comprehensive information in many areas of international legal practice.

Loislaw is a comprehensive online legal research product providing legal content to law firm practitioners of various specializations. Loislaw provides attorneys with the ability to quickly and efficiently find the necessary legal information they need, when and where they need it, by facilitating access to primary law as well as state-specific law, records, forms and treatises.

Best Case Solutions is the leading bankruptcy software product to the bankruptcy industry. It provides software and workflow tools to flawlessly streamline petition preparation and the electronic filing process, while timely incorporating ever-changing court requirements.

ftwilliam.com offers employee benefits professionals the highest quality plan documents (retirement, welfare and non-qualified) and government forms (5500/PBGC, 1099 and IRS) software at highly competitive prices.

MediRegs products provide integrated health care compliance content and software solutions for professionals in healthcare, higher education and life sciences, including professionals in accounting, law and consulting.

Wolters Kluwer Law & Business, a division of Wolters Kluwer, is head-quartered in New York. Wolters Kluwer is a market-leading global information services company focused on professionals.

Format for the Casenote® Legal Brief

Nature of Case: This section identifies the form of action (e.g., breach of contract, negligence, battery), the type of proceeding (e.g., demurrer, appeal from trial court's jury instructions), or the relief sought (e.g., damages, injunction, criminal sanctions).

Fact Summary: This is included to refresh your memory and can be used as a quick reminder of the facts.

Rule of Law: Summarizes the general principle of law that the case illustrates. It may be used for instant recall of the court's holding and for classroom discussion or home review.

Facts: This section contains all relevant facts of the case, including the contentions of the parties and the lower court holdings. It is written in a logical order to give the student a clear understanding of the case. The plaintiff and defendant are identified by their proper names throughout and are always labeled with a (P) or (D).

Palsgraf v. Long Island R.R. Co.

Injured bystander (P) v. Railroad company (D)

N.Y. Ct. App., 248 N.Y. 339, 162 N.E. 99 (1928).

NATURE OF CASE: Appeal from judgment affirming verdict for plaintiff seeking damages for personal injury.

FACT SUMMARY: Helen Palsgraf (P) was injured on R.R.'s (D) train platform when R.R.'s (D) guard helped a passenger aboard a moving train, causing his package to fall on the tracks. The package contained fireworks which exploded, creating a shock that tipped a scale onto Palsgraf (P).

🏛 **RULE OF LAW**
The risk reasonably to be perceived defines the duty to be obeyed.

FACTS: Helen Palsgraf (P) purchased a ticket to Rockaway Beach from R.R. (D) and was waiting on the train platform. As she waited, two men ran to catch a train that was pulling out from the platform. The first man jumped aboard, but the second man, who appeared as if he might fall, was helped aboard by the guard on the train who had kept the door open so they could jump aboard. A guard on the platform also helped by pushing him onto the train. The man was carrying a package wrapped in newspaper. In the process, the man dropped his package, which fell on the tracks. The package contained fireworks and exploded. The shock of the explosion was apparently of great enough strength to tip over some scales at the other end of the platform, which fell on Palsgraf (P) and injured her. A jury awarded her damages, and R.R. (D) appealed.

ISSUE: Does the risk reasonably to be perceived define the duty to be obeyed?

HOLDING AND DECISION: (Cardozo, C.J.) Yes. The risk reasonably to be perceived defines the duty to be obeyed. If there is no foreseeable hazard to the injured party as the result of a seemingly innocent act, the act does not become a tort because it happened to be a wrong as to another. If the wrong was not willful, the plaintiff must show that the act as to her had such great and apparent possibilities of danger as to entitle her to protection. Negligence in the abstract is not enough upon which to base liability. Negligence is a relative concept, evolving out of the common law doctrine of trespass on the case. To establish liability, the defendant must owe a legal duty of reasonable care to the injured party. A cause of action in tort will lie where harm,

though unintended, could have been averted or avoided by observance of such a duty. The scope of the duty is limited by the range of danger that a reasonable person could foresee. In this case, there was nothing to suggest from the appearance of the parcel or otherwise that the parcel contained fireworks. The guard could not reasonably have had any warning of a threat to Palsgraf (P), and R.R. (D) therefore cannot be held liable. Judgment is reversed in favor of R.R. (D).

DISSENT: (Andrews, J.) The concept that there is no negligence unless R.R. (D) owes a legal duty to take care as to Palsgraf (P) herself is too narrow. Everyone owes to the world at large the duty of refraining from those acts that may unreasonably threaten the safety of others. If the guard's action was negligent as to those nearby, it was also negligent as to those outside what might be termed the "danger zone." For Palsgraf (P) to recover, R.R.'s (D) negligence must have been the proximate cause of her injury, a question of fact for the jury.

▶ **ANALYSIS**

The majority defined the limit of the defendant's liability in terms of the danger that a reasonable person in defendant's situation would have perceived. The dissent argued that the limitation should not be placed on liability, but rather on damages. Judge Andrews suggested that only injuries that would not have happened but for R.R.'s (D) negligence should be compensable. Both the majority and dissent recognized the policy-driven need to limit liability for negligent acts, seeking, in the words of Judge Andrews, to define a framework "that will be practical and in keeping with the general understanding of mankind." The Restatement (Second) of Torts has accepted Judge Cardozo's view.

━■━

Quicknotes

FORESEEABILITY A reasonable expectation that change is the probable result of certain acts or omissions.

NEGLIGENCE Conduct falling below the standard of care that a reasonable person would demonstrate under similar conditions.

PROXIMATE CAUSE The natural sequence of events without which an injury would not have been sustained.

━■━

Party ID: Quick identification of the relationship between the parties.

Concurrence/Dissent: All concurrences and dissents are briefed whenever they are included by the casebook editor.

Analysis: This last paragraph gives you a broad understanding of where the case "fits in" with other cases in the section of the book and with the entire course. It is a hornbook-style discussion indicating whether the case is a majority or minority opinion and comparing the principal case with other cases in the casebook. It may also provide analysis from restatements, uniform codes, and law review articles. The analysis will prove to be invaluable to classroom discussion.

Issue: The issue is a concise question that brings out the essence of the opinion as it relates to the section of the casebook in which the case appears. Both substantive and procedural issues are included if relevant to the decision.

Holding and Decision: This section offers a clear and in-depth discussion of the rule of the case and the court's rationale. It is written in easy-to-understand language and answers the issue presented by applying the law to the facts of the case. When relevant, it includes a thorough discussion of the exceptions to the case as listed by the court, any major cites to the other cases on point, and the names of the judges who wrote the decisions.

Quicknotes: Conveniently defines legal terms found in the case and summarizes the nature of any statutes, codes, or rules referred to in the text.

Wolters Kluwer Law & Business is proud to offer *Casenote® Legal Briefs*—continuing thirty years of publishing America's best-selling legal briefs.

Casenote® Legal Briefs are designed to help you save time when briefing assigned cases. Organized under convenient headings, they show you how to abstract the basic facts and holdings from the text of the actual opinions handed down by the courts. Used as part of a rigorous study regimen, they can help you spend more time analyzing and critiquing points of law than on copying bits and pieces of judicial opinions into your notebook or outline.

Casenote® Legal Briefs should never be used as a substitute for assigned casebook readings. They work best when read as a follow-up to reviewing the underlying opinions themselves. Students who try to avoid reading and digesting the judicial opinions in their casebooks or online sources will end up shortchanging themselves in the long run. The ability to absorb, critique, and restate the dynamic and complex elements of case law decisions is crucial to your success in law school and beyond. It cannot be developed vicariously.

Casenote® Legal Briefs represents but one of the many offerings in Legal Education's Study Aid Timeline, which includes:

- *Casenote® Legal Briefs*
- *Emanuel® Law Outlines*
- Emanuel® *Law in a Flash* Flash Cards
- Emanuel® *CrunchTime®* Series
- *Siegel's Essay and Multiple-Choice Questions and Answers Series*

Each of these series is designed to provide you with easy-to-understand explanations of complex points of law. Each volume offers guidance on the principles of legal analysis and, consulted regularly, will hone your ability to spot relevant issues. We have titles that will help you prepare for class, prepare for your exams, and enhance your general comprehension of the law along the way.

To find out more about Wolters Kluwer Law & Business' study aid publications, visit us online at *www.wolterskluwerlb.com* or email us at *legaledu@wolterskluwer.com*. We'll be happy to assist you.

How to Brief a Case

A. Decide on a Format and Stick to It

Structure is essential to a good brief. It enables you to arrange systematically the related parts that are scattered throughout most cases, thus making manageable and understandable what might otherwise seem to be an endless and unfathomable sea of information. There are, of course, an unlimited number of formats that can be utilized. However, it is best to find one that suits your needs and stick to it. Consistency breeds both efficiency and the security that when called upon you will know where to look in your brief for the information you are asked to give.

Any format, as long as it presents the essential elements of a case in an organized fashion, can be used. Experience, however, has led *Casenote® Legal Briefs* to develop and utilize the following format because of its logical flow and universal applicability.

NATURE OF CASE: This is a brief statement of the legal character and procedural status of the case (e.g., "Appeal of a burglary conviction").

There are many different alternatives open to a litigant dissatisfied with a court ruling. The key to determining which one has been used is to discover *who is asking this court for what.*

This first entry in the brief should be kept as *short as possible.* Use the court's terminology if you understand it. But since jurisdictions vary as to the titles of pleadings, the best entry is the one that addresses who wants what in this proceeding, not the one that sounds most like the court's language.

RULE OF LAW: A statement of the general principle of law that the case illustrates (e.g., "An acceptance that varies any term of the offer is considered a rejection and counteroffer").

Determining the rule of law of a case is a procedure similar to determining the issue of the case. Avoid being fooled by red herrings; there may be a few rules of law mentioned in the case excerpt, but usually only one is *the* rule with which the casebook editor is concerned. The techniques used to locate the issue, described below, may also be utilized to find the rule of law. Generally, your best guide is simply the chapter heading. It is a clue to the point the casebook editor seeks to make and should be kept in mind when reading every case in the respective section.

FACTS: A synopsis of only the essential facts of the case, i.e., those bearing upon or leading up to the issue.

The facts entry should be a short statement of the events and transactions that led one party to initiate legal proceedings against another in the first place. While some cases conveniently state the salient facts at the beginning of the decision, in other instances they will have to be culled from hiding places throughout the text, even from concurring and dissenting opinions. Some of the "facts" will often be in dispute and should be so noted. Conflicting evidence may be briefly pointed up. "Hard" facts must be included. Both must be *relevant* in order to be listed in the facts entry. It is impossible to tell what is relevant until the entire case is read, as the ultimate determination of the rights and liabilities of the parties may turn on something buried deep in the opinion.

Generally, the facts entry should not be longer than three to five *short* sentences.

It is often helpful to identify the role played by a party in a given context. For example, in a construction contract case the identification of a party as the "contractor" or "builder" alleviates the need to tell that that party was the one who was supposed to have built the house.

It is always helpful, and a good general practice, to identify the "plaintiff" and the "defendant." This may seem elementary and uncomplicated, but, especially in view of the creative editing practiced by some casebook editors, it is sometimes a difficult or even impossible task. Bear in mind that the *party presently* seeking something from this court may not be the plaintiff, and that sometimes only the cross-claim of a defendant is treated in the excerpt. Confusing or misaligning the parties can ruin your analysis and understanding of the case.

ISSUE: A statement of the general legal question answered by or illustrated in the case. For clarity, the issue is best put in the form of a question capable of a "yes" or "no" answer. In reality, the issue is simply the Rule of Law put in the form of a question (e.g., "May an offer be accepted by performance?").

The major problem presented in discerning what is *the* issue in the case is that an opinion usually purports to raise and answer several questions. However, except for rare cases, only one such question is really the issue in the case. Collateral issues not necessary to the resolution of the matter in controversy are handled by the court by language known as *"obiter dictum"* or merely *"dictum."* While dicta may be included later in the brief, they have no place under the issue heading.

To find the issue, ask *who wants what* and then go on to ask *why did that party succeed or fail in getting it.* Once this is determined, the "why" should be turned into a question.

The complexity of the issues in the cases will vary, but in all cases a single-sentence question should sum up the issue. *In a few cases,* there will be two, or even more rarely, three issues of equal importance to the resolution of the case. Each should be expressed in a single-sentence question.

Since many issues are resolved by a court in coming to a final disposition of a case, the casebook editor will reproduce the portion of the opinion containing the issue or issues most relevant to the area of law under scrutiny. A noted law professor gave this advice: "Close the book; look at the title on the cover." Chances are, if it is Property, you need not concern yourself with whether, for example, the federal government's treatment of the plaintiff's land really raises a federal question sufficient to support jurisdiction on this ground in federal court.

The same rule applies to chapter headings designating sub-areas within the subjects. They tip you off as to what the text is designed to teach. The cases are arranged in a casebook to show a progression or development of the law, so that the preceding cases may also help.

It is also most important to remember to *read the notes and questions* at the end of a case to determine what the editors wanted you to have gleaned from it.

HOLDING AND DECISION: This section should succinctly explain the rationale of the court in arriving at its decision. In capsulizing the "reasoning" of the court, it should always include an application of the general rule or rules of law to the specific facts of the case. Hidden justifications come to light in this entry: the reasons for the state of the law, the public policies, the biases and prejudices, those considerations that influence the justices' thinking and, ultimately, the outcome of the case. At the end, there should be a short indication of the disposition or procedural resolution of the case (e.g., "Decision of the trial court for Mr. Smith (P) reversed").

The foregoing format is designed to help you "digest" the reams of case material with which you will be faced in your law school career. Once mastered by practice, it will place at your fingertips the information the authors of your casebooks have sought to impart to you in case-by-case illustration and analysis.

B. Be as Economical as Possible in Briefing Cases

Once armed with a format that encourages succinctness, it is as important to be economical with regard to the time spent on the actual reading of the case as it is to be economical in the writing of the brief itself. This does not mean "skimming" a case. Rather, it means reading the case with an "eye" trained to recognize into which "section" of your brief a particular passage or line fits and having a system for quickly and precisely marking the case so that the passages fitting any one particular part of

the brief can be easily identified and brought together in a concise and accurate manner when the brief is actually written.

It is of no use to simply repeat everything in the opinion of the court; record only enough information to trigger your recollection of what the court said. Nevertheless, an accurate statement of the "law of the case," i.e., the legal principle applied to the facts, is absolutely essential to class preparation and to learning the law under the case method.

To that end, it is important to develop a "shorthand" that you can use to make marginal notations. These notations will tell you at a glance in which section of the brief you will be placing that particular passage or portion of the opinion.

Some students prefer to underline all the salient portions of the opinion (with a pencil or colored underliner marker), making marginal notations as they go along. Others prefer the color-coded method of underlining, utilizing different colors of markers to underline the salient portions of the case, each separate color being used to represent a different section of the brief. For example, blue underlining could be used for passages relating to the rule of law, yellow for those relating to the issue, and green for those relating to the holding and decision, etc. While it has its advocates, the color-coded method can be confusing and time-consuming (all that time spent on changing colored markers). Furthermore, it can interfere with the continuity and concentration many students deem essential to the reading of a case for maximum comprehension. In the end, however, it is a matter of personal preference and style. Just remember, whatever method you use, underlining must be used sparingly or its value is lost.

If you take the marginal notation route, an efficient and easy method is to go along underlining the key portions of the case and placing in the margin alongside them the following "markers" to indicate where a particular passage or line "belongs" in the brief you will write:

N   (NATURE OF CASE)
RL   (RULE OF LAW)
I   (ISSUE)
HL   (HOLDING AND DECISION, relates to the RULE OF LAW behind the decision)
HR   (HOLDING AND DECISION, gives the RATIONALE or reasoning behind the decision)
HA   (HOLDING AND DECISION, applies the general principle(s) of law to the facts of the case to arrive at the decision)

Remember that a particular passage may well contain information necessary to more than one part of your brief, in which case you simply note that in the margin. If you are using the color-coded underlining method instead of marginal notation, simply make asterisks or checks in the margin next to the passage in question in the colors that indicate the additional sections of the brief where it might be utilized.

The economy of utilizing "shorthand" in marking cases for briefing can be maintained in the actual brief writing process itself by utilizing "law student shorthand" within the brief. There are many commonly used words and phrases for which abbreviations can be substituted in your briefs (and in your class notes also). You can develop abbreviations that are personal to you and which will save you a lot of time. A reference list of briefing abbreviations can be found on page x of this book.

C. Use Both the Briefing Process and the Brief as a Learning Tool

Now that you have a format and the tools for briefing cases efficiently, the most important thing is to make the time spent in briefing profitable to you and to make the most advantageous use of the briefs you create. Of course, the briefs are invaluable for classroom reference when you are called upon to explain or analyze a particular case. However, they are also useful in reviewing for exams. A quick glance at the fact summary should bring the case to mind, and a rereading of the rule of law should enable you to go over the underlying legal concept in your mind, how it was applied in that particular case, and how it might apply in other factual settings.

As to the value to be derived from engaging in the briefing process itself, there is an immediate benefit that arises from being forced to sift through the essential facts and reasoning from the court's opinion and to succinctly express them in your own words in your brief. The process ensures that you understand the case and the point that it illustrates, and that means you will be ready to absorb further analysis and information brought forth in class. It also ensures you will have something to say when called upon in class. The briefing process helps develop a mental agility for getting to the *gist* of a case and for identifying, expounding on, and applying the legal concepts and issues found there. The briefing process is the mental process on which you must rely in taking law school examinations; it is also the mental process upon which a lawyer relies in serving his clients and in making his living.

Abbreviations for Briefs

Table of Cases

Introduction

Quick Reference Rules of Law

Owens v. State

Intoxicated driver (D) v. State (P)

Md. Ct. Spec. App., 93 Md. App. 162, 611 A.2d 1043 (1992).

NATURE OF CASE: Appeal from a conviction for driving while intoxicated.

FACT SUMMARY: After Owens (D) was found asleep behind the wheel of his truck with an open can of beer between his legs and other empties in the vehicle, he was convicted of driving while intoxicated.

🏛 **RULE OF LAW**
A conviction upon circumstantial evidence alone is not to be sustained unless the circumstances are inconsistent with any reasonable hypothesis of innocence.

FACTS: After the police received a complaint about a suspicious vehicle, a truck matching the description was found parked in a private driveway with the engine running and the lights on. Owens (D), asleep in the driver's seat, had an open can of beer clasped between his legs, and two more empty beer cans were inside the truck. When awakened by a police officer, Owens (D) did not know where he was, and there was a strong odor of alcohol on his breath. His speech was slurred and very unclear. Moreover, an alcohol restriction had been placed on his license. He was convicted by a judge of driving while intoxicated. Owens (D) appealed, arguing that the evidence was not legally sufficient to support a finding of guilt.

ISSUE: Is a conviction upon circumstantial evidence alone not to be sustained unless the circumstances are inconsistent with any reasonable hypothesis of innocence?

HOLDING AND DECISION: (Moylan, J.) Yes. A conviction upon circumstantial evidence alone is not to be sustained unless the circumstances are inconsistent with any reasonable hypothesis of innocence. There are only two unstrained and likely inferences arising from the circumstances. One is that Owens (D) arrived at the driveway from somewhere else; the other is that he was about to leave for somewhere else. The first hypothesis, combined with his intoxication, is consistent with guilt, the second with innocence. One does not typically drink in the house and then carry the empties out to the car. Therefore, it may be inferred that some significant drinking took place in the car. Owens's (D) state of unconsciousness enforces that inference. It is not a reasonable inference that one would consume enough alcohol with the engine running and the car in gear to pass out on the steering wheel before starting out. Moreover, the report of a suspicious vehicle matching Owens's (D) truck also makes the first inference more likely. Affirmed.

▶ **ANALYSIS**

Here, the court of special appeals found the totality of the circumstances inconsistent with a reasonable hypothesis of innocence. The circumstances do not foreclose the hypothesis but merely make it more strained and less likely. The drawing of the inference of guilt is more rational and therefore within the proper purview of the fact finder, rather than being a mere flip of a coin between guilt and innocence.

■■■

Quicknotes

CIRCUMSTANTIAL EVIDENCE Evidence though not directly observed, supports the inference of principal facts.

■■■

State v. Ragland

State (P) v. Convicted felon (D)

N.J. Sup. Ct., 105 N.J. 189, 519 A.2d 1361 (1986).

NATURE OF CASE: Appeal from a conviction for armed robbery and possession of a weapon by a convicted felon.

FACT SUMMARY: Ragland (D), a convicted felon, argued that the judge should have informed the jury regarding its power of nullification.

🏛 RULE OF LAW
The power of the jury to acquit, despite overwhelming proof of guilt and the jury's belief, beyond a reasonable doubt, in guilt, is not one of the essential attributes of the right to trial by jury.

FACTS: At the end of Ragland's (D) trial for armed robbery and possession of a weapon by a convicted felon, among other charges, the judge instructed the jury. The instruction stated that if the jury found Ragland (D) was in possession of a weapon during the commission of the robbery, the jury "must" find him guilty of the possession charge. Ragland (D) was convicted. On appeal, he argued that the use of the word "must" in the jury instruction conflicted with the jury's power of nullification, an essential attribute of the right to trial by jury, and should have been replaced by the word "may."

ISSUE: Is the power of the jury to acquit, despite overwhelming proof of guilt and the jury's belief, beyond a reasonable doubt, in guilt, one of the essential attributes of the right to trial by jury?

HOLDING AND DECISION: (Wilentz, C.J.) No. The power of the jury to acquit, despite overwhelming proof of guilt and the jury's belief, beyond a reasonable doubt, in guilt, is not one of the essential attributes of the right to trial by jury. The power of the jury to acquit despite proof of guilt is known as the jury's power of nullification. The exercise of the jury's power of nullification, while unavoidable, is undesirable, and judicial attempts to strengthen the power are not only contrary to settled practice in this state but unwise both as a matter of governmental policy and as a matter of sound administration of criminal justice. Informing the jury of its power to nullify the law, as Ragland (D) has proposed doing, is not compelled by constitution, by statute, or by common law. Jury nullification is absolutely inconsistent with the most important value of western democracy, namely, that we should live under a government of laws and not of men. Reversed on other grounds and remanded for a new trial.

▶ ANALYSIS

It is only relatively recently that some scholars have characterized the jury's nullification power as part of a defendant's right to trial by jury and have defended it as sound policy. Supporters in the state of Oregon attempted to codify the concept by a constitutional amendment, but their initiative was voted down. Detractors, on the other hand, argue that where laws are unfair, the prevention of injustice is to be obtained through legislative revision of those laws, not through the jury's nullification power.

■══■

Quicknotes

ACQUITTAL The discharge of an accused individual from suspicion of guilt for a particular crime and from further prosecution for that offense.

RIGHT TO JURY TRIAL The right guaranteed by the Sixth Amendment to the federal constitution that in all criminal prosecutions the accused has a right to a trial by an impartial jury of the state and district in which the crime was allegedly committed.

■══■

Principles of Punishment

Quick Reference Rules of Law

The Queen v. Dudley and Stephens

Government (P) v. Stranded crew members (D)

Queen's Bench Division, 14 Q.B.D. 273 (1884).

NATURE OF CASE: Appeal of jury's special verdict finding Dudley (D) and Stephens (D) guilty of murder.

FACT SUMMARY: Dudley (D) and Stephens (D) killed Parker, with whom they were stranded on the high seas in a lifeboat, in order to survive off Parker's remains after having run out of food and water.

🏛 RULE OF LAW
Homicide may not be excused when the person killed is an innocent and unoffending victim.

FACTS: Dudley (D), Stephens (D), Brooks, and Parker, crew members of an English yacht, were cast adrift on the high seas 1,600 miles from land in an open lifeboat. They had no water and two one-pound tins of turnips. After 12 days adrift, they were without food. Dudley (D) and Stephens (D) suggested to Brooks that one of the four may be sacrificed so that the others might survive. Brooks dissented, and Parker, a 17-year-old boy, was never consulted. On the twentieth day, Dudley (D) and Stephens (D) killed Parker, who was too weak either to resist or assent. Four days after Parker's death, the surviving three were rescued. They would not have survived had they not fed off Parker's remains.

ISSUE: Was the homicide excusable by the necessity of saving some of the crewmen?

HOLDING AND DECISION: (Lord Coleridge, C.J.) No. An innocent person may not be killed in order to save the life of another. Where the victim has not assaulted or otherwise endangered the killer, the killer has not, by necessity, been placed in a position which permits him to kill the innocent victim. The extreme necessity of hunger does not justify larceny, nor can it justify murder. While, generally, the preservation of one's own life is a duty; in some cases, the highest duty may be to sacrifice it. Neither can the temptation caused by hunger be called an excuse.

▌ ANALYSIS

While this case actually discusses a defense to murder, necessity (which here did not excuse the murder), the case appears here in the casebook more for its moral discussion of why the defendants, unwillingly placed in a tragic situation, must be punished for their act. The court notes that "Law and morality are not the same, and many things may be immoral which are not necessarily illegal," but that law would be divorced from morality if the temptation to kill, which arose, could be an excuse for the actual killing. Even if the temptation were a valid excuse, who is to determine who must die so that the others might live? Note that the death sentence was later commuted by the crown to six months' imprisonment.

■═■

Quicknotes

NECESSITY DEFENSE A defense to liability for unlawful activity where the conduct is unavoidable and is justified by preventing the occurrence of a more serious harm.

■═■

People v. Superior Court (Du)

State (P) v. Lower court (D)

Cal. App. 2d Dist., 5 Cal. App. 4th 822 (1992).

NATURE OF CASE: Appeal from sentence of probation following conviction for voluntary manslaughter.

FACT SUMMARY: After Du was convicted of voluntary manslaughter for killing 15-year-old Latasha Harlins in her liquor store, the Superior Court judge gave Du a suspended sentence.

🏛 RULE OF LAW
[Rule of law not stated in casebook excerpt.]

FACTS: Du (D) and her family owned and operated two liquor stores in Los Angeles. Du (D) was working in one of the stores that was located in a crime-infested area and had been burglarized many times before. Du (D) was working in that store that day because her son had been threatened by local gang members and was afraid to work there. There were at least 40 shoplifting incidents a week at the store. Latasha Harlins, a 15-year-old customer, took a bottle of orange juice and put it in her backpack. When Latasha did not pay for the orange juice, a fight ensued, and Du (D) shot and killed Latasha. The jury found Du (D) guilty of voluntary manslaughter, rejecting the defenses that the killing was unintentional or that Du (D) had killed in self-defense. A Los Angeles County Probation Officer prepared a presentence probation report recommending that probation be denied and Du (D) be sentenced to state prison.

ISSUE: [Issue not stated in casebook excerpt.]

HOLDING AND DECISION: (Ashby, J.) The probation officer concluded that Du (D) would be most unlikely to repeat the crime and was not a person who would actively seek to harm another. Although Du (D) expressed concern for the victim and her family, this remorse was centered largely on the effect of the incident on Du (D) and her own family.

▌ ANALYSIS

The excerpt presented in the casebook does not describe the entire case. The author probably included part of the probation officer's report to provide background information.

■■■■

Quicknotes

SELF-DEFENSE The right to protect an individual's person, family or property against attempted injury by another.

VOLUNTARY MANSLAUGHTER The killing of another person without premeditation, deliberation or malice aforethought, but committed while in the "heat of passion" or upon some adequate provocation, thereby reducing the charge from murder to manslaughter.

■■■■

People v. Du

State (P) v. Convicted manslaughterer (D)

Cal. Super. Ct., Los Angeles County, No. BA037738 (1991).

NATURE OF CASE: Remarks by judge at sentencing after conviction for voluntary manslaughter.

FACT SUMMARY: Du (D) was convicted of voluntary manslaughter after she shot a young customer in her store after an altercation.

🏛 RULE OF LAW
In determining propriety of probation, a court must consider whether the crime was committed because of unusual circumstances such as great provocation.

FACTS: Du (D) was a 51-year-old Korean store owner with no criminal history who shot and killed a young customer who was leaving the store after the two had been engaged in an altercation. Over the years, Du (D) and her family had been subjected to being terrorized and victimized by gang violence. Upon being found guilty of voluntary manslaughter, Du (D) was sentenced to ten years in state prison, however the judge suspended the sentence and placed her on probation amid a public outcry since the victim was a young black girl.

ISSUE: In determining propriety of probation, must a court consider whether the crime was committed because of unusual circumstances such as great provocation?

HOLDING AND DECISION: (Karlin, J.) Yes. In determining propriety of probation, a court must consider whether the crime was committed because of unusual circumstances such as great provocation. Although here there was a presumption against probation because a firearm was used, such presumption is rebutted because this was an unusual case. First, the statutory presumption is aimed not at shopkeepers who keep firearms for their own protection but against criminals who arm themselves when they go out and commit other crimes. Second, Du (D) has no record of crimes of violence. Third, Du (D) participated in the crime under circumstances of great provocation, coercion, and duress. The statutory presumption is overcome. Although the victim was not armed with a weapon at the time of her death, she had used her fists as weapons just seconds before she was shot. Furthermore, Du (D), the shopkeeper, was a 51-year-old woman with no criminal history or history of violence, and she and her family had been consistently victimized and terrorized by gang members. There was no evidence Du (D) knew the gun had been altered in such a way as to make it an automatic weapon with a hairpin trigger. Because of the repeated robberies and gang terrorism in her store, Du's (D) over-reaction, although not appropriate, was under-

standable. The job of the court is to ensure justice, not to extract revenge. The sentence of ten years in state prison is suspended.

▶ ANALYSIS

The judge in the *Du* case made clear that in imposing a sentence, a court must consider the objectives of sentencing a defendant which are (1) to protect society; (2) to punish the defendant for committing a crime; (3) to encourage the defendant to lead a law-abiding life; (4) to deter others; (5) to isolate defendants so they cannot commit other crimes; (6) to secure restitution for the victim; and (7) to seek uniformity in sentencing. The judge explained that because of the unusual circumstances of this case, none of these objectives would have been attained by requiring Du (D) to spend time in prison.

■=■

Quicknotes

DURESS Unlawful threats or other coercive behavior by one person that causes another to commit acts that he would not otherwise do.

VOLUNTARY MANSLAUGHTER The killing of another person without premeditation, deliberation or malice aforethought, but committed while in the "heat of passion" or upon some adequate provocation, thereby reducing the charge from murder to manslaughter.

■=■

United States v. Gementera

Federal government (P) v. Convicted thief (D)

379 F.3d 596 (9th Cir. 2004).

NATURE OF CASE: Appeal from a condition of supervised release.

FACT SUMMARY: Gementera (D) argued that requiring him to wear a sign that said "I stole mail. This is my punishment," in a public place for eight hours as part of 100 hours of required public service, violated the Sentencing Reform Act.

🏛 RULE OF LAW

Requiring a convicted person to wear a sign in public stating his crime is reasonably related to the legitimate statutory objective of rehabilitation so as to render it proper under the Sentencing Reform Act.

FACTS: Gementera (D), who already had a criminal record, was convicted of stealing mail. The judge sentenced him in the lower range of the Sentencing Reform Act. As one part of Gementera's (D) condition for supervised release, the judge required that he perform 100 hours of community service to consist of standing in front of a postal facility for eight hours on one day with a sandwich board that said "I stole mail. This is my punishment." Gementera (D) appealed the signboard requirement as violating the Sentencing Reform Act.

ISSUE: Is requiring a convicted person to wear a sign in public stating his crime reasonably related to the legitimate statutory objective of rehabilitation so as to render it proper under the Sentencing Reform Act?

HOLDING AND DECISION: (O'Scannlain, J.) Yes. Requiring a convicted person to wear a sign in public stating his crime is reasonably related to the legitimate statutory objective of rehabilitation so as to render it proper under the Sentencing Reform Act. In this case, the district judge, with care and specificity, outlined a sensible logic underlying its conclusion that a set of conditions, including the signboard provision, but also including reintegration provisions, would better promote Gementera's (D) rehabilitation and amendment of life than would a lengthier term of incarceration. Criminal offenses, and the penalties that accompany them, nearly always cause shame and embarrassment. Such fact does not automatically render a condition objectionable. Furthermore, while the sandwich board condition was somewhat crude, it was coupled with more socially useful provisions, including lecturing at a high school and writing apologies, which might loosely be understood to promote the offender's social reintegration. Hence, as part of a comprehensive set of provisions tailored to the specific needs of this offender, it is concluded that the signboard condition passes the threshold of being reasonably related to rehabilitation. Affirmed.

DISSENT: (Hawkins, J.) The shaming punishment at issue was intended to humiliate Gementera (D), not to rehabilitate him or to deter him from future wrongdoing. This "crude" form of punishment is not one of the proper goals under the Sentencing Reform Act. When one shames another person, such purpose is to place them lower in the chain of being and to dehumanize them. Doing so is not a proper role of a court.

▶ ANALYSIS

There is a split of judicial and scholarly viewpoints as to whether so-called "shaming sanctions," such as, for example, requiring a person to carry a sign indicating his guilt, is a proper form of punishment. On the one hand, the punishment for criminal offenses always carries some shame and stigma which may serve to reinforce public norms against criminality, a valid objective of criminal law. This has been argued to be particularly true for white collar crime. Others contend, however, that shaming sanctions may serve to redefine a person in a negative, sometimes irreversible way and that humiliation of an individual should not be the role of courts or legislatures. In *Gementera,* the court walked a fine line because it held the judge had not gone beyond proper judicial boundaries since the shaming sanction was only one part of a comprehensive set of provisions tailored to the specific needs of this particular offender.

Quicknotes

FELONY A criminal offense of greater seriousness than a misdemeanor; felonies are generally defined pursuant to statute as any crime that is punishable by death or by a term of imprisonment exceeding one year.

MENS REA Criminal intent.

Coker v. Georgia

Death row convict (D) v. State (P)

433 U.S. 584 (1977).

NATURE OF CASE: Appeal from a sentence of death by electrocution for conviction of rape.

FACT SUMMARY: After Coker (D) escaped from prison, committing armed robbery and rape while out, he was apprehended, tried, convicted, and sentenced to death by electrocution for the commission of the rape.

> **RULE OF LAW**
> A sentence of death is grossly disproportionate and excessive punishment for the crime of rape and is therefore constitutionally forbidden as cruel and unusual punishment.

FACTS: While imprisoned for rape, murder, and attempted murder, Coker (D) escaped. He entered the Carver house and tied up the husband, taking his money and the keys to his car. Brandishing a kitchen knife, Coker (D) then raped Mrs. Carver, later driving away and taking Mrs. Carver with him. After Coker (D) was apprehended, he was charged with escape, armed robbery, motor vehicle theft, kidnapping, and rape. The jury found him guilty, sentencing him to death by electrocution. Both of the aggravating circumstances on which the court instructed the jury, i.e., whether the rape had been committed by a person with a prior record of conviction for a capital felony and whether the rape had been committed in the course of committing another capital felony, namely, the armed robbery of Mr. Carver, were found to be present by the jury. The Georgia Supreme Court affirmed. Coker (D) appealed.

ISSUE: Is a sentence of death grossly disproportionate and excessive punishment for the crime of rape and therefore constitutionally forbidden as cruel and unusual punishment?

HOLDING AND DECISION: (White, J.) Yes. A sentence of death is grossly disproportionate and excessive punishment for the crime of rape and is therefore constitutionally forbidden as cruel and unusual punishment. The legislative rejection by most states of capital punishment for rape strongly confirms the judgment that death is indeed a disproportionate penalty for the crime of raping an adult woman. This does not discount the seriousness of rape as a crime. It is highly reprehensible, both in a moral sense and in its almost total contempt for the personal integrity and autonomy of the female victim. However, the death penalty is an excessive penalty for the rapist who, as such, does not take human life. Neither of the special circumstances in this case, nor both of them together, changes the conclusion that the death sentence imposed on Coker (D) is a disproportionate punishment. Thus, the judgment of the Georgia Supreme Court upholding the death sentence is reversed.

CONCURRENCE AND DISSENT: (Powell, J.) The plurality's reasoning supports the view that ordinarily death is a disproportionate punishment for the crime of raping an adult woman. The plurality, however, ranges well beyond what is necessary, holding that capital punishment always, regardless of the circumstances, is a disproportionate penalty for the crime of rape.

DISSENT: (Burger, C.J.) The concept of disproportionality bars the death penalty for minor crimes. But rape is not a minor crime. This case reveals a chronic rapist whose continuing danger to the community is abundantly clear. The Eighth Amendment does not prevent the state from taking an individual's "well-demonstrated propensity for life-endangering behavior" into account in devising punitive measures which will prevent inflicting further harm upon innocent victims.

ANALYSIS

A punishment is excessive and unconstitutional if it makes no measurable contribution to acceptable goals of punishment and hence is nothing more than the purposeless and needless imposition of pain and suffering or is grossly out of proportion to the severity of the crime. A punishment might fail the test on either ground. These Eighth Amendment judgments should not be, or appear to be, merely the subjective view of individual justices. To this end, attention must be given to the public attitudes concerning a particular sentence.

Quicknotes

CAPITAL PUNISHMENT Punishment by death.

CRUEL AND UNUSUAL PUNISHMENT Punishment that is excessive or disproportionate to the offense committed and which is prohibited by the Eighth Amendment to the United States Constitution.

Ewing v. California

Theft convict (D) v. State (P)

538 U.S. 11 (2003).

NATURE OF CASE: Appeal from sentencing under California's "Three Strikes" law.

FACT SUMMARY: When Gary Ewing (D), after shoplifting three golf clubs, was sentenced to a prison term of 25 years to life under California's (P) "Three Strikes" law, he argued that the sentence was so grossly disproportionate to the crime that it violated the Eighth Amendment's ban against cruel and unusual punishments.

🏛 RULE OF LAW
The Eighth Amendment does not prohibit a state from sentencing a repeat felon to a prison term of 25 years to life under the state's "Three Strikes" law.

FACTS: On parole from a 9-year prison term, Gary Ewing (D) shoplifted three golf clubs. He was charged and convicted of one count of felony grand theft in excess of $400. As required by California's (P) "Three Strikes" law, the prosecutor formally alleged, and the trial court later found, that Ewing (D) had been convicted previously of four serious or violent felonies and a robbery in an apartment complex. Ewing (D) was sentenced under California's (P) "Three Strikes" law to 25 years to life. Ewing (D) appealed his sentence to the United States Supreme Court, arguing that the Eighth Amendment's ban on cruel and unusual punishments prohibits sentences which are grossly disproportionate to the crime committed.

ISSUE: Does the Eighth Amendment prohibit a state from sentencing a repeat felon to a prison term of 25 years to life under the state's "Three Strikes" law?

HOLDING AND DECISION: (O'Connor, J.) No. The Eighth Amendment does not prohibit a state from sentencing a repeat felon to a prison term of 25 years to life under the state's (P) "Three Strikes" law. As to Ewing's (D) argument that his "three strikes" sentence of 25 years to life is unconstitutionally disproportionate to his offense of shoplifting three golf clubs, this Court notes that the gravity of his offense was not merely shoplifting the three clubs, but rather it was being convicted of felony grand theft for stealing nearly $1,200 worth of merchandise after previously having been convicted of at least two violent or serious felonies. In weighing the gravity of the offense, this Court must place on the scales not only his current felony, but also his long history of felony recidivism. Any other approach would fail to accord proper deference to the state legislature's choice of sanctions. In imposing a "three strikes" sentence, the state's (P) interest is not merely punishing the offense of conviction, or the triggering of-

fense. It is, in addition, the interest in dealing in a harsher manner with those who by repeated criminal acts have shown that they are simply incapable of conforming to the norms of society as established by its criminal law. Here, Ewing's (D) sentence is justified by the state's (P) public-safety interest in incapacitating and deterring recidivist felons, and amply supported by his own long, serious criminal record. Affirmed.

CONCURRENCE: (Scalia, J.) It is difficult to speak intelligently of proportionality once deterrence and rehabilitation are given significant weight. The plurality is not applying constitutional law but evaluating policy.

CONCURRENCE: (Thomas, J.) The cruel and unusual punishment clause of the Eighth Amendment contains no proportionality principle.

DISSENT: (Breyer, J.) In the instant case, the punishment is grossly disproportionate to the crime. Ewing's (D) sentence on its face imposes one of the most severe punishments available upon a recidivist who subsequently engaged in one of the less serious forms of criminal conduct. In any ordinary case, such as one under the Federal Sentencing Guidelines, Ewing's (D) sentence would not exceed 18 months in prison. Ewing's (D) 25-year term amounts to overkill.

▶ ANALYSIS

In *Ewing*, the United States Supreme Court noted that four years after passage of California's "Three Strikes" law, the recidivism rate of parolees returned to prison for the commission of a new crime dropped by nearly 25 percent. While the "Three Strikes" law has sparked controversy and some critics have doubted the law's wisdom and effectiveness in reaching its goals, the Court explained that such criticism is appropriately directed at the legislature, which has the primary responsibility for making the difficult policy choices that underlie any criminal sentencing scheme and that the Court does not sit as a "super legislature" to second-guess these policy choices.

■══■

Quicknotes

CRUEL AND UNUSUAL PUNISHMENT Punishment that is excessive or disproportionate to the offense committed and which is prohibited by the Eighth Amendment to the U.S. Constitution.

RECIDIVIST One who repeatedly commits crimes.

■══■

Modern Role of Criminal Statutes

Quick Reference Rules of Law

Commonwealth v. Mochan

State (P) v. Morals convict (D)

Pa. Super. Ct., 177 Pa. Super. 454, 110 A.2d 788 (1955).

NATURE OF CASE: Appeal from a conviction for the common law crime of intending to debauch, corrupt, and villify another person.

FACT SUMMARY: Mochan (D) argued that since his acts did not constitute a statutory crime, he could not legally be indicted and convicted for those acts simply because they constituted a crime at common law.

RULE OF LAW

A person may be prosecuted for committing a common law crime even if such crime has not specifically been enacted into legislation.

FACTS: Mochan (D) made a series of highly obscene phone calls to Louise Zivkovich, a stranger, for which he was indicted, tried, and found guilty. The crime for which he was indicted was for intending to debauch, corrupt, embarrass and villify the person called. The conduct alleged in the indictments was not prohibited by statute. The prosecutor, however, successfully contended that the conduct did constitute a common law crime and was punishable under the common law of Pennsylvania. Mochan (D) appealed the conviction, arguing that he could not legally be indicted for acts which did not constitute a statutory crime.

ISSUE: May a person be prosecuted for committing a common law crime even if such crime has not specifically been enacted into legislation?

HOLDING AND DECISION: (Hirt, J.) Yes. A person may be prosecuted for committing a common law crime even if such crime has not specifically been enacted into legislation. Although the conduct alleged in the indictments was not prohibited by statute, the state's Penal Code provides that every offense punishable by the statutes "or common law of this Commonwealth" and not specifically provided for by statute, shall continue to be an offense punishable as heretofore. Here, the testimony establishes that Mochan (D) on numerous occasions telephoned Louise Zivkovich, a stranger to him, and used language which was obscene, lewd, and filthy. He not only suggested intercourse with her but talked of sodomy as well, in loathsome language. The test is not whether precedents for prosecution of such conduct can be found in the books, but whether the alleged crimes could have been prosecuted and the offenders punished under the state's common law. The answer is that the common law is sufficiently broad to punish as a misdemeanor, although there may be no exact precedent or statute, any act which directly injures or tends to injure the public to such an extent as to require the state to interfere and punish the wrongdoer, as in the case of acts which injuriously affect public morality, or obstruct, or pervert public justice, or the administration of government. In sum, whatever openly outrages decency and is injurious to public morals is a misdemeanor at common law. Affirmed.

DISSENT: (Woodside, J.) Under the division of powers in our constitution it is for the legislature to determine what injures or tends to injure the public. One of the most important functions of a legislature is to determine what acts require the state to interfere and punish the wrongdoer. Notwithstanding the reprehensible conduct of Mochan (D), until the legislature says that what Mochan (D) did is a crime, the courts should not declare it to be such.

ANALYSIS

Nearly all jurisdictions have statutorily abolished common law offenses, including now Pennsylvania. Some states, however, such as Rhode Island, still do authorize the prosecution of common law offenses.

Quicknotes

COMMON LAW A body of law developed through the judicial decisions of the courts as opposed to the legislative process.

COMMON LAW CRIME An activity that has been defined as a crime not by legislative enactment but by the courts through case law.

COMMON LAW STATES Those states that observe the body of law not based on statute but derived from custom and the aggregate of other tribunal's decisions.

Keeler v. Superior Court

Accused murderer (D) v. State (P)

Cal. Sup. Ct., 2 Cal. 3d 619, 470 P.2d 617 (1970).

NATURE OF CASE: Appeal from a charge of murder for the killing of a fetus.

FACT SUMMARY: After Keeler (D) assaulted his ex-wife, causing the death of her unborn infant, he was charged with murder.

🏛 RULE OF LAW
An unborn but viable fetus is not a "human being" within the meaning of the California statute defining murder.

FACTS: Mrs. Keeler divorced Keeler (D), her husband of sixteen years. Unknown to Keeler (D), Mrs. Keeler was then pregnant by Vogt, whom she had met earlier that summer. When Keeler (D) saw her approaching him on a narrow mountain road, he blocked the road with his car, causing her to pull over to the side. After telling Mrs. Keeler that he heard she was pregnant, Keeler (D) opened her car door, pushed her against the car, and shoved his knee into her abdomen. After a cesarean section was performed and the fetus examined in utero, its head was found to be severely fractured, and it was delivered stillborn. Upon delivery, the fetus weighed five pounds, and expert testimony concluded with reasonable medical certainty that the fetus had developed to the stage of viability. Keeler (D) was charged with murder of the fetus, and he appealed, arguing that he had not murdered a "human being."

ISSUE: Is an unborn but viable fetus a "human being" within the meaning of the California statute defining murder?

HOLDING AND DECISION: (Mosk, J.) No. An unborn but viable fetus is not a "human being" within the meaning of the California statute defining murder. In declaring murder to be the unlawful and malicious killing of a human being, the legislature of 1850 intended that term to have the settled common law meaning of a person who had been born alive and did not intend the act of feticide to be an offense under the laws of California. Moreover, to the charge of murder of an unborn, even though viable, fetus, there are two insuperable obstacles, one "jurisdictional" and the other constitutional. First, whether to extend liability for murder of a fetus in California is a determination solely within the province of the legislature. Second, such a ruling could only operate prospectively without violating Keeler's (D) right of due process. The first essential of due process is fair warning of the act which is made punishable as a crime. The judicial enlargement of the Penal Code now urged by the People (P) would deny Keeler (D) due process of law.

DISSENT: (Burke, C.J.) The common law reluctance to characterize the killing of a quickened fetus as a homicide was based solely upon a presumption that the fetus would have been born dead. However, based on the advancements in medical science since then, this presumption is now obsolete. If the term "human being" in the homicide statutes is a fluid concept to be defined in accordance with present conditions, then the term should include the fully viable fetus.

▶ ANALYSIS

In 1850 the legislature first defined murder as the unlawful and malicious killing of a "human being." Penal Code § 187 was enacted in 1872, and had not been amended since that date. Thus, the court looked to the common law, as established by Coke in the mid-seventeenth century and later reiterated by both Blackstone and Hale, as the accepted common law rule by the year 1850. After the California Supreme Court's decision in this case, the legislature amended Penal Code § 187 to read as follows: "Murder is the unlawful killing of a human being, or a fetus, with malice aforethought." Therapeutic abortions are expressly exempted from prosecution under the amended law.

■=■

Quicknotes

MALICE The intention to commit an unlawful act without justification or excuse.

MURDER Unlawful killing of another person either with deliberation and premeditation or by conduct demonstrating a reckless disregard for human life.

PROCEDURAL DUE PROCESS The constitutional mandate that if the state or federal government acts so as to deny a citizen of a life, liberty, or property interest the individual is first entitled to notice and the right to be heard.

■=■

In re Banks

Peeping Tom (D) v. State (P)

N.C. Sup. Ct., 295 N.C. 236, 244 S.E.2d 386 (1978).

NATURE OF CASE: Appeal from a judgment holding a state law as unconstitutionally vague and overbroad.

FACT SUMMARY: The trial court held the State's (P) "Peeping Tom" statute, under which Banks (D) was charged, to be unconstitutional.

🏛 RULE OF LAW
A criminal statute must be sufficiently definite to give notice of the required conduct to be avoided and to guide the judge in its application and the lawyer in defending one charged with its violation.

FACTS: Banks (D) was charged with violating the State's (P) so-called "Peeping Tom" statute, which made punishable, as a misdemeanor, "any person who shall peep secretly into any room occupied by a female." Banks (D) contended that the statute was unconstitutionally vague because men of common intelligence must necessarily guess at its meaning and differ as to its application. He also contended that the statute was unconstitutionally overbroad since it prohibited innocent conduct. The trial court held the statute to be unconstitutional. The State (P) appealed.

ISSUE: Must a criminal statute be sufficiently definite to give notice of the required conduct to be avoided and to guide the judge in its application and the lawyer in defending one charged with its violation?

HOLDING AND DECISION: (Moore, J.) Yes. A criminal statute must be sufficiently definite to give notice of the required conduct to be avoided and to guide the judge in its application and the lawyer in defending one charged with its violation. Here, G.S. 14-202 prohibits the wrongful spying into a room upon a female with the intent of violating the female's legitimate expectation of privacy. This is sufficient to inform a person of ordinary intelligence, with reasonable precision, of those acts the statute intends to prohibit so that he may know what acts he should avoid in order not to bring himself within its provision. Moreover, the statute is sufficiently narrowed by judicial interpretation to omit from its scope those persons who have a legitimate purpose upon another's property and those who only inadvertently glance in the window of another. Thus, the statute is not so overbroad as to proscribe legitimate conduct. Reversed.

▶ ANALYSIS

Few words possess the precision of mathematical symbols. Most statutes must deal with untold and unforeseen varia-

tions in factual situations, and the practical necessities of discharging the business of government inevitably limit the specificity with which legislators can spell out prohibitions. Consequently, no more than a reasonable degree of certainty can be demanded. It is not unfair to require that one who deliberately goes perilously close to an area of proscribed conduct shall take the risk that he may cross the line. See *Boyce Motor Lines v. United States*, 342 U.S. 337 (1952).

■===■

Quicknotes

EXPECTATION OF PRIVACY Requirement that in order to invoke the Fourth Amendment's protection against unreasonable searches and seizures, the individual must have a reasonable expectation of privacy in respect to the location searched or thing seized.

OVERBREADTH That quality or characteristic of a statute, regulation, or order which reaches beyond the problem it was meant to solve causing it to sweep within it activity it cannot legitimately reach.

■===■

City of Chicago v. Morales

Municipality (P) v. Accused gang member (D)

527 U.S. 41 (1999).

NATURE OF CASE: Supreme Court review of state court ruling on constitutionality of city ordinance.

FACT SUMMARY: Morales (D) challenged an antigang ordinance passed by the City of Chicago (P) on the basis that the wording of the statute defining "loitering" was so vague as to make the statute unconstitutional.

🏛 RULE OF LAW
A statute providing penalties for criminal conduct is unconstitutionally vague if it fails to give sufficient notice regarding the type of conduct prohibited.

FACTS: Morales (D) and others were accused as "criminal street gang members" under a new ordinance passed by the City of Chicago (P) prohibiting persons from "loitering" with one another in public places. A City of Chicago (P) commission solicited witness testimony and made a series of findings suggesting that an increase in street activity was a primary cause of the escalation in violent and drug-related crimes, and that a common function of loitering was to enable a street gang to establish control over particular areas. In addition, the commission discovered that loitering by street gang members in public places intimidated law-abiding citizens and limited access to these areas by creating a "justifiable fear for the safety of persons and property" in the areas where loitering took place. In response, the City of Chicago (P) passed the Gang Congregation Ordinance, which created a criminal offense punishable by a fine of up to $500, as well as imprisonment and community service, for "loitering" by suspected street gang members in public places. The statute defined four elements of the crime of "loitering:" first, a police officer must reasonably believe that at least one of the two or more persons present in a public place is a gang member; second, these persons must be "loitering" by remaining in one place with no apparent purpose; third, the officer must order these persons to disperse; and finally, the order to disperse is disobeyed by the suspected gang members. Morales (D) challenged the ordinance on the basis that it broadly covered a significant amount of additional activity beyond what should be interpreted as "loitering" and was therefore unconstitutionally vague. The Illinois Supreme Court concluded the ordinance was unconstitutionally vague because it did not provide specific limits on the discretion of police officers to determine what conduct constituted "loitering," and the City of Chicago (P) filed for review of that determination.

ISSUE: Is a statute which provides penalties for criminal conduct unconstitutionally vague if it fails to give sufficient notice regarding the type of conduct prohibited?

HOLDING AND DECISION: (Stevens, J.) Yes. A statute providing penalties for criminal conduct is unconstitutionally vague if it fails to give sufficient notice regarding the type of conduct prohibited. Clearly, a law directly prohibiting intimidating conduct similar to that described by the City of Chicago (P) commission is constitutional on its face. However, such a law may still be found unconstitutionally vague for two reasons: first, the law fails to provide the type of notice that permits ordinary persons to understand the conduct prohibited; and second, the wording of the law encourages arbitrary and discriminatory enforcement. Citizens should not have to speculate as to the meaning of a law. The requirement of notice is not met here because the order to disperse takes place before an officer knows whether the prohibited conduct has occurred, and is therefore an unjustifiable impairment of liberty if the loiterer is harmless and innocent. In addition, the statute establishes only minimal guidelines for law enforcement to follow. Police officers may exercise absolute discretion when assessing a group of bystanders for dispersal. The City of Chicago (P) asserts that the statute provides limitations on a police officer's discretion because it does not permit a dispersal order to issue if a person has an apparent purpose, or until the officer reasonably believes that "loitering" is taking place. However, these limitations are insufficient because they do not directly address the degree of discretion an officer may exercise. The ability to assess a "loitering" situation is only subjectively limited by the officer's own evaluation of the circumstances. The Illinois Supreme Court's ruling that the statute in question is unconstitutional was correctly concluded, and is therefore affirmed.

CONCURRENCE: (O'Connor, J.) Chicago's (P) gang ordinance is unconstitutionally vague because it lacks sufficient minimal standards to guide law enforcement officers. There remain open to Chicago (P) reasonable alternatives to combat the very real threat posed by gang intimidation and violence. For example, the Court properly and expressly distinguishes the ordinance from laws that require loiterers to have a "harmful purpose" from laws that target only gang members, and from laws that incorporate limits on the area and manner in which the law may be enforced.

DISSENT: (Scalia, J.) In recent years, Chicago (P) has been afflicted with criminal street gangs. The record indicates these gangs congregated in public places to deal drugs and to terrorize the neighborhoods. Many inner city residents felt they were prisoners in their own homes. The

Continued on next page.

minor limitation which would be placed upon the free state of nature that this prophylactic arrangement imposed upon all Chicagoans seems a small price to pay for liberation of their streets.

▶ *ANALYSIS*

Justice Stevens's opinion suggests that the Gang Congregation Ordinance could have been worded optimally to include conduct that was apparent, such as the effort by gang members to publicize the gang's dominance over a certain area. Use of this phrasing explicitly would have satisfied constitutional concerns of specificity; however, the Court ironically noted that the absence of this descriptive language not only expanded the statute's inclusion of harmless behavior, but excluded those exact circumstances where the statute would have played a critical role in addressing the intended problem.

■══■

Quicknotes

FOURTEENTH AMENDMENT Declares that no state shall make or enforce any law which shall abridge the privileges and immunities of citizens of the United States.

VAGUENESS AND OVERBREADTH Characteristics of a statute that make it difficult to identify the limits of the conduct being regulated.

■══■

Muscarello v. United States

Convicted drug trafficker (D) v. Federal government (P)

524 U.S. 125 (1998).

NATURE OF CASE: Appeal from mandatory minimum sentence under 18 U.S.C. § 924(c)(1) for "carrying" a firearm in connection with a drug trafficking crime.

FACT SUMMARY: Muscarello (D), who was convicted of drug trafficking, argued that he should not be given a mandatory five-year minimum sentence under 18 U.S.C. § 924(c)(1), which provides for such a sentence when a person "uses or carries a firearm" during and in relation to a drug trafficking crime, because the firearm was in the locked glove compartment of his vehicle at the time of the crime.

RULE OF LAW
The phrase "carries a firearm" applies to a person who knowingly possesses and conveys firearms in a vehicle, including in the locked glove compartment or trunk of a car, which the person accompanies.

FACTS: Muscarello (D), who was convicted of drug trafficking, argued that he should not be given a mandatory five-year minimum sentence under 18 U.S.C. § 924(c)(1), which provides for such a sentence when a person "uses or carries a firearm" during and in relation to a drug trafficking crime, because the firearm was in the locked glove compartment of his vehicle at the time of the crime. Muscarello (D) argued that Congress intended the term "carry" to have an "on the person" meaning, rather than a meaning equal to "transport." The United States Supreme Court granted certiorari.

ISSUE: Does the phrase "carries a firearm" apply to a person who knowingly possesses and conveys firearms in a vehicle, including in the locked glove compartment or trunk of a car, which the person accompanies?

HOLDING AND DECISION: (Breyer, J.) Yes. The phrase "carries a firearm" applies to a person who knowingly possesses and conveys firearms in a vehicle, including in the locked glove compartment or trunk of a car, which the person accompanies. The parties agree that Congress intended the phrase at issue to convey its ordinary meaning, rather than a special legal meaning. As a matter of ordinary English one can "carry firearms" in a wagon, car, truck, or other vehicle that one accompanies. The word's first, or basic, meaning in dictionaries and the word's origin make clear that "carry" includes conveying in a vehicle. The greatest of writers have used "carry" with this meaning, as has the modern press. Contrary to Muscarello's (D) and the dissent's arguments, there is no linguistic reason to think that Congress intended to limit the word to its secondary meaning, which suggests support rather than movement or transportation. Thus, in its ordinary usage, "carry" includes carrying in a car. Neither the statute's basic purpose to combat the dangerous combination of drugs and guns, nor its legislative history supports circumscribing the scope of the word "carry" by applying an "on the person" limitation. Muscarello's (D) remaining arguments to the contrary are unconvincing. First, he argues that the definition adopted here obliterates the statutory distinction between "carry" and "transport," a word used in other related statutes by Congress deliberately to signify a different, and broader, statutory coverage. However, the ordinary meaning of "carry" does not equate to "transport," as the latter term does not have a limited connotation of personal agency and some degree of possession. Muscarello (D) also argues that it would be anomalous to construe "carry" broadly when the related phrase "uses . . . a firearm," has been construed narrowly to include only the "active employment" of a firearm. The answer to that argument is that each term has its own, nonsuperfluous meaning, and the ordinary meaning of "carry" does not swallow up the term "use." Moreover, a narrow interpretation of "carry" would undercut the statute's basic objective by removing the act of carrying a gun in a car entirely from the statute's reach. Another argument made by Muscarello (D) is that the permitting "carry" to extend to a firearm in a car would extend its coverage to passengers on buses, trains, or ships, who have placed a firearm, say, in checked luggage. This argument, however, does not take account of the other limiting words in the statute that make the statute applicable only when a defendant carries a gun both "during and in relation to" a drug crime. Muscarello's (D) argument that the term "carry" should include a meaning that the arm is "immediately accessible" is not supported by the statute's history. Finally, Muscarello's (D) invocation of the "rule of lenity" because of statutory ambiguity must also be rejected because the mere existence of some statutory ambiguity is insufficient to warrant application of the rule. Most statutes are ambiguous to some degree, but application of the "rule of lenity" occurs only when there is a "grievous" ambiguity. By contrast, here, the decision is based on much more than a guess as to Congress's intention. Accordingly, Muscarello's (D) conduct falls within the statute. Affirmed.

DISSENT: (Ginsburg, J.) Although the word "carries" has many meanings, including to cart about in a vehicle, that is not the meaning intended by Congress in § 924(c)(1). In the context of that statute, the meaning of "carries a

Continued on next page.

firearm" is keeping a firearm on one's premises or in one's vehicle in such a manner as to have it ready for use as a weapon. The meaning in the context of the statute, contrary to the majority's approach, cannot be gleaned from general usage in sources such as dictionaries or the Bible or literature. Because the statute provides mandatory minimum sentences, it can be inferred that Congress intended the statute to cover the most life-jeopardizing gun-connection cases—when guns are in or at the defendant's hand when committing an offense. Finally, because it is clear that the statute is at best ambiguous, and because ambiguity in criminal statutes is resolved in favor of defendants, the ambiguity of § 924(c)(1) must be resolved in favor of Muscarello (D).

▶ ANALYSIS

Even if the Court had ruled that § 924(c)(1) was inapplicable, the fact that a gun was in the car would have been taken into account under the federal sentencing guidelines, under which extra punishment for drug-related gun possession varies with the seriousness of the drug crime. Thus, as the dissent concludes, there would have been no "gap," no relevant conduct "ignored," if the Court rejected the Government's (P) broad reading of the term "carries" in § 924(c)(1). Under the more nuanced sentencing guidelines, in this particular case, the sentence would have been increased by four months to account for the gun being in the car, versus the mandatory five years under § 924(c)(1).

■═■

Quicknotes

RULE OF LENITY The doctrine that where a statute is ambiguous as to the term of punishment imposed, it will be construed in favor of the less severe punishment.

■═■

Actus Reus

Quick Reference Rules of Law

Martin v. State

Public drunk (D) v. State (P)

Ala. Ct. App., 31 Ala. App. 334, 17 So. 2d 427 (1944).

NATURE OF CASE: Appeal of a conviction for drunkenness on a public highway.

FACT SUMMARY: Martin (D), after being arrested at his home, was taken by officers on to the highway, where he manifested a drunken condition.

🏛 RULE OF LAW
Criminal liability must be based on conduct which includes a voluntary act or omission to act which was physically possible to have performed.

FACTS: Martin (D), who was convicted of being drunk on a public highway, was arrested at his home by officers who then took him on to the highway, where he allegedly used loud and profane language and otherwise manifested a drunken condition. He was charged with violation of a statute which proscribed such acts in a public place where more than one person is present.

ISSUE: Did Martin's (D) conduct include a voluntary act or omission to act which was physically possible to have performed?

HOLDING AND DECISION: (Simpson, J.) No. The statute presupposes that the violator voluntarily appears drunk in public. When one is drunk, being involuntarily and forcibly brought into a public place by an arresting officer is not a voluntary breach of the law and is not punishable. Reversed and rendered.

▶ ANALYSIS

This case introduces the concept of actus reus, or wrongful conduct. For conduct to be wrongful, it must either be a voluntary act or omission to act. This in itself is not sufficient to establish liability, but is an essential element for liability to arise. The law rests on the supposition that only voluntary acts or omissions are punishable, and while involuntary acts may be threatening, they are not of such nature so as to require correction by the penal system.

■══■

Quicknotes

ACTUS REUS The unlawful act, that gives rise to criminal liability, as distinguished from the required mental state.

■══■

State v. Utter

State (P) v. Convicted murderer (D)

Wash. Ct. App., 4 Wash. App. 137, 479 P.2d 946 (1971).

NATURE OF CASE: Appeal from a conviction of manslaughter.

FACT SUMMARY: After Utter (D) stabbed his son to death, he asserted the defense of conditioned response, contending that he was incapable of committing a culpable act because he was in an automatistic state.

🏛 RULE OF LAW
An "act," within the definition of homicide, must be a willed movement.

FACTS: After drinking large amounts of wine and whiskey all day, Utter (D) fatally stabbed his son upon his son's return home. Utter (D) remembered sitting around drinking with a friend and then being in jail but had no recollection of any intervening events. He was charged with murder in the second degree. During the trial, Utter (D), a combat infantryman during World War II, introduced evidence regarding conditioned response. He contended that he was incapable of committing a culpable act when he killed his son because he was in an "automatistic," or unconscious, state at the time that caused him to react violently toward people who came up behind him unexpectedly. The trial court, ruling that conditioned response was not a defense in Washington, instructed the jury to disregard all evidence introduced on this subject. The jury convicted Utter (D) of manslaughter. Utter (D) appealed.

ISSUE: Must an "act" within the definition of homicide be a willed movement?

HOLDING AND DECISION: (Farris, J.) Yes. An "act" within the definition of homicide must be a willed movement. Homicide is the killing of a human being by the act, procurement, or omission of another. An "act" involves an exercise of the will and signifies something done voluntarily. An act committed while one is unconscious is in reality no act at all. It is merely a physical event or occurrence for which there can be no criminal liability. However, when the state of unconsciousness is voluntarily induced by using alcohol or drugs, then that state of unconsciousness may fall short of a complete defense. Thus, in this case, Utter's (D) theory of the case should have been presented to the jury if there was substantial evidence in the record to support it, although the trial court should also have given a cautionary instruction with respect to voluntarily induced unconsciousness. However, the evidence presented was insufficient to present to the jury the issue of Utter's (D) unconscious or automatistic state at the time of the act. There is no evidence, circumstantial or otherwise, from which the jury could determine or reasonably infer what happened in the room at the time of the stabbing. Affirmed.

▶ ANALYSIS

According to the Model Penal Code, the following are not voluntary acts: a reflex or convulsion; a bodily movement during unconsciousness or sleep; conduct during hypnosis; and any bodily movement that otherwise is not a product of the effort of the actor, either conscious or habitual. From the facts given in the above case, it is probable that Utter (D) was a victim of posttraumatic stress disorder, a diagnosis that gained impetus following the Vietnam War. Most defendants in Utter's (D) position would probably choose to proceed as he did since the defense of unconsciousness is a complete defense, resulting in an acquittal with no follow-up consequences. A finding of not guilty by reason of insanity, on the other hand, ordinarily results in a commitment to a mental institution.

■■■

Quicknotes

ACTUS REUS The unlawful act, that gives rise to criminal liability, as distinguished from the required mental state.

INSANITY (DEFENSE) An affirmative defense to a criminal prosecution that the defendant suffered from a mental illness, thereby relieving him of liability for his conduct.

■■■

People v. Beardsley

State (P) v. Casual companion (D)

Mich. Sup. Ct., 150 Mich. 206, 113 N.W. 1128 (1907).

NATURE OF CASE: Appeal from conviction of manslaughter.

FACT SUMMARY: Beardsley (D), who was spending the night with a woman other than his wife, failed to get medical treatment for his companion when she took a fatal overdose of morphine.

RULE OF LAW
While it is the moral duty of every person to extend to others assistance when in danger, a person who fails to act to save the life of someone to whom he does not stand in the legal relation of protector is not chargeable with manslaughter.

FACTS: While his wife was out of town, Beardsley (D) took Blanche Burns, a woman accustomed to visiting saloons and with whom he had previously slept, to his apartment. Both became intoxicated. During the visit, Blanche took an overdose of morphine. Beardsley (D) prevented her from taking more morphine. An hour later, Beardsley (D) had Blanche, who was by this time in a stupor, taken downstairs into a room in the basement which was occupied by Skoba. Beardsley (D) asked Skoba to look after her and to let her out the back way when she awakened. Skoba became alarmed at Blanche's condition, and called a doctor who pronounced Blanche dead from the morphine overdose. Beardsley (D) was tried for failing to secure medical treatment for Blanche at the time he discovered the overdose, and was convicted of manslaughter.

ISSUE: Does a man's failure to act to save the life of a mistress over whom he had assumed no care or control constitute manslaughter if the omission was the immediate and direct cause of death?

HOLDING AND DECISION: (McAlvay, C.J.) No. The duty neglected to save the life of another, when doing so can be done without jeopardizing one's own life, or the lives of others, must be a legal duty, and not a mere moral obligation. A failure to act when the only duty imposed is a purely moral one will not make one liable for manslaughter. Thus, only when one person sustains to another the legal relation of protector—as husband to wife, parent to child, or master to servant—will omission of the duty to save the life of the other give rise to criminal sanctions. In the absence of some domestic relationship, public duty or voluntary choice, where one has assumed the care of another, an omission will not be punished as manslaughter. Here, applying this rule, Beardsley (D) was under no legal duty to save Blanche's life. The fact that Blanche was a woman cannot change the applicable rule of law. Had Beardsley (D) been carousing with another man who had attempted suicide, no one would suggest that Beardsley (D) was criminally responsible for omitting to make an effort to save his companion. Beardsley (D) may have violated a moral duty, but he is certainly not liable for manslaughter. The conviction is set aside.

ANALYSIS

Criminal liability for an omission to act will usually be imposed in the following situations: (1) a duty founded upon a special relationship: e.g., a parent has the legal obligation to protect his child from the elements, sickness, starvation, third persons, etc.; (2) a duty based upon statute: e.g., a driver must stop and give assistance to all those injured in an accident; (3) a contractual duty: e.g., a lifeguard, hired by the city, must rescue those who are drowning; (4) a duty arising from a voluntary assumption of care: e.g., a person who stops, and initially administers care to someone on the road, may not thereafter abandon the injured party; (5) placing another in a condition of peril; (6) controlling the acts of a charge: e.g., a parent must protect others against the known and dangerous propensities of his child; or (7) a duty of a landowner.

Quicknotes

DUTY TO RESCUE The duty to take some action to assist another in danger; such a duty is only imposed under certain circumstances.

MANSLAUGHTER The killing of another person without premeditation, deliberation, or with the intent to kill or to commit a felony, which may be reasonably expected to result in death or serious bodily injury; manslaughter is characterized by reckless conduct or by some adequate provocation on the part of the actor, as determined by a subjective standard.

Barber v. Superior Court

Physician (D) v. State (P)

Cal. Ct. App., 147 Cal. App. 3d 1006 (1983).

NATURE OF CASE: Appeal from reinstatement of dismissal of murder charges.

FACT SUMMARY: When Clarence Herbert, permanently comatose following surgery, was taken off of artificial respiration and nutrition, leading to death, Barber (D), his physician, was charged with murder.

🏛 RULE OF LAW
Absent objection from the spouse of one permanently comatose, a doctor is under no legal duty to keep the patient alive through forced respiration and nutrition.

FACTS: Clarence Herbert underwent surgery following a heart attack and lapsed into a coma from which medical authorities gave virtually no chance of his recovering. He was not completely brain-dead. His family expressed a desire that he be taken off all life support equipment, including nutrition. This was done, and Herbert died. The Government (P) then charged Barber (D), the attending physician, with murder. The complaint was dismissed, and then reinstated. Barber (D) appealed.

ISSUE: Absent objection from the spouse of one permanently comatose, is a doctor under a legal duty to keep the patient alive through forced respiration and nutrition?

HOLDING AND DECISION: (Compton, J.) No. Absent objection from the spouse of one permanently comatose, a doctor is under no legal duty to keep the patient alive through forced respiration and nutrition. As Herbert was not clinically dead at the time support was withdrawn, the court must decide whether such withdrawal was unlawful. The best way to analyze this is in terms of benefits versus burdens analysis. Where there is a reasonable chance of recovery, the benefits outweigh the burdens. Where, as here, there is no such chance, extraordinary measures confer no such benefit. Both respiration and nutrition are medical procedures that can be classified as extraordinary support. Thus, a doctor may, without objection from the patient's survivor, cease such support. Reversed.

▶ ANALYSIS

The issue here has been grappled with by courts for some time, and they have understandably had difficulty with it. Criminal law was developed in times when such situations were unthinkable. This area is appropriate for legislative action, but as yet there has been little.

Mens Rea

Quick Reference Rules of Law

United States v. Cordoba-Hincapie

Federal government (P) v. [Party not identified] (D)

825 F. Supp. 485 (E.D.N.Y. 1993).

NATURE OF CASE: [Nature of case not stated in casebook excerpt.]

FACT SUMMARY: [Fact summary not stated in casebook excerpt.]

🏛 RULE OF LAW
An act does not make the doer of it guilty, unless the mind is guilty; that is, unless the intent be criminal.

FACTS: [Facts not stated in casebook excerpt.]

ISSUE: Does an act make the doer of it guilty, if the mind is not guilty; that is, if the intent is not criminal?

HOLDING AND DECISION: (Weinstein, J.) No. An act does not make the doer of it guilty, unless the mind is guilty; that is, unless the intent be criminal. This doctrine of criminal responsibility and the theories that support it are deeply rooted in our legal tradition as one of our first principles of law.

▌ ANALYSIS

The court in this case discussed the origins of the requirement of a "mens rea" or guilty mind and its relationship to criminal law. The modern trend has been to narrow the meaning of "mens rea." Note that mens rea refers to the mental state expressly required in the definition of an offense, not to any morally blameworthy state of mind.

■■■

Quicknotes

CULPA Fault.

MENS REA Criminal intent.

■■■

Regina v. Cunningham

Municipality (P) v. Gas meter thief (D)

Ct. Crim. App., 41 Crim. App. 155, 2 Q.B. 396, 2 All. Eng. Rep. 412 (1957).

NATURE OF CASE: Appeal from a conviction for offenses against the person.

FACT SUMMARY: When Wade was partially asphyxiated by seeping gas after Cunningham (D) stole the gas meter from the basement of her building, Cunningham (D) was charged and convicted for the injury to Wade.

🏛 RULE OF LAW
Malice requires either an actual intention to do the particular kind of harm that was in fact done or recklessness as to whether such harm should occur or not.

FACTS: When Cunningham (D) stole the gas meter and its contents from the basement of a building by wrenching the meter from the gas pipes, gas escaped from the pipes, partially asphyxiating Sarah Wade. Cunningham (D) was charged with larceny of the meter and with the violation of § 23 of the Offences against the Person Act because of the injury to Wade. In instructing the jury, the trial judge told the jury that they could convict Cunningham (D) under the Act, even if he did not intend to harm Wade, as long as he acted unlawfully and maliciously. The judge then defined malicious as meaning "wicked." Cunningham (D) was convicted on both charges and appealed.

ISSUE: Does malice require either an actual intention to do the particular kind of harm that was in fact done or recklessness as to whether such harm should occur or not?

HOLDING AND DECISION: (Byrne, J.) Yes. Malice requires either an actual intention to do the particular kind of harm that was in fact done or recklessness as to whether such harm should occur or not. Cunningham's (D) act was clearly unlawful, but the question for the jury was whether it was also malicious within the meaning of the Act. It is incorrect to say that the word "malicious" in a statutory offense merely means wicked. It should have been left to the jury to decide whether, even if Cunningham (D) did not intend the injury to Wade, he foresaw that the removal of the gas meter might cause injury to someone but chose to remove it anyway. It is not possible to say that a reasonable jury, properly directed as to the meaning of the word "maliciously" in the context of § 23, would, without doubt, have convicted. Appeal allowed and conviction quashed.

▶ ANALYSIS

Under § 23 of the Offences against the Person Act, a person must act unlawfully and maliciously in administering to or causing to be administered to another person any poison or other destructive or noxious thing which endangers the life of the person. The court of criminal appeal thought that the trial judge was, by his instruction, telling the jury that if they were satisfied that Cunningham (D) acted wickedly, they ought to find that he had acted maliciously in causing the gas to be taken by Wade so as to endanger her life. The court declared that Cunningham (D) had clearly acted wickedly in stealing the gas meter and its contents.

■■■

Quicknotes

MALICE The intention to commit an unlawful act without justification or excuse.

RECKLESSNESS The conscious disregard of substantial and justifiable risk.

■■■

People v. Conley

State (P) v. Convicted batterer (D)

Ill. App. Ct., 187 Ill. App. 3d 234, 543 N.E.2d 138 (1989).

NATURE OF CASE: Appeal from a conviction on one count of aggravated battery.

FACT SUMMARY: In a fight outside a large party, Conley (D) hit Sean O'Connell in the face with a wine bottle, breaking his upper and lower jaws, other facial bones, and some of his teeth.

RULE OF LAW
A person who, in committing a battery, intentionally or knowingly causes great bodily harm or permanent disability or disfigurement commits aggravated battery.

FACTS: While Sean O'Connell and his friends were walking to their car, they were accosted by a group of people. One of the accosters, Conley (D), demanded a can of beer from Sean. When Sean refused, Conley (D) struck Sean in the face with a wine bottle, breaking both his upper and lower jaws and four facial bones. Conley (D) was charged with two counts of aggravated battery based on permanent disability and great bodily harm. Expert testimony revealed that Sean had a permanent condition called mucosal mouth and permanent partial numbness in one lip. Conley (D) was found guilty of aggravated battery based solely on permanent disability. Conley (D) appealed, arguing that Sean was not disabled by his injuries and, alternatively, that he did not intend to inflict any permanent disability.

ISSUE: Does a person who, in committing a battery, intentionally or knowingly causes great bodily harm or permanent disability or disfigurement commit aggravated battery?

HOLDING AND DECISION: (Cerda, J.) Yes. A person who, in committing a battery, intentionally or knowingly causes great bodily harm or permanent disability or disfigurement commits aggravated battery. For an injury to be disabling, it must only be shown that the injured bodily portion no longer serves the body in the same manner as it did before the injury. Applying that standard, the injuries Sean suffered are sufficient to constitute a permanent disability. Although the State (P) must establish specific intent, problems of proof are alleviated by the ordinary presumption that one intends the natural and probable consequences of his actions. Intent can be inferred from the surrounding circumstances, the offender's words, the weapon used, and the force of the blow. From the totality of the circumstances, the jury in this case could reasonably infer the intent to cause permanent disability. Affirmed.

ANALYSIS

The rule applied here, Ill. Rev. Stat. 1983, Ch. 38, Par. 12-4(a), incorporates the old offense of mayhem. While mayhem formerly required the dismemberment or disablement of some bodily part, what is important today is the integrity of the victim's person. Because the offense is defined in terms of result, the prosecution must prove beyond a reasonable doubt that a defendant either had a conscious objective to achieve the harm defined or was consciously aware that the harm defined was practically certain to be caused by his conduct.

Quicknotes

MAYHEM At common law, the unlawful dismemberment or disfigurement of another.

SPECIFIC INTENT The intent to commit a specific unlawful act which is a required element for criminal liability for certain crimes.

State v. Nations

State (P) v. Disco operator (D)

Mo. Ct. App., 676 S.W.2d 282 (1984).

NATURE OF CASE: Appeal from a conviction for child endangerment.

FACT SUMMARY: Nations (D) owned and operated a bar where police found a 16-year-old girl dancing for tips.

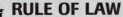 **RULE OF LAW**
To "knowingly" engage in criminal conduct, a defendant must have actual knowledge of the existence of the attendant circumstances which constitute the crime.

FACTS: Police learned that a disco owned and operated by Nations (D) employed a 16-year-old girl who "danced" for "tips." After observing the girl dancing with another female, the police questioned Nations (D), believing that at least one of the girls appeared to be "young." Nations (D) told them she had verified the girl as being of legal age through identification before she hired her, a statement that was untrue since the young girl in question lacked proper identification the day Nations (D) hired her. The police took the child into custody, and Nations (D) was charged with endangering the welfare of a child "less than 17 years old" under § 568.050 of the State's (P) Criminal Code, which provided that a person be found guilty of endangering the welfare of a child if she "knowingly encourages, aids, or causes" a child less than 17 years old to be exposed to an environment injurious to the child's welfare. Nations (D) was convicted and on appeal, contended that the State (P) failed to show she possessed the requisite intent since it was not shown that she actually knew the child was under 17.

ISSUE: Must a defendant have actual knowledge of the existence of the attendant circumstances which constitute the crime to "knowingly" engage in criminal conduct?

HOLDING AND DECISION: (Satz, J.) Yes. To "knowingly" engage in criminal conduct, a defendant must have actual knowledge of the existence of the attendant circumstances which constitute the crime. The applicable Criminal Code, when literally read, defines "knowingly" as actual knowledge with respect to attendant circumstances, excluding those cases where a defendant has "willfully shut his eyes" to avoid knowing. The Model Penal Code (MPC) expands the definition of "knowingly" to include even willful blindness, but the state legislature chose to enact the narrower definition, limiting "knowingly" to only actual knowledge. Although Nations (D) did not properly check the young girl's identification when she was hired, that does not prove that Nations (D) actually knew the girl

was less than 17 years old. At best, it proves that Nations (D) either did not know, or willfully shut her eyes to, the young girl's real age. Thus, Nations (D) was only aware of a "high probability" that the child was under 17 years old which does not amount to actual knowledge under the Criminal Code. Reversed.

ANALYSIS

The court further notes that the Model Penal Code (MPC) definition of "knowingly" is more akin to a definition of "recklessly." This similarity is intentional, since the MPC proposes that a standard of "knowingly" only be applied to a defendant's present actions, which are existing facts, and not to the results of the defendant's conduct, which are future circumstances yet unproven. In addition, like the MPC many states have chosen to include the "willfully blind" activity of a defendant as the equivalent of actual knowledge.

Quicknotes

KNOWINGLY Intentionally; willfully; an act that is committed with knowledge as to its probable consequences.

MENS REA Criminal intent.

RECKLESSNESS The conscious disregard of substantial and justifiable risk.

Flores-Figueroa v. United States

Illegal alien convicted of aggravated identity theft (D) v. Federal government (P)

556 U.S. 646 (2009).

NATURE OF CASE: Appeal from affirmance of conviction under 18 U.S.C. § 1028A(a)(1) for aggravated identity theft.

FACT SUMMARY: Flores-Figueroa (Flores) (D) was convicted of the predicate crimes of entering the United States without inspection and misusing immigration documents, as well as of aggravated identity theft. Flores (D) contended that his conviction for aggravated identity theft had to be overturned because the Government (P) failed to prove that he knew that the identification he used while committing the predicate crimes belonged to someone else.

🏛 RULE OF LAW

Before an individual may be convicted of the crime of aggravated identity theft under 18 U.S.C. § 1028A(a)(1), the Government must prove that he knew that the identification he used to commit predicate crimes belonged to someone else.

FACTS: Figueroa-Flores (Flores) (D), a Mexican citizen, was convicted of the predicate crimes of entering the United States without inspection and misusing immigration documents, as well as of aggravated identity theft under 18 U.S.C. § 1028A(a)(1), which imposes a mandatory consecutive two-year prison term on an individual convicted of certain predicate crimes if, during (or in relation to) the commission of those other crimes, the offender "knowingly . . . uses, without lawful authority, a means of identification of another person." He was convicted of the aggravated identity theft charge because he had given his employer counterfeit social security and alien registration cards containing his name but other people's identification numbers. Flores (D) moved for acquittal on this charge, claiming that the Government (P) could not prove that he knew that the documents' numbers were assigned to other people. The district court found Flores (D) guilty on all counts and the court of appeals affirmed. The United States Supreme Court granted certiorari.

ISSUE: Before an individual may be convicted of the crime of aggravated identity theft under 18 U.S.C. § 1028A(a)(1), must the Government prove that he knew that the identification he used to commit predicate crimes belonged to someone else?

HOLDING AND DECISION: (Breyer, J.) Yes. Before an individual may be convicted of the crime of aggravated identity theft under 18 U.S.C. § 1028A(a)(1), the Government must prove that he knew that the identification he used to commit predicate crimes belonged to someone else. As a matter of ordinary English grammar, "knowingly" is naturally read as applying to all the subsequently listed elements of the crime. Where a transitive verb has an object, listeners in most contexts assume that an adverb (such as "knowingly") that modifies the verb tells the listener how the subject performed the entire action, including the object. The Government (P) does not provide a single example of a sentence that, when used in typical fashion, would lead the hearer to a contrary understanding. Courts ordinarily interpret criminal statutes consistently with ordinary English usage and read a phrase in a criminal statute that introduces the elements of a crime with the word "knowingly" as applying that word to each element. The Government (P) argues that this position is incorrect because it would either require the same language to be interpreted differently in a neighboring provision relating to terrorism, or would render the language in that provision superfluous. This argument fails because the Government's (P) reasoning is faulty and the use of the word "knowingly" as applied to "other person" in the terrorism statute would not be surplus. Finally, the Government's (P) arguments based on the statute's purpose and on the practical problems of enforcing it are not sufficient to overcome the ordinary meaning, in English or through ordinary interpretive practice, of Congress's words. The purpose of the statute is to provide enhanced protection for individuals whose identifications are used to commit crimes, but the Government (P) has failed to show that Congress intended to achieve such protection by permitting the conviction of those who do not know the identification they are using belongs to a real person. Also, had Congress placed conclusive weight upon practical enforcement of the statute, the statute would likely not read the way it now reads—by using the word "knowingly" followed by a list of offense elements. Reversed.

▶ ANALYSIS

The Justices concurring in this opinion cautioned that the Court's reliance on the principle that "courts ordinarily read a phrase in a criminal statute that introduces the elements of a crime with the word 'knowingly' as applying that word to each element," should not be construed as a per se rule that a specified mens rea applies to all the elements of an offense. Justice Scalia indicated that while this principle may be descriptive of what courts generally do, it should not be construed as a rule of law as to what courts should do. Justice Alito also would not construe the Court's use of this principle as adopting an overly rigid rule of statutory construction, and instead would begin with a

Continued on next page.

general presumption that the specified mens rea applies to all the elements of an offense, but would recognize that there are instances in which context could well rebut that presumption.

■═■

Quicknotes

KNOWINGLY Intentionally; willfully; an act that is committed with knowledge as to its probable consequences.

PER SE By itself; not requiring additional evidence for proof.

■═■

United States v. Cordoba-Hincapie

Federal government (P) v. [Party not identified] (D)

825 F. Supp. 485 (E.D.N.Y. 1993).

NATURE OF CASE: [Nature of case not stated in casebook excerpt.]

FACT SUMMARY: [Fact summary not stated in casebook excerpt.]

🏛 RULE OF LAW
Criminal liability is permitted to attach without regard to fault in instances in which the actor's conduct involves minor violations of public welfare laws.

FACTS: [Facts not stated in casebook excerpt.]

ISSUE: Is criminal liability permitted to attach without regard to fault in instances in which the actor's conduct involves minor violations of public welfare laws?

HOLDING AND DECISION: (Weinstein, J.) Yes. Criminal liability has been permitted to attach without regard to fault in instances in which the actor's conduct involves minor violations of public welfare laws. The mens rea requirement in modern criminal law has many distinctions and limited exceptions. The most common exception has been in cases involving minor violations of the liquor laws, the pure food laws, the anti-narcotics laws, motor vehicle and traffic regulations, sanitary, building and factory laws and the like. If punishment of the wrongdoer far outweighs regulation of the social order as a purpose of the law in question, then mens rea is probably required. If the penalty is light, involving a relatively small fine and not including imprisonment, then mens rea probably is not required. Strict liability has been permitted in the criminal law in a number of other instances, such as the crime of "statutory rape."

▶ ANALYSIS

The court in this case discussed the evolution of the mens rea requirement and its exceptions. The other major exception to the mens rea requirement in a majority of states is for the crime of statutory rape. There is no allowance made for ignorance of the law or on the basis of a mistake in cases involving a strict liability offense.

Quicknotes

MENS REA Criminal intent.

STRICT LIABILITY Liability for all injuries proximately caused by a party's conducting of certain inherently dangerous activities without regard to negligence or fault.

Staples v. United States

Gun owner (D) v. Federal government (P)

511 U.S. 600 (1994).

NATURE OF CASE: Appeal from a criminal conviction for violating the National Firearms Act.

FACT SUMMARY: When Staples (D) was convicted because he had not registered in the National Firearms Registration and Transfer Record a rifle which had been modified to be capable of fully automatic fire, he claimed that he did not know of the rifle's automatic firing capability.

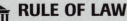 **RULE OF LAW**
When construing a statute as dispensing with mens rea would require the defendant to have knowledge only of traditionally lawful conduct, a severe penalty is a further factor tending to suggest that Congress did not intend to eliminate a mens rea requirement.

FACTS: Upon executing a search warrant at Staples's (D) home, local police and agents of the Bureau of Alcohol, Tobacco and Firearms (BATF) recovered an AR-15 rifle. The AR-15 is the civilian version of the military's M-16 [BBL1] rifle, and is, unless modified, a semiautomatic weapon. Suspecting that the AR-15 had been modified to be capable of fully automatic fire, BATF agents seized the weapon. The metal stop that prevents an installed M-16 selector switch from rotating to the fully automatic position had been filed away, and the rifle had been assembled with an M-16 selector switch and several other M-16 internal parts. Staples (D), was indicted for unlawful possession of an unregistered machine gun in violation of § 5861(d) of the National Firearms Act. The district court rejected Staples's (D) request for a jury instruction that the Government (P) must prove beyond a reasonable doubt that he knew that the gun would fire fully automatically. When found guilty and sentenced to five years' probation and a fine, Staples (D) appealed, claiming that his alleged ignorance of the gun's automatic firing capability should have shielded him from criminal liability for his failure to register the weapon.

ISSUE: When construing a statute as dispensing with mens rea would require the defendant to have knowledge only of traditionally lawful conduct, is a severe penalty a further factor tending to suggest that Congress did not intend to eliminate a mens rea requirement?

HOLDING AND DECISION: (Thomas, J.) Yes. When construing a statute as dispensing with mens rea would require the defendant to have knowledge only of traditionally lawful conduct, a severe penalty is a further factor tending to suggest that Congress did not intend to

eliminate a mens rea requirement. In such a case, the usual presumption that a defendant must know the facts that make his conduct illegal should apply. Determining the mental state required for commission of a federal crime requires construction of the statute and inference of the intent of Congress. Offenses that require no mens rea generally are disfavored and some indication of congressional intent, express or implied, is required to dispense with mens rea as an element of a crime. Generally, offenses punishable by imprisonment cannot be understood to be public welfare offenses, but must require mens rea. If Congress had intended to make outlaws of ignorant gun owners, and subject them to lengthy prison terms, it would have spoken more clearly to that effect. Reversed and remanded.

DISSENT: (Stevens, J.) This case involves a semiautomatic weapon that was readily convertible into a machine gun, not a gun that can be owned in perfect innocence. The Act contains no knowledge requirement and it does not describe a common law crime, so the background rules of common law do not apply. The National Firearms Act unquestionably is a public welfare statute.

▶ **ANALYSIS**

There is no allowance made for a mistake of fact or of law if an offense is strict liability in nature. The common law rule requiring mens rea can be dispensed with only when a statute expressly says so. Only public welfare or regulatory offenses are generally understood to impose a form of strict criminal liability.

━■

Quicknotes

MENS REA Criminal intent.

STRICT LIABILITY Liability for all injuries proximately caused by a party's conducting of certain inherently dangerous activities without regard to negligence or fault.

━■

Garnett v. State

Alleged rapist (D) v. State (P)

Md. Ct. App., 332 Md. 571, 632 A.2d 797 (1993).

NATURE OF CASE: Appeal from a rape conviction.

FACT SUMMARY: Garnett (D), a 20-year-old retarded man, was convicted of second degree statutory rape for having intercourse with a 13-year-old girl.

🏛 RULE OF LAW
The state statute prohibiting sexual intercourse with underage persons makes no reference to the actor's knowledge, belief, or other state of mind.

FACTS: Garnett (D), a young retarded man, had sexual intercourse with a 13-year-old girl who later gave birth to a child of which he was the biological father. Garnett (D) was tried and convicted under the state statutory rape law, despite his proffer of evidence that the girl herself and friends had told him that she was 16 years old. Garnett (D) appealed, arguing that the criminal law exists to assess and punish morally culpable behavior and that such culpability was absent here.

ISSUE: Does the state statute prohibiting sexual intercourse with underage persons make any reference to the actor's knowledge, belief, or other state of mind?

HOLDING AND DECISION: (Murphy, C.J.) No. The state statute prohibiting sexual intercourse with underage persons makes no reference to the actor's knowledge, belief, or other state of mind. This silence as to mens rea results from legislative design since another section of the statute does explicitly require mens rea. An examination of the drafting history of the statute during the 1976 revision of Maryland's sexual offense laws reveals that the statute was viewed as one of strict liability from its inception and throughout the amendment process. Affirmed.

DISSENT: (Eldridge, J.) The penalty provision for a violation of § 463(a)(3), namely making the offense a felony punishable by a maximum of 20 years imprisonment, is strong evidence that the state legislature did not intend to create a pure strict liability offense. There is no indication that the legislature intended that criminal liability attach to one who, because of his or her mental impairment, was unable to appreciate the risk involved.

DISSENT: (Bell, J.) To hold, as a matter of law, that § 463(a)(3) does not require the state to prove that a defendant possessed the necessary mental state to commit the crime, i.e., knowingly engaged in sexual relations with a female under the age of 14, or that the defendant may not litigate that issue in defense, offends a principle of justice so rooted in the traditions of conscience of our people as to be ranked as fundamental and is, therefore, inconsistent with due process.

▶ ANALYSIS

The Model Penal Code attacks absolute or strict liability in the penal law. Strict liability is generally condemned on two grounds. First, there is no deterrent effect, since the actor is not aware of the dangerousness of his act. Secondly, a person who is not morally culpable is being condemned.

Quicknotes

MARYLAND CODE ART. 27, § 463 Defined second degree rape as the act of vaginal intercourse with another person by force or threat of force against the will and without the consent of the other person who is under 14 years of age and the person performing the act is at least four years older than the victim.

MENS REA Criminal intent.

STATUTORY RAPE Unlawful sexual intercourse by a man with a woman, either consensual or nonconsensual, under an age specified by statute.

STRICT LIABILITY Liability for all injuries proximately caused by a party's conducting of certain inherently dangerous activities without regard to negligence or fault.

People v. Navarro

State (P) v. Petty theft convict (D)

Cal. App. Dep't. Super. Ct., 99 Cal. App. 3d Supp. 1, 160 Cal. Rptr. 692 (1979).

NATURE OF CASE: Appeal from a conviction under state law of petty theft.

FACT SUMMARY: When Navarro (D) was charged with grand theft for taking four wooden beams from a construction site, he unsuccessfully requested the court to instruct the jury that if he in good-faith believed he had the right to take the beams, he should be acquitted, even if his belief is unreasonable.

⬛ RULE OF LAW
If one takes personal property with the good-faith belief that the property has been abandoned or discarded by the true owner, he is not guilty of theft, even where such good-faith belief is unreasonable.

FACTS: Navarro (D) was charged with grand theft under California Penal Code § 487.1. At trial, Navarro (D) requested two jury instructions which the court modified so that the instructions stated that if one takes personal property in the reasonable and good-faith belief that the owner has consented, he is entitled to acquittal. The state of the evidence was such that the jury could have found that Navarro (D) believed either that the beams had been abandoned as worthless and the owner had no objection to his taking them or that they had substantial value, had not been abandoned, and he had no right to take them. Navarro (D) was convicted of petty theft and appealed.

ISSUE: If one takes personal property with the good-faith belief that the property has been abandoned or discarded by the true owner, is he guilty of theft, even where such good-faith belief is unreasonable?

HOLDING AND DECISION: (Dowds, J.) No. If one takes personal property with the good-faith belief that the property has been abandoned or discarded by the true owner, he is not guilty of theft, even where such good-faith belief is unreasonable. In this case, evidence was presented from which the jury could have concluded that Navarro (D) believed, albeit unreasonably, that the wooden beams had been abandoned and that the owner had no objection to his taking them, i.e., that he lacked the specific criminal intent required to commit the crime of theft. Cases in other jurisdictions also hold that where the law requires a specific criminal intent, it is not enough merely to prove that a reasonable man would have had that intent, without meeting the burden of proof that the defendant himself also entertained it. Here, the trial court in effect instructed the jury that even though Navarro (D) lacked the specific intent required for the crime of theft, he should be convicted unless such belief was "reasonable." In doing so it erred. Reversed.

▶ ANALYSIS

California Penal Code § 484(a) stated in pertinent part that: Every person who shall feloniously steal the personal property of another is guilty of theft. The statute codified the common law definition of larceny, the trespassory taking and carrying away of the personal property of another with the intent to steal the property. Quoting LaFave & Scott, *Handbook on Criminal Law* (1972), the court stated that an honest mistake of fact or law is a defense when it negates a required mental element of the crime.

■══■

Quicknotes

LARCENY The illegal taking of another's property with the intent to deprive the owner thereof.

MISTAKE OF FACT An unintentional mistake in knowing or recalling a fact without the will to deceive.

SPECIFIC INTENT The intent to commit a specific unlawful act which is a required element for criminal liability for certain crimes.

■══■

People v. Marrero

State (P) v. Possessor of an illegal firearm (D)

N.Y. Ct. App., 69 N.Y.2d 382, 507 N.E.2d 1068 (1987).

NATURE OF CASE: Appeal of conviction for illegal firearms possession.

FACT SUMMARY: Marrero (D), charged with illegal firearms possession, argued that he mistakenly believed himself exempt from the ambit of the statute proscribing possession.

🏛 RULE OF LAW
A good-faith mistaken belief as to the meaning of a criminal statute is no defense to a violation of the statute.

FACTS: Marrero (D) was a corrections officer in a federal prison. He was found to be carrying a handgun in public and was charged with violating a statute criminalizing such possession. He argued that he mistakenly believed that a subdivision exempting state correctional officers also applied to him. He was convicted, and the appellate division affirmed. He appealed.

ISSUE: Is a good-faith mistaken belief as to the meaning of a criminal statute a defense to a violation of the statute?

HOLDING AND DECISION: (Bellacosa, J.) No. A good-faith mistaken belief as to the meaning of a criminal statute is no defense to a violation of the statute. To admit the excuse of ignorance of law would work to encourage ignorance when policy should favor knowledge. While this rule will no doubt result in occasional unfair outcomes, the larger societal interest in promoting knowledge of the law is more important. Here, Marrero (D) was ignorant of the law, and this will not excuse him. Affirmed.

DISSENT: (Hancock, J.) The ancient rule, "ignorance of the law is no excuse," may have been proper in times when almost all laws proscribed conduct *malum in se*. Today, however, a vast array of laws prohibits conduct only *malum prohibitum*, and an arbitrary rule disallowing a good-faith mistake defense is unfair.

▶ ANALYSIS

"Ignorance of the law is no excuse" is something of a cliché and is generally true. It is not universal, however. The Model Penal Code rule, accepted in numerous jurisdictions, permits the defense when mistake negates the purpose or belief necessary to establish a material element.

Quicknotes

MALUM IN SE An act that is wrong in accordance with natural law, without respect to whether it is prohibited by statute.

MALUM PROHIBITUM An action that is not inherently wrong, but which is prohibited by law.

MISTAKE OF FACT An unintentional mistake in knowing or recalling a fact without the will to deceive.

Cheek v. United States

Tax evader (D) v. Federal government (P)

498 U.S. 192 (1991).

NATURE OF CASE: Appeal from affirmance of a conviction for tax evasion and other tax-related felonies.

FACT SUMMARY: When Cheek (D) was charged with willfully failing to file a federal income tax return and willfully attempting to evade his income tax, he argued that because he sincerely believed that the tax laws were invalid, he had acted without the willfulness required for conviction.

🏛 RULE OF LAW
A good-faith misunderstanding of the law or a good-faith belief that one is not violating the law negates willfulness, whether or not the claimed belief or misunderstanding is objectively reasonable.

FACTS: After attending various seminars, and based on his own study, Cheek (D) concluded that the income tax laws were being unconstitutionally enforced. He increased his allowances, thereby reducing the amount of tax his employer withheld from his wages. He then ceased to file any income tax returns at all. As a result, he was indicted and charged with willfully failing to file a federal income tax and willfully attempting to evade his income tax. Cheek (D) represented himself at trial. Evidence showed that he had been involved in at least four civil cases that unsuccessfully challenged various aspects of the federal income tax system, and that the courts had informed him and the other plaintiffs that many of their arguments were frivolous. An attorney had also advised Cheek (D) that the courts had rejected as frivolous the claim that wages are not income. Cheek (D) defended by asserting that based on what he learned from the seminars he attended, as well as his own study, he sincerely believed that the tax laws were being unconstitutionally enforced, and that, therefore, his actions were lawful. In instructing the jury, the district court stated that an honest but unreasonable belief is not a defense and does not negate willfulness. The jury returned a verdict of guilty on all counts. The court of appeals affirmed. Cheek (D) appealed, and the United States Supreme Court granted certiorari.

ISSUE: Does a good-faith misunderstanding of the law or a good-faith belief that one is not violating the law negate willfulness, whether or not the claimed belief or misunderstanding is objectively reasonable?

HOLDING AND DECISION: (White, J.) Yes. A good-faith misunderstanding of the law or a good-faith belief that one is not violating the law negates willfulness, whether or not the claimed belief or misunderstanding is objectively reasonable. The common law presumes that every person knows the law. Hence, ignorance of the law or mistake of law under the common law is no defense to criminal prosecution. In the case of federal tax laws, which are very complex, Congress wanted to soften the impact of this common-law presumption by making specific intent to violate the law an element of certain federal tax crimes. Statutory willfulness, which protects the average citizen from prosecution for innocent mistakes made due to the complexity of the tax laws, is the voluntary, intentional violation of a known legal duty. Thus, if the jury credited Cheek's (D) assertion that he truly believed that the Internal Revenue Code (Code) did not treat wages as income, the Government (P) would not have carried its burden to prove willfulness, however unreasonable a court might deem such a belief. Of course, in deciding whether to credit Cheek's (D) claim, the jury was free to consider any admissible evidence showing that he had knowledge of his legal duties to file a return and treat wages as income. Thus, the court of appeals erred by requiring that a claimed good-faith belief must be objectively reasonable before it can negate the Government's (D) evidence as to willfulness. Accordingly, it was error to instruct the jury to disregard evidence of Cheek's (D) understanding that, within the meaning of the tax laws, he was not a person required to file a tax return or to treat wages as taxable income—as incredible as such misunderstandings of and beliefs about the law might be.

DISSENT: (Blackmun, J.) The majority's opinion will encourage taxpayers to cling to frivolous views of the law in the hope of convincing a jury of their sincerity. If that ensues, the majority's holding will have gone beyond the limits of common sense.

▶ ANALYSIS

While the court holds that the jury must consider such a tax-crime defendant's beliefs or misunderstandings—no matter how unreasonable—in determining whether the defendant acted willfully, the more unreasonable the asserted beliefs or misunderstandings are, the more likely the jury will consider them to be nothing more than simple disagreement with known legal duties imposed by the tax laws and will find that the Government (D) has carried its burden of proving knowledge.

■▬■

Quicknotes

FELONY A criminal offense of greater seriousness than a misdemeanor; felonies are generally defined pursuant to

Continued on next page.

statute as any crime that is punishable by death or by a term of imprisonment exceeding one year.

MENS REA Criminal intent.

WILLFULLY An act that is undertaken intentionally, knowingly, and with the intent to commit an unlawful act without a justifiable excuse.

■—■

Causation

Quick Reference Rules of Law

Oxendine v. State

Child abuser (D) v. State (P)

Del. Sup. Ct., 528 A.2d 870 (1987).

NATURE OF CASE: Appeal from a conviction for manslaughter in the beating death of a child.

FACT SUMMARY: When Oxendine's (D) six-year-old son died after being beaten first by Oxendine's (D) girlfriend, Tyree (D), and then by Oxendine (D), Oxendine (D) and Tyree (D) were convicted of manslaughter in the same trial.

⚖ RULE OF LAW
To obtain a conviction for manslaughter, the state is required to show that the defendant's conduct hastened or accelerated the victim's death.

FACTS: Oxendine (D) lived with his girlfriend, Leotha Tyree (D), and his six-year-old son, Jeffrey. When Oxendine (D) returned home from work one evening, he saw bruises on Jeffrey and knew that Tyree (D) had beaten the child during the day. The beating caused microscopic tears in the child's intestines, which led to peritonitis. The next morning, Oxendine (D) beat Jeffrey while screaming at him to get up. Jeffrey's abdomen became swollen later that day, and he died en route to the hospital. At trial, the evidence established that Oxendine (D) inflicted a nonlethal injury upon Jeffrey 24 hours after Tyree (D) had inflicted a lethal injury. Tyree (D) and Oxendine (D) were both convicted of manslaughter in the same trial. Oxendine (D) appealed.

ISSUE: To obtain a conviction for manslaughter is the state required to show that the defendant's conduct hastened or accelerated the victim's death?

HOLDING AND DECISION: (Horsey, J.) Yes. To obtain a conviction for manslaughter, the state is required to show that the defendant's conduct hastened or accelerated the victim's death. In this case, however, the evidence established that Oxendine (D) inflicted a nonlethal injury upon Jeffrey after he had sustained a lethal injury from a previous beating by Tyree (D). Thus, the State (P) was required to show for purposes of causation that Oxendine's (D) conduct hastened or accelerated the child's death. The State's (P) expert medical testimony, even when viewed in the light most favorable to the State (P), was insufficient to sustain the State's (P) ultimate theory of causation ("acceleration"). The trial court, however, properly denied Oxendine's (D) motion for judgment of acquittal at the close of the State's (D) case because its expert medical testimony was sufficient for a rational trier of fact to conclude beyond a reasonable doubt that Oxendine (D) was guilty of the lesser included offense of assault in the second degree. Reversed and remanded for entry of judgment of conviction and resentence on the lesser included offense.

▶ ANALYSIS

As the court declared, it is extremely difficult to be objective about the death of a child. Those responsible ought to be punished. Nevertheless, there must be proof as to whom, (if anyone), inflicted the injuries that resulted in death. Where two individuals inflict injuries on another person, it is often difficult to determine which of those injuries actually caused the individual's death.

■═■

Quicknotes

ACTUAL CAUSE Also known as cause-in-fact; the event or instrumentality which sets in motion the chain of events resulting in the injury and to which the injurious result can be directly traced.

MANSLAUGHTER The killing of another person without premeditation, deliberation, or with the intent to kill or to commit a felony, which may be reasonably expected to result in death or serious bodily injury; manslaughter is characterized by reckless conduct or by some adequate provocation on the part of the actor, as determined by a subjective standard.

■═■

People v. Rideout

State (P) v. Driver convicted of causing death while intoxicated/impaired (D)

Mich. Ct. App., 272 Mich. App. 602, 727 N.W.2d 630 (2006).

NATURE OF CASE: Appeal from conviction of causing death while intoxicated or visibly impaired.

FACT SUMMARY: Rideout (D) argued that the accident he caused while driving intoxicated (OWI) or visibly impaired (OWVI) was not the proximate cause of Keiser's death, since Keiser, who had been a passenger in the car struck by Rideout's (P) vehicle, had reached a point of safety on the side of the road, but then decided to check on the unlit car he had been in, which was in the middle of the road, and was struck by an oncoming vehicle.

🏛 RULE OF LAW

A defendant may not be convicted of a crime where the defendant's conduct, although the cause-in-fact of a victim's injury, is not the proximate cause of that injury as the result of a superseding intervening cause, which may be the victim's own decision to place himself in a position of danger.

FACTS: Rideout (D) was intoxicated when he drove his sport utility vehicle (SUV) into Reichelt's car, causing that car to come to rest on the centerline of the road. Reichelt, and his passenger, Keiser, were not seriously hurt and left their car. After getting to the side of the road to check on Rideout (D), and acknowledging the danger that oncoming cars could hit the darkened car, Reichelt and Keiser went to the car to determine if they could turn on the car's flashers. As Reichelt and Keiser stood by the car, an oncoming car hit Keiser, killing him. Rideout (D) was convicted of operating a motor vehicle while intoxicated (OWI) or while visibly impaired (OWVI) and thereby causing death. During the jury trial, the court gave extensive instructions on factual causation, but almost none on proximate cause or superseding intervening causes. The court did instruct the jury that one of several causes "is a substantial factor in causing a death if, "but for" that cause's contribution, the death would not have occurred, unless the death was an utterly unnatural result of whatever happened." The instructions also told the jury that another cause could be a superseding cause only if it was the sole cause. Rideout (D), contending that the trial court's instructions were erroneous, and that he was not the proximate cause of Keiser's death, appealed, and the state's intermediate appellate court granted review.

ISSUE: May a defendant be convicted of a crime where the defendant's conduct, although the cause-in-fact of a victim's injury, is not the proximate cause of that injury as the result of a superseding intervening cause, which may be the victim's own decision to place himself in a position of danger?

HOLDING AND DECISION: (Sawyer, J.) No. A defendant may not be convicted of a crime where the defendant's conduct, although the cause-in-fact of a victim's injury, is not the proximate cause of that injury as the result of a superseding intervening cause, which may be the victim's own decision to place himself in a position of danger. First, the trial court's instructions were erroneous, since a superseding intervening cause does not need to be the only cause. The effect of this erroneous instruction was the jury could convict Rideout (D) if it found him to be a factual cause of Keiser's death, and could find a superseding intervening cause only if that cause was the only cause of the death. While this alone is enough to set aside the conviction, even if the jury had been properly instructed, there was insufficient evidence that Rideout's (D) driving OWI or OWVI was the proximate cause of the second accident. Here, the second accident occurred only after Keiser had reached a position of safety, but then decided to reenter the roadway. While foreseeability is the linchpin of the superseding causation analysis, and it is at least arguably foreseeable that a person involved in an accident would check on his or her vehicle even if it remains on the road, the analysis does not end there. First, there is no universal test for determining if an intervening cause is also a superseding cause. However, there are several factors that aid a fact finder in making that determination. One of these is foreseeability. As Professor Dressler [the author of the Casebook] points out, a responsive intervening cause will establish proximate cause, while a coincidental intervening cause will not unless it was foreseeable. Here, whether the intervening cause is responsive or coincidental in the case at bar is arguable at best. On the one hand, Keiser's reentering the roadway to check on the vehicle was in direct response to the accident, though not in direct response to Rideout's (D) having driven. On the other hand, it was entirely coincidental that the car that struck Keiser was going down the road when it did. Keiser's decision to reenter the roadway renders the foreseeability factor of little value to the analysis. Rather, that decision directly involves the two remaining factors identified by Professor Dressler that are present here: the apparent-safety doctrine and voluntary human intervention. These two factors compel the conclusion that the intervening cause of the second accident was also a superseding cause. The apparent-safety doctrine provides that when a defendant's active force has come to rest in a position of apparent safety, the court will no longer follow it. Here, Keiser had reached a point of apparent safety, on the side of the road.

Continued on next page.

He was able to get out of harm's way, but then made the decision to place himself in a more dangerous position. That decision ended the initial causal chain and started a new one for which Rideout (D) was not responsible. The voluntary human intervention factor provides that a defendant will be relieved of criminal liability where the intervention is "free, deliberate, and informed" human intervention. Here Keiser made the voluntary decision to reenter the roadway, despite the danger that it posed and of which he was aware. For these reasons, there was insufficient evidence that Rideout's (D) conduct was the proximate cause of Keiser's death. Vacated.

► ANALYSIS

According to the reasoning of this case, if Keiser had been unable to leave Reichelt's car and get to a point of safety, and the second accident occurred while Keiser was still in the car, the causal chain would have been intact since neither the apparent-safety doctrine nor the voluntary human intervention factors would have been applicable, and the factual causality or Rideout's (D) driving would merge with proximate causality.

■═■

Quicknotes

FORESEEABILITY A reasonable expectation that an act or omission would occur.

INTERVENING CAUSE A cause, not anticipated by the initial actor, which is sufficient to break the chain of causation and relieve him of liability.

PROXIMATE CAUSE The natural sequence of events without which an injury would not have been sustained.

VOLUNTARY ACT An act that is undertaken pursuant to an individual's free will and without the influence of another.

■═■

Velazquez v. State

Drag racer (D) v. State (P)

Fla. Dist. Ct. App., 561 So. 2d 347 (1990).

NATURE OF CASE: Appeal from a conviction for vehicular homicide.

FACT SUMMARY: When Velazquez (D) was convicted of vehicular homicide for the death of a co-participant in a drag race, he argued that his conduct was not the cause-in-fact of the co-participant's death.

🏛 RULE OF LAW
There can be no criminal liability for result-type offenses unless it can be shown that the defendant's conduct was a cause-in-fact of the prohibited result.

FACTS: Velazquez (D) met the deceased at a restaurant where both agreed to "drag race" with their respective automobiles. Upon completing the course without incident, the deceased suddenly turned his vehicle 180 degrees and began another race with Velazquez (D) at which time the deceased was traveling at an estimated 123 m.p.h., was not wearing a seat belt, and had a blood alcohol level between .11 and .12. The deceased crashed through a guard rail, his car propelled into the air. When it landed, the deceased was ejected from the car and died when his car landed on him. Velazquez (D) was convicted of vehicular homicide for the death of the co-participant in the drag race and appealed.

ISSUE: Can there be criminal liability for a result-type offense if it cannot be shown that the defendant's conduct was a cause-in-fact of the prohibited result?

HOLDING AND DECISION: (Hubbart, J.) No. There can be no criminal liability for a result-type offense if it cannot be shown that the defendant's conduct was a cause-in-fact of the prohibited result. Courts throughout the country have uniformly followed the traditional "but for" test in determining whether a defendant's conduct was a cause-in-fact of a prohibited consequence in result-type offenses such as vehicular homicide. If the result would not have occurred "but for" the defendant's conduct, that conduct is a cause-in-fact. In relatively rare cases, the "but for" test has been abandoned in favor of the "substantial factor" test when two defendants, acting independently and not in concert, commit two separate acts, each of which alone is sufficient to bring about the prohibited result. In such an anomalous case, the defendant's conduct is a cause-in-fact if it was a "substantial factor" in bringing about the prohibited result. The "proximate cause" element embraces more, however, than the "but for" causation-in-fact test as modified by the "substantial factor" exception. Even where a defendant's conduct is a cause-in-fact of a prohibited result, such as vehicular homicide, courts throughout the country

have for good reason declined to impose criminal liability where the prohibited result of the defendant's conduct is beyond the scope of any fair assessment of the danger created by the defendant's conduct or where it would otherwise be unjust based on fairness and policy consideration, to hold the defendant criminally responsible for the prohibited result. Here, no one forced the deceased to participate in the drag race or to turn around after the agreed-on race was over, return to the starting line, proceed toward the canal at 123 m.p.h. and vault the canal, killing himself on impact. Thus, the evidence indicates he was the major cause of his own death. Reversed and remanded.

▶ ANALYSIS

Section 2.03 of the Model Penal Code codified the "but for" test as follows: "conduct is the cause of a result when: (a) it is an antecedent but for which the result in question would not have occurred; and (b) the relationship between the conduct and result satisfies any additional causal requirements imposed . . . by the law." When recklessly causing a particular result is an element of an offense, as in the above case, the Code states that the element is not established if the actual result is not within the risk of which the actor is aware, unless the actual result is similar to the probable result and not too remote or accidental. The *Velazquez* court here stressed that the deceased in effect killed himself by his own volitional reckless driving and that, therefore, it would be unjust to hold the defendant criminally liable for this death.

■■■■

Quicknotes

"BUT FOR" TEST For purposes of determining tort liability the test for the element of causation is whether the plaintiff would not have suffered the injury "but for" the defendant's conduct.

CAUSE IN FACT The event without which an injury would not have been incurred.

PROXIMATE CAUSE The natural sequence of events without which an injury would not have been sustained.

SUBSTANTIAL FACTOR TEST In determining whether one of several joint acts was the proximate cause of an injury for purposes of tort liability, the inquiry is whether the act or omission was a substantial factor in causing the damage and whether the damage was the direct or probable result of the act or omission.

■■■■

State v. Rose

State (P) v. Hit and run driver (D)

R.I. Sup. Ct., 112 R.I. 402, 311 A.2d 281 (1973).

NATURE OF CASE: Appeal from a manslaughter conviction.

FACT SUMMARY: McEnery was struck by Rose's (D) car. The car sped away from the scene without its driver attempting to assist McEnery, whose dead body was later found lodged beneath Rose's (D) car.

🏛 RULE OF LAW
A defendant cannot be convicted of manslaughter unless the evidence establishes beyond a reasonable doubt that his victim was still alive at the time the defendant's culpable conduct commenced.

FACTS: Rose (D) was charged with manslaughter in the death of McEnery. Trial testimony established that Rose's (D) car struck McEnery at an intersection, then immediately drove off without any effort being made to aid McEnery. A witness to the incident was unable to find McEnery's body at the scene. About ten minutes later, Rose's (D) car was located some 200 yards away. McEnery's dead body was wedged beneath the vehicle. Rose (D) was convicted of manslaughter but appealed. He contended that the only culpable negligence with which he had been charged was in driving away after impact. But, Rose (D) argued expert medical testimony had been inconclusive as to whether McEnery had died immediately upon impact or some time later, from which it followed that the State (P) had not proved that Rose's (D) negligence had contributed to McEnery's death.

ISSUE: May a party be convicted of manslaughter if it cannot be established that his negligence preceded his victim's death?

HOLDING AND DECISION: (Roberts, C.J.) No. A defendant cannot be convicted of manslaughter unless the evidence established beyond a reasonable doubt that his victim was still alive at the time the defendant's culpable conduct commenced. Rose's (D) negligence consisted of his driving away after the accident. But the expert medical testimony creates a reasonable doubt that McEnery was still alive when Rose (D) drove away. It follows that Rose's (D) motion for a directed verdict of acquittal should have been granted.

▶ ANALYSIS

State v. Rose clearly turns upon an issue of causation. Even an intentional act which would be sufficient to cause death cannot be deemed culpable unless the actor's conduct actually contributed to the victim's demise. Thus, it has been held that a deliberate attack with a gun cannot result in a murder conviction absent proof that the victim would not have died "but for" the gunshot wounds. At common law, a defendant could not be convicted of homicide if a victim survived more than a year and a day because after that time the causal connection between the defendant's act and the eventual death was deemed too tenuous. The "year and a day rule" still enjoys popular acceptance.

■■■

Quicknotes

CULPA Fault.

MANSLAUGHTER The killing of another person without premeditation, deliberation or with the intent to kill or to commit a felony, which may be reasonably expected to result in death or serious bodily injury; manslaughter is characterized by reckless conduct or by some adequate provocation on the part of the actor, as determined by a subjective standard.

PROXIMATE CAUSE The natural sequence of events without which an injury would not have been sustained.

■■■

Criminal Homicide

Quick Reference Rules of Law

People v. Eulo

State (P) v. Convicted murderer (D)

N.Y. Ct. App., 63 N.Y.2d 341, 472 N.E.2d 286 (1984).

NATURE OF CASE: Appeal from convictions for manslaughter.

FACT SUMMARY: After shooting their victims in the head, Eulo (D) and Bonilla (D) were tried and convicted of manslaughter in separate prosecutions when the victims were declared brain-dead and taken off their life-support systems.

🏛 RULE OF LAW
Where victims are properly diagnosed as dead, no subsequent medical procedure constitutes a superseding cause of death relieving a defendant of liability.

FACTS: Both Eulo (D) and Bonilla (D) shot their victims in the head. The victims did not die immediately but were taken to hospitals where they were placed on life-support systems. Because each victim's brain had irreversibly ceased to function, the families consented to having the victims declared dead. The families also consented to each victim's removal from life-support systems and to the removal of their organs for transplant purposes. Eulo (D) and Bonilla (D) were tried and convicted of manslaughter in separate prosecutions. The cases were consolidated on appeal.

ISSUE: Where victims are properly diagnosed as dead, do subsequent medical procedures constitute a superseding cause of death relieving a defendant of liability?

HOLDING AND DECISION: (Cooke, C.J.) No. Where victims are properly diagnosed as dead, no subsequent medical procedure constitutes a superseding cause of death relieving a defendant of liability. As it became clear that breathing and heartbeat are not independent indicia of life but are part of an integration of functions in which the brain is dominant, the medical community began to consider the cessation of brain activity as indicative of death. Certainly where respiratory and circulatory functions are maintained by mechanical means, their significance is ambiguous. The law also followed this medical trend. Thus, the state's homicide statute may be construed to provide for criminal responsibility for homicide when a defendant causes injury leading to a victim's total loss of brain functions consistent with the legislature's concept of death. Under these facts, there was sufficient evidence for a rational juror to conclude beyond a reasonable doubt that Eulo's (D) and Bonilla's (D) conduct caused each victim's death and that the following medical transplant procedures were not superseding causes of death. Affirmed.

▶ ANALYSIS

Where a victim's death is prematurely pronounced due to a doctor's negligence, the subsequent medical procedures may be a cause of death, but that negligence would not be a superseding cause relieving a defendant of liability. However, if premature pronouncements of death were due to gross negligence or intentional wrongdoing of doctors, the intervening medical procedure would be such a superseding cause of death. The propriety of medical procedures is thus integral to the question of causation.

Quicknotes

INTERVENING CAUSE A cause not anticipated by the initial actor, which is sufficient to break the chain of causation and relieve him of liability.

PROXIMATE CAUSE The natural sequence of events without which an injury would not have been sustained.

SUPERVENING CAUSE An independent cause, which is the proximate cause of an act.

State v. Guthrie

State (P) v. Convicted murderer (D)

W.Va. Sup. Ct. App., 194 W.Va. 657, 461 S.E.2d 163 (1995).

NATURE OF CASE: Murder case.

FACT SUMMARY: Guthrie (D) stabbed a co-worker who poked fun at him.

🏛 RULE OF LAW
There must be some evidence that the defendant considered and weighed his decision to kill in order for the state to establish premeditation and deliberation under the West Virginia first-degree murder statute.

FACTS: Farley, a co-worker of defendant, poked fun at Guthrie (D) who appeared to be in a bad mood. Farley snapped him with a dishtowel several times on the nose and Guthrie (D) became enraged. He stabbed Farley in the neck and killed him. He appealed the jury verdict finding him guilty of first-degree murder on the basis that the jury instructions were improper because the terms willful, deliberate, and premeditated were equated with a mere intent to kill.

ISSUE: Must there be some evidence that the defendant considered and weighed his decision to kill in order for the state to establish premeditation and deliberation under the West Virginia first-degree murder statute?

HOLDING AND DECISION: (Cleckley, J.) Yes. There must be some evidence that the defendant considered and weighed his decision to kill in order for the state to establish premeditation and deliberation under the West Virginia first-degree murder statute. Here the jury instructions confuse premeditation with the intent to kill. Although premeditation and deliberation are not measured by any particular time period, there must be some period between the formation of the intent to kill and the actual killing, which indicates that the killing is by prior calculation and design. Reversed and remanded.

▶ ANALYSIS

Compare this case with the decision in *Commonwealth v. Carroll*, 412 Pa. 525 (1963). There the court concluded that "no time is too short" to form the requisite premeditation for a finding of first-degree murder.

■■■

Quicknotes

DELIBERATION Reflection; the pondering and weighing of the consequences of an action.

FIRST-DEGREE MURDER The willful killing of another person with deliberation and premeditation; first-degree murder also encompasses those situations in which a person is killed within the perpetration of, or attempt to perpetrate, specified felonies.

PREMEDITATION The contemplation of undertaking an activity prior to action; any length of time is sufficient.

■■■

Midgett v. State

Child abuser (D) v. State (P)

Ark. Sup. Ct., 292 Ark. 278, 729 S.W.2d 410 (1987).

NATURE OF CASE: Appeal from a conviction for murder in the first degree.

FACT SUMMARY: After the death of Midgett's son, Midgett (D) was tried and convicted of first-degree murder when an autopsy attributed death to intra-abdominal bleeding due to blunt force trauma consistent with having been delivered by a human fist.

⚖ RULE OF LAW
Where a person is accused of first-degree murder, it must be shown by substantial evidence that the killing was premeditated and deliberate.

FACTS: Midgett (D) had abused his eight-year-old son by brutal beatings over a substantial period of time. The last beating Midgett (D) administered to his son consisted of four blows, two to the stomach and two to the back. Several days later, Midgett (D) appeared at the hospital carrying his son's body. An autopsy showed the son to be very poorly nourished and underdeveloped and showed numerous recent and old bruises, as well as older, healed rib fractures. The medical examiner concluded that the death resulted from intra-abdominal hemorrhage caused by a blunt force trauma consistent with having been delivered by a human fist. Midgett (D) argued that there was no evidence that his son's death was premeditated and deliberate. The jury found him guilty of first-degree murder. This appeal followed.

ISSUE: Where a person is accused of first-degree murder, must it be shown by substantial evidence that the killing was premeditated and deliberate?

HOLDING AND DECISION: (Newbern, J.) Yes. Where a person is accused of first-degree murder, it must be shown by substantial evidence that the killing was premeditated and deliberate. The evidence in this case supports only the conclusion that Midgett (D) intended to further abuse his son or that his intent, if it was to kill the child, was developed in a drunken, heated rage while disciplining the child. Neither supports a finding of premeditation or deliberation, the required elements of first-degree murder. There is, however, sufficient evidence to sustain a conviction of second-degree murder since Midgett (D) caused his son's death by delivering a blow to his abdomen or chest with the purpose of causing serious physical injury. The conviction is thus modified to second-degree murder and affirmed as modified.

DISSENT: (Hickman, J.) The State (P) proved Midgett (D) starved the boy, choked him, and struck him several times in the stomach and back. The jury could easily conclude that such repeated treatment was intended to kill the child. According to the law, there is substantial evidence to support that verdict. That should end the matter. The judgment should be affirmed.

▶ ANALYSIS

Perhaps because they wish to punish more severely child abusers who kill their children, other states have created laws permitting them to go beyond second-degree murder. Illinois has made aggravated battery one of the felonies qualifying for felony murder, allowing a child abuser to be convicted of murder if the child dies as a result of aggravated battery. California has adopted a "murder by torture" statute, making the offense murder in the first degree without regard to the intent to kill.

■■■

Quicknotes

FIRST-DEGREE MURDER The willful killing of another person with deliberation and premeditation; first-degree murder also encompasses those situations in which a person is killed within the perpetration of, or attempt to perpetrate, specified felonies.

PREMEDITATION The contemplation of undertaking an activity prior to action; any length of time is sufficient.

SECOND-DEGREE MURDER The unlawful killing of another person, without premeditation, and characterized by either intent to kill, or by a reckless disregard for human life.

■■■

State v. Forrest

State (P) v. Murdering-son (D)

N.C. Sup. Ct., 321 N.C. 186, 362 S.E.2d 252 (1987).

NATURE OF CASE: Appeal from a conviction for murder in the first degree.

FACT SUMMARY: After Forrest (D) shot his terminally ill father in the head four times, he was tried and convicted of first-degree murder.

🏛 RULE OF LAW
First-degree murder is the intentional and unlawful killing of a human being with malice and with premeditation and deliberation.

FACTS: When Forrest's (D) critically ill father was admitted to the hospital, his medical condition was determined to be untreatable and terminal. While visiting his father in the hospital, Forrest (D) became very upset and was seen crying. When his father coughed, emitting a gurgling and rattling noise, Forrest (D) put a small pistol to his father's temple, firing four times. Forrest (D) then walked out into the hospital corridor and dropped the gun, neither running nor threatening anyone. He never denied shooting his father and told police that he promised his dad he wouldn't let him suffer. The exact cause of death was determined to be the four bullet wounds to the head. Forrest (D) argued that the trial court's submission of the first-degree murder charge was improper because there was insufficient evidence of premeditation and deliberation. Forrest (D), tried and convicted of first-degree murder, was sentenced to life imprisonment. Forrest (D) appealed.

ISSUE: Is first-degree murder the intentional and unlawful killing of a human being with malice and with premeditation and deliberation?

HOLDING AND DECISION: (Meyer, J.) Yes. First-degree murder is the intentional and unlawful killing of a human being with malice and with premeditation and deliberation. Before the issue of a defendant's guilt may be submitted to the jury, the trial court must be satisfied that substantial evidence has been introduced tending to prove each essential element of the offense charged. Here, many of the circumstances that establish a factual basis for a finding of premeditation and deliberation are present. Forrest's (D) father did nothing to provoke Forrest's (D) action but was lying helpless at the time he was shot, and Forrest's (D) revolver had to be cocked each time before it could be fired. Most persuasive of all are Forrest's (D) own statements following the incident. Among these, Forrest (D) said he thought about putting his father out of his misery because he was suffering. His statements, together with the above circumstances, make it clear that the trial court did not err in submitting to the jury the issue of first-

degree murder based upon premeditation and deliberation. Affirmed.

▶ ANALYSIS

Premeditation and deliberation relate to mental processes and ordinarily are not readily susceptible to proof by direct evidence. Instead, they usually must be proved by circumstantial evidence. Among other things considered, the nature and number of the victim's wounds is a circumstance from which premeditation and deliberation can be inferred.

Quicknotes

FIRST-DEGREE MURDER The willful killing of another person with deliberation and premeditation; first-degree murder also encompasses those situations in which a person is killed within the perpetration of, or attempt to perpetrate, specified felonies.

MALICE The intention to commit an unlawful act without justification or excuse.

PREMEDITATION The contemplation of undertaking an activity prior to action; any length of time is sufficient.

Girouard v. State

Murdering husband (D) v. State (P)

Md. Ct. App., 321 Md. 532, 583 A.2d 718 (1991).

NATURE OF CASE: Appeal from conviction of murder.

FACT SUMMARY: When Girouard (D) was convicted of the murder of his wife, he appealed on the basis that because she provoked him, the charge of murder should have been mitigated to manslaughter.

🏛 RULE OF LAW
Words cannot constitute adequate provocation to mitigate a charge of murder to manslaughter unless the words are accompanied by conduct indicating a present intention and ability to cause the defendant bodily harm.

FACTS: Girouard (D) was married to the deceased, Joyce, for three months. Both were in the army. One night she informed him that she wanted a divorce, that she never loved him, and that she had reported that he had abused her so that he would be court-martialed. She taunted him for some time and climbed on top of him, pulling his hair. Girouard (D) stabbed his wife and then attempted, but failed, to commit suicide. He was arrested and tried for murder. At trial, Girouard (D) attempted to have the charge of murder reduced to manslaughter on the basis that he was so provoked by Joyce's taunting and threats that the provocation should have mitigated the murder. The trial court rejected this theory, and Girouard (D) was convicted of second-degree murder. He appealed.

ISSUE: Can words constitute provocation adequate to mitigate a charge of murder into manslaughter, if the words are not accompanied by conduct indicating a present intention and ability to cause the defendant bodily harm?

HOLDING AND DECISION: (Cole, J.) No. Voluntary manslaughter is an intentional homicide done in a sudden heat of passion, caused by adequate provocation before there is a reasonable opportunity to cool down, and committed without the malice aforethought required for murder. To determine whether a murder charge should be mitigated to manslaughter, one must look to see if there was adequate provocation by the victim, if the killing was in the heat of passion, if there was no reasonable opportunity to cool down, and if there was a causal connection between the provocation, the passion, and the act. Provocation is adequate if it is calculated to inflame the passion of a reasonable man and tends to cause him to act for the moment from passion instead of reason. It is generally held that mere words, however offensive, are not adequate provocation to reduce a charge of murder. Words can only be adequate provocation if accompanied by conduct indicating that the victim will harm the defendant. Although Joyce climbed on Girouard (D) and pulled his hair, he could not have been afraid that she would cause him bodily harm. Therefore, her words alone did not constitute legally sufficient provocation enough to mitigate the charge of murder into manslaughter. Affirmed.

▶ ANALYSIS

At early common law, only a few types of provocation were considered to be adequate. These included assault and battery, mutual combat, and a husband observing the adultery of his wife. However, the modern trend is to treat the question of whether the provocation was adequate as one for the jury. The court may allow a jury not just to decide if a reasonable man would have been provoked but also might allow it to consider the defendant's personal characteristics.

━■━

Quicknotes

ADEQUATE PROVOCATION Provocation such that would cause an ordinary reasonable man to set aside his judgment; a defense to a claim of premeditation.

COOLING PERIOD A sufficient period, after provocation, for an individual to regain his composure and after which he is presumed to understand the consequences of his actions.

VOLUNTARY MANSLAUGHTER The killing of another person without premeditation, deliberation or malice aforethought, but committed while in the "heat of passion" or upon some adequate provocation, thereby reducing the charge from murder to manslaughter.

━■━

Director of Public Prosecutions v. Camplin

Prosecutor (P) v. 15-year-old convicted of murder (D)

House of Lords, 2 All E.R. 168, 2 W.L.R. 679 (1978).

NATURE OF CASE: Certified appeal from reduction of murder conviction to one of manslaughter.

FACT SUMMARY: Camplin (D), a 15-year-old boy who killed Khan after Khan allegedly sodomized Camplin (D) and then laughed at him, contended that the jury, when considering his affirmative defense of provocation, should not have been instructed that the "reasonable person" standard does not account for the defendant's age and sex.

RULE OF LAW

Where a defendant who is a minor is being prosecuted for murder, and the defendant asserts the affirmative defense of provocation, the jury must be instructed to consider whether the provocation was sufficient to have made a reasonable person of the same age and sex as the defendant, under the same circumstances, act as the defendant acted.

FACTS: Camplin (D), a 15-year-old boy killed Khan with a fry pan after Khan allegedly sodomized Camplin (D) and then laughed at him. At trial, the judge instructed the jury that, contrary to Camplin's (D) attorney's suggestion, when considering Camplin's (D) affirmative defense of provocation, they could not consider Camplin's (D) age or sex, saying that they had to consider whether "the provocation was sufficient to make a reasonable man in like circumstances act as [Camplin (D)] did. Not a reasonable boy . . . or a reasonable lad; it is an objective test—a reasonable man." The jury convicted Camplin (D) of murder. The intermediate appellate court reduced the conviction to manslaughter on the ground that the judge's instruction was erroneous. The appellate court held that the proper instruction would have been to have the jury consider whether the provocation was sufficient to have made a reasonable person of the same age as the defendant, under the same circumstances, act as the defendant acted. The issue was certified to England's highest court.

ISSUE: Where a defendant who is a minor is being prosecuted for murder, and the defendant asserts the affirmative defense of provocation, must the jury be instructed to consider whether the provocation was sufficient to have made a reasonable person of the same age and sex as the defendant, under the same circumstances, act as the defendant acted?

HOLDING AND DECISION: (Lord Diplock, J.) Yes. Where a defendant who is a minor is being prosecuted for murder, and the defendant asserts the affirmative defense of provocation, the jury must be instructed to

consider whether the provocation was sufficient to have made a reasonable person of the same age and sex as the defendant, under the same circumstances, act as the defendant acted. For purposes of the provocation defense, the "reasonable man" standard has never been confined to an adult male. It means an ordinary person of either sex, who is not particularly sensitive or violent, and who has a degree of self-control that everyone in society may expect from each other. Additionally, the proportionality between the gravity of the provocation and the response thereto must be judged by current social norms. The common law has been statutorily changed to permit mere words or taunts to be considered provocation when reducing murder to manslaughter. Hence, the gravity of such provocation may depend on the particular characteristics or circumstances of the person at whom the taunt or insult is directed. Otherwise, the mitigation of the common law's severity in not permitting verbal provocation as a defense would be undone. Here, Camplin's (D) age, as it related to temperament and self-control, was the particular characteristic that the jury should have been able to consider—as a fact matter, rather than as a matter of law—in assessing his provocation defense, based on their experience of how ordinary people behave. Therefore, the jury should have been instructed that the reasonable person they were to consider was an ordinary person of the same sex and age as Camplin (D), but otherwise sharing his characteristics that would affect the gravity of provocation to him, as well as his response to that provocation. Affirmed.

CONCURRENCE: (Lord Simon, J.) A defendant's individual characteristics, including their sex, may be taken into account by a jury considering the provocation defense. The provocation defense was motivated by common sense to account for human infirmity, but the law placed limits on the defense through the use of the reasonable person standard. While that standard must still be met before murder can be reduced to manslaughter, in determining whether a person of reasonable self-control would lose his or her self-control in circumstances faced by the defendant, all the circumstances, including the defendant's characteristics, must be considered.

▶ ANALYSIS

The "reasonable man" or "reasonable person" standard is not fixed. At one end—rejected by the court in this case—is the purely objective standard, devoid of any of the defendant's characteristics. At the other end is the purely subjective standard, taking into account all of the

Continued on next page.

defendant's characteristics. In this case, the court attempts to strike what it believes is an appropriate balance between these extremes by identifying the characteristics of the defendant relevant to the provocation defense, both as to the gravity of the provocation sufficient to cause the "reasonable person" to lose control, as well as the level of self-control such a reasonable person would have.

■━■

Quicknotes

ADEQUATE PROVOCATION Provocation such that would cause an ordinary reasonable man to set aside his judgment; a defense to a claim of premeditation.

AFFIRMATIVE DEFENSE A manner of defending oneself against a claim not by denying the truth of the charge, but by the introduction of some evidence challenging the plaintiff's right to bring the claim.

VOLUNTARY MANSLAUGHTER The killing of another person without premeditation, deliberation or malice aforethought, but committed while in the "heat of passion" or upon some adequate provocation, thereby reducing the charge from murder to manslaughter.

■━■

People v. Casassa

State (P) v. Disturbed murderer (D)

N.Y. Ct. App., 49 N.Y.2d 668, 404 N.E.2d 1310 (1980).

NATURE OF CASE: Appeal of conviction for second-degree murder.

FACT SUMMARY: Casassa (D), charged with murder, contended that whether he was under extreme disturbance should be analyzed subjectively.

RULE OF LAW
Whether a defendant was so emotionally disturbed as to lessen murder to manslaughter involves both an objective and subjective analysis.

FACTS: Casassa (D) became romantically obsessed with a neighbor. After she consistently rejected his advances, he confronted her with a knife, stabbing her to death. He was charged with murder. The trial court rejected his argument that whether he was under an extreme emotional disturbance sufficient to mitigate the homicide to manslaughter should be viewed from an entirely subjective viewpoint. Instead, the court, sitting without a jury, found the reaction to have been so peculiar to Casassa (D) that it would have been unreasonable to mitigate the crime. The court therefore convicted Casassa (D) of second-degree murder. Casassa appealed.

ISSUE: Does the question of whether a defendant was so emotionally disturbed as to lessen murder to manslaughter involve both an objective and subjective analysis?

HOLDING AND DECISION: (Jasen, J.) Yes. Whether a defendant was so emotionally disturbed as to lessen murder to manslaughter involves both an objective and subjective analysis. The applicable penal code permits the affirmative defense where "the defendant acted under the influence of extreme emotional disturbance for which there was a reasonable explanation or excuse." This language clearly introduces both subjective and objective elements into the analysis. It is subjective as to whether or not the defendant was in fact under an extreme emotional disturbance. It is objective as to whether or not the disturbance was reasonable. The court here appears to have used this standard, and found Casassa's (D) disturbance not to have been based on reasonable grounds. This was a proper analysis. Affirmed.

▶ ANALYSIS

The language adopted by the New York Legislature here basically comports with the Model Penal Code. The test here can be seen to have grown out of the classic "heat of passion" manslaughter test. The test here differs from heat of passion mainly in that the homicide does not necessarily have to be basically contemporaneous to the triggering event, as heat of passion almost always requires.

■═■

Quicknotes

ADEQUATE PROVOCATION Provocation such that would cause an ordinary reasonable man to set aside his judgment; a defense to a claim of premeditation.

SECOND-DEGREE MURDER The unlawful killing of another person, without premeditation, and characterized by either intent to kill or by a reckless disregard for human life.

■═■

People v. Moore

State (P) v. Reckless driver (D)

Cal. Ct. App., 187 Cal. App. 4th 937, 114 Cal. Rptr. 3d 540 (2010).

NATURE OF CASE: Action for second-degree murder, resisting arrest, and other crimes and violations. [Procedural posture not stated in casebook excerpt.]

FACT SUMMARY: Moore (D) was charged with second-degree murder, resisting arrest, and other crimes and violations after he drove 70 miles per hour in a 35-mile-per-hour zone, crossed into the opposing traffic lane, caused oncoming drivers to avoid him, ran a red light, struck a car in the intersection without even attempting to apply his brakes—which caused death to one victim and serious injury to another—and then failed to stop for police and resisted arrest.

 RULE OF LAW
[Rule of law not stated in casebook excerpt.]

FACTS: Moore (D), who was angry, drove 70 miles per hour in a 35-mile-per-hour zone, crossed into the opposing traffic lane, caused oncoming drivers to avoid him, ran a red light, and struck a car in the intersection without even attempting to apply his brakes. The accident caused death to one victim and serious injury to another. Moore (D) did not stop to check on the victims, nor did he stop when police pursued him. He also resisted being arrested. When he was finally subdued, he admitted he was merely going too fast, but had not intended to kill anyone. When asked why he resisted arrest, he replied, "I don't know. I just went wacky from Tobacky." Moore (D) was charged with second-degree murder, leaving the scene of an accident, evading a peace officer, reckless driving with bodily injury, and resisting a police officer.

ISSUE: [Issue not stated in casebook excerpt.]

HOLDING AND DECISION: (Gilbert, J.) [Holding and decision not stated in casebook excerpt.]

▶ **ANALYSIS**

The casebook presents only the facts of this case, and leaves it to the student to decide whether Moore (D) was guilty of murder. Arguably, there was ample evidence here to support Moore's (D) second-degree murder conviction based on implied malice. His actions went well beyond gross negligence, and it seems he acted with wanton disregard of the near certainty that someone would be killed. A jury certainly could conclude that because anyone would be aware of the risk of death under such circumstances, Moore (D) was aware of the risk, but willfully ignored it.

People v. Knoller

State (P) v. Convicted second-degree murderer (D)

Cal. Sup. Ct., 41 Cal. 4th 139, 158 P.3d 731 (2007).

NATURE OF CASE: [Appeal in action for second-degree murder.]

FACT SUMMARY: [Fact summary not stated in casebook excerpt.]

> ## 🏛 RULE OF LAW
> Malice is implied when a killing is proximately caused by an act, the natural consequences of which are dangerous to life, which act was deliberately performed by a person who knows that his conduct endangers the life of another and who acts with conscious disregard for life.

FACTS: [Facts not stated in casebook excerpt.]

ISSUE: Is malice implied when a killing is proximately caused by an act, the natural consequences of which are dangerous to life, which act was deliberately performed by a person who knows that his conduct endangers the life of another and who acts with conscious disregard for life?

HOLDING AND DECISION: (Kennard, J.) Yes. Malice is implied when a killing is proximately caused by an act, the natural consequences of which are dangerous to life, which act was deliberately performed by a person who knows that his conduct endangers the life of another and who acts with conscious disregard for life. Second-degree murder is the unlawful killing of a human being with malice aforethought but without the additional elements, such as willfulness, premeditation, and deliberation, that would support a conviction of first-degree murder. The malice required to convict for second-degree murder can be express or implied. Malice is implied when it can be inferred from the circumstances. Statutorily, implied malice is defined as a killing by one with an "abandoned and malignant heart." This definition is far from clear and two lines of cases have developed to translate this "amorphous anatomical characterization" into a standard that a jury can apply. Under both lines of cases, implied malice requires that a defendant be aware of the risk of death to another. Under one of these lines of cases, and the one that has the clearer standard, a jury should be instructed that malice is implied when the killing is proximately caused by an act, the natural consequences of which are dangerous to life, which act was deliberately performed by a person who knows that his conduct endangers the life of another and who acts with a conscious disregard for life.

▶ ANALYSIS

As in California, where this case was adjudicated, most jurisdictions require proof that a defendant subjectively knew he was taking an unjustifiable risk to human life for a murder conviction based on implied malice, also known as "depraved-heart murder." A minority of states, however, require only a showing that the defendant should have known of such a risk.

■━■

Quicknotes

IMPLIED MALICE The intention to commit an unlawful act as implied from the commission of wrongful actions.

SECOND-DEGREE MURDER The unlawful killing of another person, without premeditation, and characterized by either intent to kill or by a reckless disregard for human life.

■━■

State v. Williams

State (P) v. Negligent parents (D)

Wash. Ct. App., 4 Wash. App. 908, 484 P.2d 1167 (1971).

NATURE OF CASE: Appeal of manslaughter conviction.

FACT SUMMARY: Mr. and Mrs. Williams (D) failed to obtain medical aid for their 17-month-old child and, as a result, he died.

🏛 RULE OF LAW
Where the failure of a person to act while under the duty to do so is the proximate cause of the death of another, that person may be convicted of involuntary manslaughter, even though his conduct was no more than ordinary negligence.

FACTS: Mrs. Williams (D) had a son by a previous marriage before she married Mr. Williams (D). When the lad, only 17 months old, developed a toothache, neither she nor her husband considered it serious enough to seek out medical help. As the tooth became worse and abscessed, however, the Williamses (D) became apprehensive but did not seek medical (or dental) care for the boy, fearing that the welfare department might take him away if they saw how bad he looked. Eventually, the boy developed gangrene (the smell from which was clearly noticeable), and pneumonia, from which he died about ten days later. The Williamses (D) were convicted of manslaughter on these facts. They appealed.

ISSUE: May ordinary negligence, serve as the basis for convicting someone of involuntary manslaughter?

HOLDING AND DECISION: (Horowitz, C.J.) Yes. Where the failure of a person to act while under a duty to do so is the proximate cause of the death of another, that person may be convicted of involuntary manslaughter, even though his conduct was no more than ordinary negligence. There is no question but that the Williamses (D) were under a duty to obtain medical care for their seriously ill son, and their fear of the welfare department does not excuse this duty. The tough question here is whether the seriousness of the child's illness became sufficiently apparent to them early enough for their failure to do anything about it to be declared the proximate cause of the boy's death. Medical experts, however, testified that the gangrenous condition of the boy's cheek must have been apparent (both by sight and smell) to his parents for some ten days before he died. Clearly, they were on notice as to the seriousness of their son's illness in time to prevent him from dying of it. Affirmed.

▶ ANALYSIS

This case points up a modern departure from the common-law rule that involuntary manslaughter required an act of gross negligence (i.e., criminal negligence). Ordinary negligence may arise either by act or, as above, by omission while under a duty to act. As in tort, its general formulation is the "failure of a man of reasonable prudence to exercise due care under the circumstances." Note, however, that this "objective" (i.e., what a reasonable man would do) standard runs the risk of undermining individualized justice by sanctioning punishment, regardless of the subjective knowledge of the wrongdoer. In *Williams*, for example, it appeared that the parents were illiterates—wholly ignorant of the most rudimentary principles of health care—who honesty did not know their son was in trouble.

Quicknotes

INVOLUNTARY MANSLAUGHTER The killing of another person without premeditation or deliberation or with the intent to kill or to commit a felony, which may be reasonably expected to result in death or serious bodily injury; involuntary manslaughter is characterized by reckless conduct in the commission of a lawful act, or by the commission of an unlawful act that is not a felony, but which leads to the killing of another.

PROXIMATE CAUSE The natural sequence of events, without which an injury would not have been sustained.

People v. Fuller

State (P) v. Tire thief (D)

Cal. Ct. App., 86 Cal. App. 3d 618,150 Cal. Rptr. 515 (1978).

NATURE OF CASE: Appeal from dismissal of first-degree murder charges.

FACT SUMMARY: Fuller (D) and his accomplice (D) were charged with first-degree murder after their car struck another car and killed the driver while they were fleeing the scene after stealing tires from vans parked on a car lot.

🏛 RULE OF LAW
An accidental death occurring during flight subsequent to a theft from a vehicle will support first-degree murder charges.

FACTS: A police officer noticed Fuller (D) and another man (D) rolling four tires toward their car. The vehicle sped away with the officer in pursuit, ran a red light, and collided with another vehicle. The other vehicle's occupant was killed. It was later discovered that Fuller (D) and his accomplice (D) had broken into four vans and stolen spare tires. Fuller (D) and his accomplice (D) were charged with first-degree murder under the felony-murder rule. The trial court dismissed the murder charge, and the State (P) appealed.

ISSUE: Will an accidental death occurring during flight subsequent to a theft from a vehicle support first-degree murder charges?

HOLDING AND DECISION: (Franson, J.) Yes. A theft from a vehicle leading to an accidental death will support first-degree murder charges. Penal Code § 189, California's felony-murder rule, provides that all murder occurring in the perpetration of, among other things, burglary is first-degree murder. The Penal Code includes breaking into a locked auto within the definition of burglary. Since Fuller (D) and his accomplice (D) were fleeing from a burglary, and a homicide occurred, the felony-murder rule applies, and first-degree murder charges were appropriate. Reversed.

▶ ANALYSIS

The felony-murder rule has been subject to much criticism. It does not require a specific intent, other than that required for the underlying felony, as do all other classifications of murder. The California Supreme Court has repeatedly emphasized that felony murder, although law of the state, is a disfavored doctrine. Consequently, it has given the rule the narrowest possible application con-

sistent with its purpose—which is to deter those engaged in felonies from killing negligently or accidentally.

■═■

Quicknotes

BURGLARY Unlawful entry of a building at night with the intent to commit a felony therein.

FELONY MURDER The unlawful killing of another human being while in the commission of, or attempted commission of, specified felonies.

FIRST-DEGREE MURDER The willful killing of another person with deliberation and premeditation; first-degree murder also encompasses those situations in which a person is killed within the perpetration of, or attempt to perpetrate, specified felonies.

SPECIFIC INTENT The intent to commit a specific unlawful act which is a required element for criminal liability for certain crimes.

■═■

People v. Howard

State (P) v. Convicted felony murderer (D)

Cal. Sup. Ct., 34 Cal. 4th 1129, 104 P.3d 107 (2005).

NATURE OF CASE: Appeal from a felony-murder conviction.

FACT SUMMARY: Howard (D) was convicted of felony murder when, while he was fleeing from the police during a high speed chase, he ran into and killed another motorist.

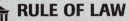 **RULE OF LAW**
Driving with willful or wanton disregard for the safety of persons or property, while fleeing from a pursuing police officer, is not an inherently dangerous felony for purposes of the felony-murder rule.

FACTS: Howard (D) was stopped by a police car for driving without a rear license plate. When the officer and his partner got out of their car to walk over, Howard (D) restarted his vehicle and sped to a nearby freeway. The officers gave chase at speeds up to 90 miles per hour. The chase then continued on dirt roads when Howard (D) left the freeway. Fearing an accident might result from the high speeds, the officers gave up the chase. A minute later they saw Howard (D) run a red light and collide with a car driven by Jeanette Rodriguez who was killed by the crash. Howard (D) was tried and convicted for second-degree felony murder. The court of appeals affirmed, and Howard (D) appealed.

ISSUE: Is driving with willful or wanton disregard for the safety of persons or property while fleeing from a pursuing police officer an inherently dangerous felony for purposes of the felony-murder rule?

HOLDING AND DECISION: (Kennard, J.) No. Driving with willful or wanton disregard for the safety of persons or property, while fleeing from a pursuing police officer, is not an inherently dangerous felony for purposes of the felony-murder rule. Nothing in this decision should be read as saying that a motorist who kills an innocent person in a hazardous, high-speed flight from a police officer should not be convicted of murder. However, the prosecution may not, as it did here, resort to the second-degree felony-murder rule to remove from the jury's consideration the question whether the killing which occurred during a violation of the felony-murder statute was done with malice. In determining whether the felony is inherently dangerous for purposes of the rule, the court must look to the elements of the felony in the abstract, not the particular facts of the case. That is, the court determines whether the felony "by its very nature" cannot be committed without creating a substantial risk that someone will be killed. A violation of the statutory provision here at issue,

namely, attempting to elude a pursuing police officer, is not, in the abstract, inherently dangerous to human life. Therefore, the second-degree felony-murder rule does not apply when a killing occurs during a violation of the statute. Reversed.

CONCURRENCE AND DISSENT: (Brown, J.) The majority is correct in holding that the conviction must be reversed; however, the majority should not continue its allegiance to the dubious felony-murder doctrine. The court should go further and abrogate the felony-murder rule entirely. As the facts of this case conclusively demonstrate, application of this rule remains irredeemably arbitrary.

DISSENT: (Baxter, J.) The statute at issue gives clear and specific notice that one who, in order to elude police pursuit, drives with reckless indifference to safety is guilty of a felony. Such reckless driving is inherently dangerous. By definition, it creates a substantial risk that someone will be killed.

▶ *ANALYSIS*

In the *Howard* decision, the California Supreme Court pointed out that because the felony-murder rule is a court-made rule, it has no statutory definition. Because the felony-murder rule has been criticized by legal scholars as incorporating an artificial concept of strict criminal liability, most courts have stressed that the rule deserves no extension beyond its required application.

■■■

Quicknotes

FELONY MURDER The unlawful killing of another human being while in the commission of, or attempted commission of, specified felonies.

WANTON AND RECKLESS Unlawful intentional or reckless conduct without regard to the consequences.

■■■

People v. Smith

State (P) v. Convicted second-degree murderer (D)

Cal. Sup. Ct., 35 Cal. 3d 798, 678 P.2d 886 (1984).

NATURE OF CASE: Appeal from conviction for second-degree murder and felony child abuse.

FACT SUMMARY: Smith (D), who had been convicted of second-degree murder that was based on her being convicted of felony child abuse, contended that the second-degree murder charge had to be overturned because the felony was an integral part of the homicide and merged therewith.

> ## 🏛 RULE OF LAW
> The felony-murder rule is barred where the underlying felony is assaultive felony child abuse.

FACTS: Smith (D) regularly disciplined her two daughters by beating them. When Smith's (D) two-year-old, Amy, refused to sit on the couch instead of the floor to eat a snack, Smith (D) hit her repeatedly, knocking her to the floor. Eventually, Smith (D) knocked Amy backwards. Amy hit her head, went into respiratory arrest, and died. Smith (D) was convicted of second-degree murder and felony child abuse. The second-degree murder charge was based on the underlying felony, i.e., was a felony-murder charge. Smith (D) contended that the second-degree murder charge had to be overturned because the felony was an integral part of the homicide and merged therewith. The state's highest court granted review.

ISSUE: Is the felony-murder rule barred where the underlying felony is assaultive felony child abuse?

HOLDING AND DECISION: (Mosk, J.) Yes. The felony-murder rule is barred where the underlying felony is assaultive felony child abuse. Although the state recognizes felony murder, it is a disfavored doctrine that may be used only in the most circumscribed circumstances, where it cannot be extended beyond any rational function that it is designed to serve—to deter those engaged in felonies from killing negligently or accidentally. Thus, the felony-murder rule has been held inapplicable to felonies that are an integral part of and included in fact within the homicide. Part of the rationale for this limitation is that permitting the rule in such circumstances would effectively preclude the jury from considering the issue of malice aforethought in all cases where homicide has been committed as a result of a felonious assault. This limitation has been applied to the underlying felony of assault with a deadly weapon; burglary with the intent to assault with a deadly weapon; and discharging a firearm at an inhabited dwelling. Those cases where the limitation on felony murder has not been applied are cases that did not involve an underlying felony that has as its principal purpose an assault on the victim (e.g., furnishing narcotics; kidnapping; armed robbery, etc.), or includes an "independent felonious purpose," such as obtaining money (e.g., armed robbery). Applying these principles here, it is clear that the felony-murder rule should not apply because it is plain that the purpose of the child abuse was the "very assault which resulted in death." Moreover, it would be illogical to permit such assaultive child abuse to be bootstrapped into felony murder merely because the victim is a child. The homicide in this case was the result of assaultive child abuse, so that the underlying felony was an integral part of and included in the fact of the homicide. There was no independent purpose for the conduct; the purpose was the assault, which resulted in death. Finally, application of the felony-murder rule would not further deter an assaultive child abuser from killing negligently or accidentally, since the abuser is already willfully inflicting unjustifiable pain on the child.

⏵ ANALYSIS

The court's holding in this case that the underlying felony is an integral part of and included in fact in the homicide—that the felony has merged into the homicide—is known as the merger doctrine. Not all states recognize the merger doctrine. Those that do, like California in this case, look to the elements of the crime and not the facts of the case, to determine if the felony merges with the homicide. Accordingly, if the elements of the crime have an assaultive aspect, the crime merges with the underlying homicide even if the elements also include conduct that is not assaultive.

■═■

Quicknotes

FELONY MURDER The unlawful killing of another human being while in the commission of, or attempted commission of, specified felonies.

MALICE AFORETHOUGHT The intention to commit an unlawful act without justification or excuse.

MERGER DOCTRINE A rule of law whereby, if a defendant committed a single criminal act that constitutes two separate offenses, the lesser-included offense merges into the higher offense; the defendant may only be charged with the higher offense.

■═■

State v. Sophophone

State (P) v. Convicted felon (D)

Kan. Sup. Ct., 270 Kan. 703, 19 P.3d 70 (2001).

NATURE OF CASE: Appeal from a felony-murder conviction.

FACT SUMMARY: Sanexay Sophophone (D) was prosecuted for felony murder when a law enforcement officer attempting to apprehend a co-felon, killed the co-felon.

🏛 RULE OF LAW
When a killing results from lawful acts of a law enforcement officer attempting to apprehend a felon, a co-felon is not responsible for the death under the felony-murder doctrine.

FACTS: Sanexay Sophophone (D) and three other individuals broke into a house. The police responded, observed the individuals, and ordered them to stop. An officer chased Sophophone (D), handcuffed him, and placed him in a police car. Meanwhile, another officer chased another of the intruders, placed him on the ground and directed him not to move. This intruder, however, rose up and fired at the officer, who returned fire and killed him. Sophophone (D) was charged and convicted of felony murder and appealed.

ISSUE: When a killing results from lawful acts of a law enforcement officer attempting to apprehend a felon, is a co-felon responsible for the death under the felony-murder doctrine?

HOLDING AND DECISION: (Larson, J.) No. When a killing results from lawful acts of a law enforcement officer attempting to apprehend a felon, a co-felon is not responsible for the death under the felony-murder doctrine. The applicable statute defines murder in the first degree as, among other things, the killing of a human being committed in the commission of, attempt to commit, or flight from an inherently dangerous felony as elsewhere defined in the statute. Sophophone's (D) argument that his being in custody at the time his co-felon was killed by the officer constituted a break in circumstances, or intervening cause, sufficient to insulate him from further criminal responsibility, is of no merit since the killing in fact took place "during flight" from the aggravated burglary, an inherently dangerous felony. Here, however, to impute the act of killing to Sophophone (D) when the act was a lawful and courageous one of a law enforcement officer acting in the line of his duties, would be contrary to the strict construction courts are required to give criminal statutes. There is considerable doubt as to the meaning of our jurisdiction's felony-murder statute as applied to the facts of the instant case, but clearly making one criminally

responsible for lawful acts of a law enforcement officer is not the intent of the statute as it is currently written. Reversed.

DISSENT: (Abbott, J.) When an issue requires statutory analysis and the statute is unambiguous, as here, the court is limited by the wording chosen by the legislature. The court is not free to alter the statutory language, regardless of the result. Here, there is nothing in the statute which establishes an agency approach. The statute simply does not contain the limitations indicated by the majority. This case is exactly the type of case the legislature had in mind when it adopted the felony-murder rule.

▶ ANALYSIS

It is not enough to prove felony murder that the killing occurs, as a temporal matter, during the commission of the offense. There must also be a causal relationship between the felony and the killing. Under the so-called "agency approach," adopted in some jurisdictions, the felony-murder doctrine does not apply if the person who directly causes the death is, as in the *Sophophone* case, a non-felon. An alternative theory, sometimes adopted, holds the felon may be responsible under the felony-murder doctrine for a killing committed by a nonfelon if the felon "set in motion" the acts which resulted in the victim's death.

■=■

Quicknotes

CAUSATION The aggregate effect of preceding events that bring about a tortious result; the causal connection between the actions of a tortfeasor and the injury that follows.

FELONY MURDER The unlawful killing of another human being while in the commission of, or attempted commission of, specified felonies.

INTERVENING CAUSE A cause, not anticipated by the initial actor, which is sufficient to break the chain of causation and relieve him of liability.

■=■

Gregg v. Georgia

Convicted murderer (P) v. State (D)

428 U.S. 153 (1976).

NATURE OF CASE: Review of verdict imposing the death penalty.

FACT SUMMARY: Gregg (P) contended that the death penalty was per se violative of the Eighth Amendment.

🏛 RULE OF LAW
The death penalty is not per se violative of the Eighth Amendment.

FACTS: Gregg (P) was convicted of premeditated murder. Under Georgia law, six categories of murder merited exposure to capital punishment. The law provided for a series of specific aggravating circumstances and mitigating circumstances. The jury, finding two categories of capital murder applicable to Gregg (P), also found two aggravating circumstances. The jury recommended the death penalty, which the court imposed. Gregg (P), after his state appeals concluded unsuccessfully, filed a federal habeas action. The district court and court of appeals denied the writ, and the Supreme Court granted review.

ISSUE: Is the death penalty per se violative of the Eighth Amendment?

HOLDING AND DECISION: (Stewart, J.) No. The death penalty is not per se violative of the Eighth Amendment. The Eighth Amendment prohibits cruel and unusual punishment. A penalty is cruel and unusual if it is out of favor with public attitudes, is inconsistent with human dignity, or is excessive for the crime. However, the death penalty clearly is supported by the public and was envisioned by the Amendment's framers. Capital punishment, though grim, is an expression of society's outrage at particularly heinous crimes. It serves the purposes of deterrence and retribution. Although the deterrent effect of the death penalty is open to question, it serves a retributive function that is needed to prevent citizens from resorting to self-help. For these reasons, the death penalty is not per se violative of the Eighth Amendment. [The Court went on to hold the Georgia statute constitutional as applied to Gregg (D) because it did not give juries unbridled discretion to impose capital punishment.]

CONCURRENCE: (White, J.) The fact that mistakes will inevitably occur in what is an imperfect justice system does not in itself make the death penalty unconstitutional.

DISSENT: (Brennan, J.) Our society and legal system has evolved to the point where the death penalty, like the rack and the wheel, cannot be considered anything other than cruel and unusual.

DISSENT: (Marshall, J.) The death penalty is an affront to human dignity. This, combined with its lack of demonstrable utility, renders it in violation of the Eighth Amendment.

▶ ANALYSIS

The Supreme Court's jurisprudence on the applicability of the Eighth Amendment to the death penalty has been somewhat inconsistent. On the one hand, juries cannot have unbridled discretion to impose the death penalty. On the other hand, they must have some discretion. Accordingly, the Supreme Court has struck down mandatory death penalty statutes that eliminate jury discretion completely. See, e.g., *Woodson v. North Carolina,* 428 U.S. 280 (1976).

━━▪

Quicknotes

CAPITAL PUNISHMENT Punishment by death.

CRUEL AND UNUSUAL PUNISHMENT Punishment that is excessive or disproportionate to the offense committed and which is prohibited by the Eighth Amendment to the United States Constitution.

PREMEDITATION The contemplation of undertaking an activity prior to action; any length of time is sufficient.

━━▪

McCleskey v. Kemp

[Parties not identified.]

481 U.S. 279 (1987).

NATURE OF CASE: Appeal from sentence of death following murder conviction.

FACT SUMMARY: McCleskey (D) contended that the capital sentencing process in Georgia was administered in a racially discriminatory manner because black defendants, who killed white victims, had the greatest likelihood of receiving the death penalty.

🏛 RULE OF LAW
Capital punishment is constitutional even though statistics indicate a risk that racial considerations may enter into capital sentencing determinations.

FACTS: Professor Baldus conducted a statistical study analyzing 2,000 Georgia murder cases from the 1970s. Using computer modeling, Baldus concluded that defendants charged with killing white victims were 4.3 times as likely to receive a death sentence as those defendants charged with killing blacks. Furthermore, black defendants were 1.1 times as likely to receive a death sentence when compared to other defendants. Based on the Baldus study, McCleskey (D), a black man convicted of killing a white police officer, challenged the sentencing process as a violation of the Eighth and Fourteenth Amendments to the U.S. Constitution. The court of appeals rejected his claim, and the Supreme Court granted review.

ISSUE: Is capital punishment constitutional even though statistics indicate a risk that racial considerations may enter into capital sentencing determinations?

HOLDING AND DECISION: (Powell, J.) Yes. Capital punishment is constitutional even though statistics indicate a risk that racial considerations may enter into capital sentencing determinations. Because a defendant who alleges an equal protection violation must prove "purposeful" discrimination, McCleskey (D) must prove that the decision-makers in his case acted with discriminatory purpose. However, he has not presented any evidence specific to his own case but instead relies solely on the Baldus study. Although such studies may be used as proof of intent in certain limited circumstances, such as jury selection, they are not appropriate in this case, where so many entities and variables are involved. Furthermore, Georgia's sentencing system does not violate the prohibition against cruel and unusual punishment. The Baldus study indicates a discrepancy that may correlate with race, but apparent disparities in sentencing are inevitable in a justice system that values discretion, equity, and flexibility. In light of the safeguards designed to minimize racial bias and the value

of jury trial, the Baldus study does not demonstrate a constitutionally significant risk of bias in the Georgia capital sentencing process. Affirmed.

DISSENT: (Brennan, J.) Enhanced willingness to impose the death sentence on black defendants reflects a devaluation of the lives of black persons and is completely at odds with the concern for rationality and for the evaluation of an individual as a human being.

▶ ANALYSIS

The *Durham* decision, [*Durham v. United States*, 214 F.2d 862 (1954)], though it may seem morally reprehensible, is well grounded in precedent. Prior to 1988, no defendant had ever succeeded in challenging his sentencing on grounds of racial discrimination. The most significant factor in this universal judicial resistance is probably the reluctance to interfere in sentencing determinations for defects that have no bearing on individual culpabilities.

Quicknotes

CAPITAL PUNISHMENT Punishment by death.

DISCRIMINATORY PURPOSE Intent to discriminate; must be shown to establish an Equal Protection violation.

Payne v. Tennessee

Convicted murderer (D) v. State (P)

501 U.S. 808 (1991).

NATURE OF CASE: Review of death sentence imposed for first-degree murder.

FACT SUMMARY: Payne (D), convicted of first-degree murder, contended that the prosecution (P) had improperly presented testimony of the emotional impact of Payne's (D) crime on the victim's family.

RULE OF LAW
Victim impact evidence may constitutionally be offered during the sentencing phase of a capital murder trial.

FACTS: Payne (D) went on a rampage in the apartment of a neighbor. He stabbed a woman 84 times and inflicted multiple stab wounds on her two children. The woman and her daughter died, but her son survived. Payne (D) was charged with murder and assault and was convicted on all counts. During the sentencing phase of the trial, the prosecution offered evidence of the consequences of the attack on the surviving son, as testified to by the victim's mother. The jury returned a sentence of death. The sentence was affirmed on appeal, and the United States Supreme Court granted review to reconsider its prior holding that the Eighth Amendment prohibited a jury from considering victim impact evidence.

ISSUE: May victim impact evidence, be offered during the sentencing phase of a capital murder trial?

HOLDING AND DECISION: (Rehnquist, C.J.) Yes. Victim impact evidence may constitutionally be offered during the sentencing phase of a capital murder trial. Prior decisions of this Court have held to the contrary. These decisions were based on the notion that the only relevant issue at sentencing is the defendant's blameworthiness, and victim impact evidence is not probative of this issue. The Court now rejects this analysis. To arrive at a conclusion regarding a victim's blameworthiness, a jury should know what harm he has caused. Since a defendant is entitled to introduce mitigating evidence, the state has an equal right to introduce aggravating evidence of the effect of a murder on the victim's family. For these reasons, victim impact evidence is not barred by the Eighth Amendment. Affirmed.

CONCURRENCE: (Souter, J.) A murderer should realize that there will be consequences to persons beyond his immediate victim. It is not unfair that evidence regarding these indirect victims be admitted.

DISSENT: (Marshall, J.) The present decision is a violation of stare decisis occasioned by nothing more than Court personnel changes.

DISSENT: (Stevens, J.) Evidence that has no purpose other than to appeal to jurors' emotions has no place in so crucial a proceeding as a capital sentencing hearing.

ANALYSIS

Justice Marshall was essentially correct in his observations regarding the reason for its change of position. Only two years before, the Court had, by a five-to-four majority, rejected the rule adopted here. In 1991, with liberal William Brennan gone, the Court reversed itself using this case. It should be noted that, as a general rule, the Court is considered to have more leeway in changing constitutional law than statutory construction.

Quicknotes

CAPITAL PUNISHMENT Punishment by death.

CRUEL AND UNUSUAL PUNISHMENT Punishment that is excessive or disproportionate to the offense committed and which is prohibited by the Eighth Amendment to the United States Constitution.

FIRST-DEGREE MURDER The willful killing of another person with deliberation and premeditation; first-degree murder also encompasses those situations in which a person is killed within the perpetration of, or attempt to perpetrate, specified felonies.

Tison v. Arizona

Jailbreak brothers (D) v. State (P)

481 U.S. 137 (1987).

NATURE OF CASE: Review of death sentence imposed subsequent to conviction under the felony-murder rule.

FACT SUMMARY: Ricky and Raymond Tison (D), charged with felony murder after they orchestrated a jailbreak to free their father that resulted in four homicides, contended that the imposition of the death penalty was unconstitutional since they had not actually taken a life themselves.

RULE OF LAW
The death penalty may be imposed upon a felony-murder defendant whose acts constituted reckless disregard for life.

FACTS: Raymond Tison (D) and Ricky Tison (D) participated in the violent jailbreak of their father, Gary. After smuggling a cache of guns into the prison, Raymond (D), Ricky (D), and several others shot their way out and fled by automobile. Their getaway car broke down. Several members of the gang then flagged down a vehicle and killed the occupants. Neither Raymond (D) nor Ricky (D) participated in the murders. After a shootout with police, Raymond (D) and Ricky (D) were apprehended. They were charged and convicted of felony murder and sentenced to die. The Arizona Supreme Court affirmed. The United States Supreme Court granted review.

ISSUE: May the death penalty, be imposed upon a felony-murder defendant whose acts constituted reckless disregard for life?

HOLDING AND DECISION: (O'Connor, J.) Yes. The death penalty may be imposed upon a felony-murder defendant whose acts constituted reckless disregard for life. The Eighth Amendment requires some proportionality between a crime and a sentence. The Tisons (D) argue that the death penalty is commensurate only with intent to kill and, therefore, cannot be imposed in a felony-murder rule. This is incorrect. Reckless indifference to human life can be just as threatening and blameworthy as intent to kill. The present case is an excellent example. The Tisons (D) purposefully entered into a situation where a death was not only possible but quite likely. The level of their blameworthiness is not materially less than that of a defendant who intends to kill, so the imposition of the death penalty was permissible. Affirmed.

DISSENT: (Brennan, J.) The felony-murder rule is an anachronism from a time when all felonies carried a death sentence; it is no longer legally acceptable.

▶ ANALYSIS

The Eighth Amendment has put some limitations on the felony-murder rule. In *Enmund v. Florida*, 458 U.S. 782 (1982), a defendant whose role in a robbery resulting in death was tangential (he drove the getaway car) was sentenced to death for felony murder. The United States Supreme Court reversed, holding the penalty disproportionate to the crime.

■==■

Quicknotes

FELONY MURDER The unlawful killing of another human being while in the commission of, or attempted commission of, specified felonies.

MALICE The intention to commit an unlawful act without justification or excuse.

RECKLESSNESS The conscious disregard of substantial and justifiable risk.

■==■

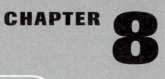
Quick Reference Rules of Law

State v. Alston

State (P) v. Rapist (D)

N.C. Sup. Ct., 310 N.C. 399, 312 S.E.2d 470 (1984).

NATURE OF CASE: Appeal from rape conviction.

FACT SUMMARY: Alston (D) contended that his rape conviction had been improper because the prosecution (P) had not proven that he used force against his ex-girlfriend.

🏛 RULE OF LAW
Use of actual or constructive force to procure victim compliance is an element of rape.

FACTS: Alston (D) had had a consensual sexual relationship with Brown for about six months. The relationship had been punctuated several times by violence and episodes of Brown leaving and later being coaxed into returning. After Alston (D) struck her, Brown at one point left again intending not to return. Alston (D) later showed up at the school Brown was attending. He grabbed her arm and forced her to walk with him. They talked about the relationship, with Brown telling Alston (D) that she wished to terminate the arrangement. Alston (D) then said he had a "right" to have sex with her one more time. Eventually they came to the house of a friend of Alston (D). Alston (D) and the friend talked for a while, but Brown did not try to leave. Alston (D) asked Brown for sex. She said "no," but Alston (D) pulled her out of her chair. He told her to lie down on the bed, which she did. Alston (D) undressed her and then had intercourse with her. This was not the first time they had had sex in this manner. Brown filed a criminal complaint later that day. Alston (D) was convicted of rape and appealed.

ISSUE: Is use of actual or constructive force to procure victim compliance an element of rape?

HOLDING AND DECISION: (Mitchell, J.) Yes. Use of actual or constructive force to procure victim compliance is an element of rape. If the act of intercourse is both by force and against the victim's will, the offense is rape, regardless of whether the victim has consented to prior acts of intercourse with the defendant. However, when the victim and alleged offender have had a history of consensual sexual relations, proof of the victim's state of mind is quite problematic. To establish a lack of consent by proof beyond a reasonable doubt, it must be proven that the victim clearly communicated a lack of consent to the perpetrator, who then used force to overcome her. Such proof was not adduced here. Although Brown's general fear of Alston (D) may have been justified by his prior conduct, Alston's (D) behavior was not so threatening on the day in question that it can be said to have clearly overcome Brown's will. For these reasons, the case should not have gone to the jury. Reversed.

▶ ANALYSIS

Abusive relationships have become a hot political topic in the mid-1990s. Interest in the issue began fomenting around the time of the Anita Hill—Clarence Thomas hearings (although that did not deal with relationships per se) and really came to the forefront in the wake of the *O.J. Simpson* case [*State of California v. O.J. Simpson*, (1995)]. It would seem fair to call the present case a "close call" in terms of reversibility. It seems unlikely the case would have been decided the same had it come down ten years later.

Quicknotes

CONSENT A voluntary and willful agreement by an individual possessing sufficient mental capacity to undertake an action suggested by another.

RAPE Unlawful sexual intercourse with a woman by a man by means of fear or force and without her consent.

Rusk v. State

Rapist (D) v. State (P)

Md. Ct. Spec. App., 43 Md. App. 476, 406 A.2d 624 (1979).

NATURE OF CASE: Appeal from rape conviction.

FACT SUMMARY: A woman pressed rape charges against Rusk (D), contending that, although she did not resist him, she feared for her safety if she did not consent to sex with him.

🏛 RULE OF LAW
To commit rape, a perpetrator must obtain the victim's compliance by force or threats.

FACTS: Rusk (D) met a woman at a bar. He asked for a ride home, which she gave him. When they got to his residence, he asked her to come upstairs. She refused. He then took her car keys and repeated the request. Because she was afraid, she went with him. In his apartment, he asked for sex and began touching her and removing her blouse. After at first refusing, she complied after Rusk (D) lightly choked her, then said he'd let her go if she gave him sex. Rusk (D) was charged and convicted of rape and assault. He appealed the rape conviction.

ISSUE: To commit rape, must a perpetrator obtain the victim's compliance by force or threats?

HOLDING AND DECISION: (Thompson, J.) Yes. To commit rape, a perpetrator must obtain the victim's compliance by force or threats. Force is an element of rape. Force requires evidence that the victim resisted and that such resistance was overcome by force or threats. A subjective fear by the victim, unaccompanied by physical force or specific threats by the perpetrator, does not support a rape conviction. Here, no evidence of physical force or threats by Rusk (D) sufficient to cause reasonable fear in the victim was adduced, so a rape conviction was improper. Reversed.

DISSENT: (Wilner, J.) The majority confuses the concepts of force and lack of consent, but these are separate and distinct elements and should not be treated as one. Consent is not the issue here, only whether there was sufficient evidence of force or the threat of force. The majority erroneously believes that if the victim fails to offer sufficient resistance it can find that there was no force or threat of it. The focus is not on the assailant's act but that of the victim's. It is not on the wrongful stimulus, but the victim's reaction to it. This raises the question of how much resistance the victim must offer and where the line is to be drawn between requiring that she either risk serious physical harm, maybe even death, or be termed a willing, consenting partner. Most victims do not resist because they are much more likely to be injured if they do. The jury and trial court found that the victim's fear was reasonable and that Rusk (D) used force or a threat of it. By concluding that her fear was not reasonable, or that there was no fear at all, the majority here has invaded the province of judge and jury.

▶ ANALYSIS

It is has been shown, based on statistical studies, that rape victims who resist are more likely to suffer death or serious bodily injury than those who do not. The view taken by the court here puts a rape victim in the position of having to take life-threatening steps to later prevail in a prosecution. It should be noted that the Maryland Supreme Court later reversed this decision in *State v. Rusk,* 424 A.2d 720 (1981), concluding that the reasonableness of the victim's apprehension of fear was a jury question.

■■■

Quicknotes

CONSENT A voluntary and willful agreement by an individual possessing sufficient mental capacity to undertake an action suggested by another.

RAPE Unlawful sexual intercourse with a woman by a man by means of fear or force and without her consent.

■■■

State v. Rusk

State (P) v. Alleged rapist (D)

Md. Ct. App., 289 Md. 230, 424 A.2d 720 (1981).

NATURE OF CASE: Appeal from reversal of rape conviction.

FACT SUMMARY: The Court of Special Appeals overturned Rusk's (D) rape conviction because it found the victim's fear was unreasonable.

⚖ RULE OF LAW
The reasonableness of a victim's apprehension of fear is a question of fact for the jury to determine.

FACTS: Pat agreed to drive Rusk (D) home after meeting him in a bar. When they got to his neighborhood, part of the city with which Pat was not familiar, Rusk (D) took her car keys and demanded that she accompany him to his apartment, implying she would be stranded if she refused. Once in his apartment, she begged him to let her go. After he choked her lightly, she had intercourse with him. The jury found Rusk (D) guilty of rape and assault. However, the appellate court overturned the rape conviction, having concluded that there was not enough evidence for the jury to find that Pat's fear of harm was reasonable. The State (P) appealed.

ISSUE: Is the reasonableness of a victim's apprehension of fear a question of fact for the jury to determine?

HOLDING AND DECISION: (Murphy, C.J.) Yes. The reasonableness of a victim's apprehension of fear is a question of fact for the jury to determine. Reversed and remanded.

DISSENT: (Cole, J.) To constitute coercion sufficient to vitiate consent, a woman's apprehension of fear must be generated by something of substance. A mere "I was really scared" does not constitute evidence of coercion.

▶ ANALYSIS

In reinstating Rusk's (D) rape conviction, the majority in the above case adopted the dissenting opinion in *Rusk v. State*, 406 A.2d 624 (1979). In that dissent, Judge Wilner severely criticized the majority for not only invading the jury's province but also for giving new life to myths about rape. He cited a Battelle Study which found that, contrary to the majority's expectations, the most common type of resistance by victims was verbal and that rape victims who resisted were more likely to be injured than those who did not.

Quicknotes

CONSENT A voluntary and willful agreement by an individual possessing sufficient mental capacity to undertake an action suggested by another.

RAPE Unlawful sexual intercourse with a woman by a man by means of fear or force and without her consent.

Commonwealth v. Berkowitz

State (P) v. Rapist (D)

Pa. Super. Ct., 415 Pa. Super. 505, 609 A.2d 1338 (1992).

NATURE OF CASE: Appeal from a rape conviction.

FACT SUMMARY: Berkowitz (D) was alleged to have raped a fellow student when she visited his college dormitory.

🏛 RULE OF LAW
Whether there is sufficient evidence to demonstrate that an accused engaged in sexual intercourse by forcible compulsion is a determination that will be made in each case based on the totality of the circumstances.

FACTS: When a fellow student was looking for her boyfriend at a dorm on campus, Berkowitz (D) was alleged to have raped her. The victim claimed that throughout the encounter, she repeatedly said, "no." Berkowitz (D) claimed that the sex was consensual. After hearing the accounts of both students, the jury convicted Berkowitz (D) of rape and indecent assault and he was sentenced to a term of imprisonment of one to four years. Berkowitz (D) appealed, asking the court to define the parameters between what may have been unacceptable social conduct and the criminal conduct necessary to support the charge for forcible rape.

ISSUE: Is a determination to be made in each case based on the totality of the circumstances on whether there is sufficient evidence to demonstrate that an accused engaged in sexual intercourse by forcible compulsion?

HOLDING AND DECISION: (Per curiam) Yes. Whether there is sufficient evidence to demonstrate that an accused engaged in sexual intercourse by forcible compulsion is a determination that will be made in each case based on the totality of the circumstances. In Pennsylvania, a person commits a felony of the first degree when he engages in a sexual intercourse with another person not his spouse by forcible compulsion or by threat of forcible compulsion that would prevent resistance by a person of real resolution. Upon review, the facts show no more than what legal scholars refer to as "reluctant submission." The complainant herself admits that she was neither hurt nor threatened at any time during the encounter. She admits she never screamed or attempted to summon help. The uncontroverted evidence fails to establish forcible compulsion. Reversed and remanded.

▸ ANALYSIS

The court in this case determined that there was no evidence that the victim, if she had wanted to do so, could not have removed herself from Berkowitz's (D) bed and walked out of the room without any risk of harm or danger to herself whatsoever. These circumstances could not be bootstrapped into sexual intercourse by forcible compulsion, according to the court. Since rape is based on a finding of "forcible compulsion" and was not defined simply as nonconsensual intercourse, the lower court was found to have erred in adducing that verbal resistance, without more, was sufficient for a rape conviction.

■══■

Quicknotes

COMPULSION Imminent threat of great bodily harm or death by one party so as to induce the other to commit a criminal offense.

RAPE Unlawful sexual intercourse with a woman by a man by means of fear or force and without her consent.

■══■

State of New Jersey in the Interest of M.T.S.

State (P) v. Juvenile (D)

N.J. Sup. Ct., 129 N.J. 422, 609 A.2d 1266 (1992).

NATURE OF CASE: Appeal from reversal of finding of juvenile delinquency.

FACT SUMMARY: M.T.S. (D) contended that, because he had not used force to have nonconsensual intercourse with a 15-year-old, he could not be guilty of sexual assault.

RULE OF LAW

Force necessary to constitute sexual assault need not use more force than that necessary to perform the sex act.

FACTS: The State of New Jersey (P) instituted a delinquency action against M.T.S. (D), a juvenile, arising out of an alleged sexual assault. According to the alleged victim, he had penetrated her vagina while she was asleep. According to M.T.S. (D), the two had been petting heavily, whereupon he penetrated her without first asking. The trial court held that sexual assault had occurred and made a finding of delinquency. The appellate division reversed. The New Jersey Supreme Court granted review.

ISSUE: Must the force necessary to constitute a sexual assault involve more force than that necessary to perform the sex act?

HOLDING AND DECISION: (Handler, J.) No. Force necessary to constitute sexual assault need not involve more force than that necessary to perform the sex act. New Jersey statutory law defines "sexual assault" as "sexual penetration" with another person with the use of "physical force or coercion." The statute itself provides no help with respect to the issue of whether "physical force" requires more than the force used to complete the act, and reference to the dictionary likewise does not clear up the issue. However, a look at the legislative history does provide some insight. Prior to 1979 revisions, resistance by the victim was considered indispensable to proving force. Changes in 1979 were designed to shift the focus away from the victim's behavior and to emphasize consent. Any penetration, absent consent, was to be considered rape. To impose a rule that "physical force" involves force beyond that needed for penetration would run counter to legislative purposes. The appellate division was therefore incorrect in holding that penetration alone was insufficient force to constitute rape. Reversed.

▶ ANALYSIS

Traditionally, a rape conviction required a high level of resistance by the victim. Circumstances such as delays in reporting the situation and a lack of physical bruising were tantamount to consent in most situations. Reforms such as these enacted in New Jersey reflected changing public perceptions of the nature of rape.

■═■

Quicknotes

ASSAULT The intentional placing of another in fear of immediate bodily injury.

RAPE Unlawful sexual intercourse with a woman by a man by means of fear or force and without her consent.

SEXUAL HARASSMENT An employment practice subjecting persons to oppressive conduct on account of their gender.

■═■

Commonwealth v. Sherry

State (P) v. Convicted rapist (P)

Mass. Sup. Jud. Ct., 386 Mass. 682, 437 N.E.2d 224 (1982).

NATURE OF CASE: Appeal of rape conviction.

FACT SUMMARY: Sherry (D), charged with rape, argued that he had believed the victim to have consented to intercourse.

> ## 🏛 RULE OF LAW
> A subjective belief that the victim has consented is no defense to a rape charge.

FACTS: Sherry (D) and two male companions left a party with a woman. Whether she left voluntarily or was coerced was unclear. When the four arrived at the home of one of the men, they smoked marijuana and conversed for a while. Eventually the woman had intercourse with the three men, sequentially. The woman pressed charges, and the three were charged with rape. Sherry (D) and the other two defendants claimed that the woman had consented. The court refused to offer an instruction permitting a subjective belief in consent to be a defense. Sherry (D) et al. were convicted and appealed.

ISSUE: Is a subjective belief that the victim has consented, a defense to a rape charge?

HOLDING AND DECISION: (Liacos, J.) No. A subjective belief that the victim has consented is not a defense to a rape charge. It has never been held that the subjective mindset of an alleged perpetrator was crucial in passing upon consent; the prosecution would have a serious burden of proof were this so. Rather, it is proper for the jury to consider the entire sequence of events from an objective perspective. Here, the instruction the court gave did in fact create an objective standard, and this was proper. Affirmed.

▶ ANALYSIS

There is no uniform rule on this issue among the jurisdictions. A fully subjective approach is found in few, if any, jurisdictions. Some permit a good-faith-belief-in-consent defense, but those that do require the good-faith belief to be reasonable.

Quicknotes

OBJECTIVE STANDARD A standard that is not personal to an individual but is dependent on some external source.

RAPE Unlawful sexual intercourse with a woman by a man by means of fear or force and without her consent.

SUBJECTIVE BELIEF A belief that is personal to an individual.

Boro v. Superior Court

Fraudulent persuader (D) v. State (P)

Cal. Ct. App., 163 Cal. App. 3d 1224 (1985).

NATURE OF CASE: Motion to dismiss rape charge.

FACT SUMMARY: Boro (D) convinced Ms. R. that she would die unless she had sexual intercourse with him to cure her of a fatal disease.

🏛 RULE OF LAW
Intercourse induced by fraud does not constitute rape.

FACTS: Ms. R. received a call from "Dr. Stevens." "Dr. Stevens" told her that she had contracted a deadly disease and that the only way to cure it other than an expensive surgical procedure was to have intercourse with a person who had been injected with a serum that would cure the disease. Boro (D), who had been masquerading as Dr. Stevens, of course turned out to be the person with whom Ms. R. had intercourse. Boro (D) was later charged with a § 261 rape, where the victim is not conscious of the nature of the act. He moved to dismiss the charges. The trial court denied the motion. Boro (D) appealed.

ISSUE: Does intercourse induced by fraud constitute rape?

HOLDING AND DECISION: (Newsom, J.) No. Intercourse induced by fraud does not constitute rape. Fraud that induces a lack of understanding of an act (fraud in the factum) does vitiate consent. However, fraud that does not induce such a lack of understanding of the nature of an act does not vitiate consent. In the situation here, Ms. R. knew the nature of the act she was committing; fraud was in the inducement and related not to the act itself but to some collateral matter. Consequently, her consent, although fraudulently induced, was consent nonetheless. Boro's (D) act, though reprehensible, was not rape pursuant to § 261. Writ issued.

▶ ANALYSIS

An example of fraud in the factum may be found in *People v. Minkowski*, 204 Cal. App. 2d 832 (1962). There, a doctor purported to treat several women for menstrual cramps by inserting an object into their vaginas from the rear. The "object" turned out to be his penis. Since the fraud went to what the women thought they were experiencing, consent was held not to be present.

∎▬∎

Quicknotes

FRAUD IN THE FACTUM Occurs, when a testator is induced to execute a testamentary instrument as a result of a misrepresentation as to the nature of the document or its provisions.

RAPE Unlawful sexual intercourse with a woman by a man by means of fear or force and without her consent.

∎▬∎

State v. Herndon

State (P) v. Rapist (D)

Wis. Ct. App., 145 Wis. 2d 91, 426 N.W.2d 347 (1988).

NATURE OF CASE: Appeal from rape conviction.

FACT SUMMARY: [Fact summary not stated in casebook excerpt.]

 RULE OF LAW
Sixth Amendment rights usually must give way to rape shield laws.

FACTS: [Facts not stated in casebook excerpt.]

ISSUE: Must Sixth Amendment rights usually give way to rape shield laws?

HOLDING AND DECISION: (Moser, J.) Yes. Sixth Amendment rights usually must give way to rape shield laws. Because the probativeness of the evidence is so miniscule when weighed against the potential prejudice to the complaining witness that the receipt of such evidence may engender to the fact finders, the Sixth Amendment rights usually must bend to protect the innocent victims. A victim will more readily report and testify in sexual assault cases if she does not fear that her prior sexual conduct will be brought before the public. Sometimes, however, if the issues of a witness's bias and credibility are not collateral, the rape shield laws must give way to the defendant's Sixth Amendment rights.

▶ ANALYSIS

Rape shield laws have been enacted by every state. Such laws generally deny a defendant in a sexual assault case the opportunity to examine the complainant concerning her prior sexual conduct with third parties or reputation for sexual conduct. They also usually deny the defendant an opportunity to offer extrinsic evidence of the prior sexual conduct or reputation of the complainant.

■═■

Quicknotes

RAPE SHIELD LAW Law conferring a privilege on rape victims against harassing examination at trial regarding past sexual conduct.

SIXTH AMENDMENT Provides the right to a speedy and public trial by impartial jury, the right to be informed of the accusation, the right to confront witnesses, and the right to have the assistance of counsel in all criminal prosecutions.

■═■

People v. Wilhelm

State (P) v. Person convicted of criminal sexual conduct (D)

Mich. Ct. App., 190 Mich. App. 574, 476 N.W.2d 753 (1991).

NATURE OF CASE: Appeal from conviction for criminal sexual conduct.

FACT SUMMARY: Wilhelm (D) argued that he was wrongfully precluded from introducing evidence of the victim's sexual conduct with another.

> ## 🏛 RULE OF LAW
> A rape shield statute may properly prohibit evidence of the victim's sexual conduct with another.

FACTS: Wilhelm (D) and the victim were in a bar but were not together. At his trial for criminal sexual conduct, Wilhelm (D) claimed he had earlier observed the victim lift her shirt and expose her breasts to two men who were sitting at her table. He also alleged that the victim allowed one of the two men to "fondle" her breasts. The trial court disallowed such evidence on grounds that the state's rape shield law prohibited evidence of the victim's sexual conduct with another. Wilhelm (D) was found guilty and appealed on the grounds the rape shield law violated his Sixth Amendment rights.

ISSUE: May a rape shield law properly prohibit evidence of the victim's sexual conduct with another?

HOLDING AND DECISION: (Per curiam) Yes. A rape shield law may properly prohibit evidence of the victim's sexual conduct with another. Here, the public nature of the victim's activities did not remove her from the protection of the statute. One of the purposes of the law is to encourage victims to report and testify without fear that the trial court's proceedings would veer from an impartial examination of the accused's conduct on the date in question and instead take on the aspects of an inquisition during which the victim would be required to acknowledge and justify her sexual past. Moreover, this court fails to see how a woman's consensual conduct with another in public indicates to third parties that the woman would engage in similar behavior with them. Affirmed.

▶ ANALYSIS

In *Wilhelm*, the court explained that preclusion of the prohibited evidence under a rape shield law does not deprive the defendant of the constitutional right of confrontation since evidence of a victim's sexual conduct with a third party is irrelevant to the issue whether she consented to sexual intercourse with the defendant.

Quicknotes

RAPE SHIELD LAW Law conferring a privilege on rape victims against harassing examination at trial regarding past sexual conduct.

SIXTH AMENDMENT Provides the right to a speedy and public trial by impartial jury, the right to be informed of the accusation, the right to confront witnesses, and the right to have the assistance of counsel in all criminal prosecutions.

■■■

General Defenses to Crimes

Quick Reference Rules of Law

Patterson v. New York

Murder defendant (D) v. State (P)

432 U.S. 197 (1977).

NATURE OF CASE: Review of second-degree murder conviction.

FACT SUMMARY: Patterson (D) contended that he should not be burdened with proving the affirmative defense of extreme emotional disturbance in order to reduce murder to manslaughter.

🏛 RULE OF LAW
A state may constitutionally impose upon a murder defendant the burden of proving the affirmative defense of extreme emotional disturbance.

FACTS: Patterson (D) shot and killed a man he found with his estranged wife. At trial, he raised the affirmative defense of extreme emotional disturbance, seeking a lesser conviction of manslaughter. A jury convicted him of murder. Patterson (D) appealed, contending that the State (P) could not constitutionally place upon him the burden of proving emotional disturbance. The conviction was affirmed, and the United States Supreme Court granted review.

ISSUE: May a state constitutionally impose upon a murder defendant the burden of proving an affirmative defense?

HOLDING AND DECISION: (White, J.) Yes. A state may constitutionally impose upon a murder defendant the burden of proving the affirmative defense of extreme emotional disturbance. Due process requires that the state prove every element of a crime beyond a reasonable doubt. It requires no more with respect to proof. When a state creates an affirmative defense to a crime, where proof of the defense is not tantamount to disproving an element of the crime, the state may place the burden of persuasion on the defendant. Here, emotional disturbance, or the lack thereof, was not an element of murder. Therefore, the State (P) could constitutionally impose upon Patterson (D) the burden of proving it. Affirmed.

DISSENT: (Powell, J.) The majority has established a test that allows a legislature to shift the burden of proof on an element of a crime merely by redrafting the penal statute, renaming what once was an element as an affirmative defense.

▶ ANALYSIS

The Court, without so holding, essentially overruled *Mullaney v. Wilbur*, 421 U.S. 684 (1975), which involved a similar allocation of proof. The statute there was worded somewhat differently, but the result was the same. While *Mullaney* was not overruled, it would appear to have little vitality left.

■=■

Quicknotes

AFFIRMATIVE DEFENSE A manner of defending oneself against a claim not by denying the truth of the charge but by the introduction of some evidence challenging the plaintiff's right to bring the claim.

BURDEN OF PROOF The duty of a party to introduce evidence to support a fact that is in dispute in an action.

■=■

United States v. Peterson

Federal government (P) v. Property owner (D)

483 F.2d 1222 (D.C. Cir. 1973).

NATURE OF CASE: Appeal from manslaughter conviction.

FACT SUMMARY: Peterson (D) contended that self-defense had justified his use of lethal force when he shot Keitt after inciting Keitt to an encounter.

RULE OF LAW
Self-defense is not an excuse for homicide if the person claiming it created the situation necessitating it.

FACTS: Keitt came onto Peterson's (D) property and attempted to steal the windshield wipers from Peterson's (D) wrecked auto. Peterson (D) shouted at him and ran into his house to get a pistol. Keitt began to drive away. After Peterson returned, Keitt alighted from his car, grabbed a lug wrench, and began advancing on Peterson (D). Peterson (D) shot and killed him. Peterson (D) was charged with murder and claimed self-defense. At trial, the court instructed the jury that one creating a deadly situation could not invoke self-defense. Peterson (D) was convicted. He appealed, contending that the instruction constituted reversible error.

ISSUE: Is self-defense an excuse for homicide if the person claiming it created the situation necessitating it?

HOLDING AND DECISION: (Robinson, J.) No. Self-defense is not an excuse for homicide if the person claiming it created the situation necessitating it. The unifying element running through the various situations where homicide is excused is necessity: the use of deadly force was necessary under the circumstances. When the person claiming self-defense created the situation calling for it, however, this element breaks down: necessity occasioned by one's own actions is not necessity in any real sense. Here, it is true that Keitt was trespassing on Peterson's (D) property. However, the situation grew into a lethal confrontation only when Peterson (D), who had been in no physical peril, went to get his gun. From this, a jury could have found the need by Peterson (D) to use deadly force to have been self-generated and therefore no defense to murder. Peterson (D) may not invoke the "castle" doctrine, wherein one who through no fault of his own is attacked in his home is under no duty to retreat. Affirmed.

▶ ANALYSIS

As a matter of common law and majority doctrine in the United States, defense of property alone is never a justification for deadly force. A small number of states have changed this by statute but usually only in very specific situations, such as defense of a home. Nor can deadly force be employed to arrest or prevent the escape of a misdemeanor.

Quicknotes

DEADLY FORCE That degree of force which is likely to result in death or great bodily injury.

MISDEMEANOR Any offense that does not constitute a felony, which is generally less severe and for which a lesser punishment is imposed.

SELF-DEFENSE The right to protect an individual's person, family or property against attempted injury by another.

People v. Goetz

State (P) v. Subway rider (D)

N.Y. Ct. App., 68 N.Y.2d 96, 497 N.E.2d 41 (1986).

NATURE OF CASE: Appeal from dismissal of attempted murder charges.

FACT SUMMARY: Goetz (D) contended that he was justified in shooting his assailants if he alone reasonably believed he was in danger, and not if a reasonable man believed so.

🏛 **RULE OF LAW**
A person is justified in the use of deadly force if, objectively, a reasonable man would, in his position, believe he was in danger of life or physical being.

FACTS: Goetz (D) was approached on a subway by several youths who asked him for money. Goetz (D), who had been attacked years before, subjectively believed he was being robbed and pulled a gun. He shot at the youths several times, even though they ran away. In one case, Goetz (D) approached an unarmed youth and shot him. Goetz (D) admitted he wanted to kill the youths. The prosecution instructed the Grand Jury that self-defense could be found only if Goetz (D) objectively, as a reasonable man, could have concluded his life was in danger. Indictments were handed down, yet the trial court dismissed them because it held the prosecution erroneously instructed that an objective rather than a subjective standard applied. The State (P) appealed.

ISSUE: Does an objective test apply to the determination of the availability of self-defense?

HOLDING AND DECISION: (Wachtler, C.J.) Yes. A person is justified in the use of self-defense by deadly force if, objectively, a reasonable man would believe he was in danger of life. Subjective basis for the use of such force cannot be the standard a civilized society uses. It is too easy to fabricate a justification for the use of force. The situation must objectively require the use of such force, and the factors must be identifiable by the trier of fact. Reversed and dismissed counts of the indictment should be reinstated.

▌ *ANALYSIS*

A common thread that runs through the defense of self-defense and the defense of insanity is the objective test. As seen above in *Goetz*, an objective reasonable person test was applied to determine whether the defendant was justified in taking the action he did to protect his own life. In insanity defense cases, the preferred approach is similar. If objectively viewed, the defendant cannot appreciate the illegality of his conduct, then the insanity defense, can be assessed.

■■■

Quicknotes

DEADLY FORCE That degree of force which is likely to result in death or great bodily injury.

INSANITY DEFENSE An affirmative defense to a criminal prosecution that the defendant suffered from a mental illness, thereby relieving him of liability for his conduct.

SELF-DEFENSE The right to protect an individual's person, family or property against attempted injury by another.

■■■

State v. Wanrow

State (P) v. Convicted murderer (D)

Wash. Sup. Ct., 88 Wash. 2d 221, 559 P.2d 548 (1977).

NATURE OF CASE: Appeal from reversal of a second-degree murder conviction.

FACT SUMMARY: A reversal of Wanrow's (D) second-degree murder conviction had been obtained on the grounds that the jury instructions regarding the law of self-defense were improper.

🏛 RULE OF LAW
In determining if a defendant engaged in what is legally permissible self-defense, his or her actions are to be judged against his or her own subjective impressions, and not those which a detached jury might determine to be objectively reasonable.

FACTS: Yvonne Wanrow (D) was convicted of second-degree murder, although she claimed to have acted in self-defense when she killed the man she suspected had molested her daughter and other neighborhood children. The evidence indicated that her friend, Chuck Michel, had gone to talk to the victim and that they went to the house in which Mrs. Wanrow (D) was staying to supposedly try to straighten out the situation; that he entered the house alone, and that he declined to leave when Mrs. Wanrow (D) asked him to upon seeing him. At the time, Mrs. Wanrow (D), who was 5'4" tall and used a crutch because of a broken leg, testified that she went to the door and shouted for Chuck Michel's aid. She then turned around to find the suspected molester directly behind her. Whereupon, Mrs. Wanrow (D) testified, she became gravely startled and shot him in a reflex action. In reversing her conviction for second-degree murder, the court of appeals held that the jury instructions regarding self-defense had been improper. First of all, they instructed the jury to consider only those acts and circumstances occurring at or immediately before the killing in deciding whether Mrs. Wanrow (D) had been under the apprehension of death or serious bodily harm when she fired the fatal shot. This meant the jury could not consider Mrs. Wanrow's (D) knowledge of the victim's reputation for aggressive acts based upon events that had occurred over a period of years. The jury instructions also continuously used the masculine gender in setting up an objective standard for determining if the defendant had acted in self-defense.

ISSUE: When the issue of self-defense is raised, are a defendant's actions to be judged against his or her own subjective impressions?

HOLDING AND DECISION: (Utter, J.) Yes. When, as in this case, self-defense is raised as an issue, the defendant's actions are to be judged against his or her own subjective impressions and not those which a detached jury might determine to be objectively reasonable. The vital question is the reasonableness of the defendant's apprehension of danger, but only in the sense that the jury must stand, as nearly as practicable, in the shoes of the defendant; and from this point of view, determine if the act was the result of the defendant's reasonable apprehension of death or serious bodily harm. It is thus apparent that the jury should have considered Mrs. Wanrow's (D) knowledge of the victim's prior reputation for aggressive acts and not just those circumstances "at or immediately before the killing." Under the law of this state, the jury should have been allowed to consider this information in making the critical determination of the "degree of force which ... a reasonable person in the same situation ... seeing what (s)he sees and knowing what (s)he knows then would believe to be necessary." Another fatal flaw in the instructions is that they did not make clear that the defendant's actions are to be judged against her own subjective impressions and not those which a detached jury might determine to be objectively reasonable. A defendant's conduct is to be judged by the condition appearing to her at the time, not by the condition as it might appear to the jury in light of testimony before it. The instructions clearly misstated our law in creating an objective standard of "reasonableness." They then compounded that error by utilizing the masculine gender and thus suggesting that the defendant's conduct should be measured against that of a reasonable male individual finding himself in the same circumstances. Furthermore, the impression created—that a 5'4" woman with a cast on her leg and using a crutch must, under the law, somehow repel an assault by a 6'2" intoxicated man without employing weapons in her defense, unless the jury finds her determination of the degree of danger to be objectively reasonable—constituted a separate and distinct misstatement of the law. The defendant was entitled to have the jury consider her actions in the light of her own perceptions of the situation, including those perceptions which were the product of our nation's "long and unfortunate history of sex discrimination." Until such time as the effects of that history are eradicated, care must be taken to assure that our self-defense instructions afford women the right to have their conduct judged in the light of the individual physical handicaps which are the product of sex discrimination. Reversed and remanded.

▶ ANALYSIS

In many states where the objective reasonableness of the defendant's apprehension and response must still be

Continued on next page.

shown when self-defense is claimed, the ultimate question becomes what to do with those people whose apprehension and response was honest but not objectively reasonable. Many jurisdictions have solved this dilemma by making such parties guilty of the crime of "voluntary manslaughter" instead of murder.

■══■

Quicknotes

SECOND-DEGREE MURDER The unlawful killing of another person, without premeditation, and characterized by either intent to kill or by a reckless disregard for human life.

SELF-DEFENSE The right to protect an individual's person, family or property against attempted injury by another.

VOLUNTARY MANSLAUGHTER The killing of another person without premeditation, deliberation or malice aforethought, but committed while in the "heat of passion" or upon some adequate provocation, thereby, reducing the charge from murder to manslaughter.

■══■

State v. Norman

State (P) v. Murdering-wife (D)

N.C. Ct. App., 89 N.C. App. 384, 366 S.E.2d 586 (1988).

NATURE OF CASE: Appeal from murder conviction.

FACT SUMMARY: Norman (D), charged with murdering her husband while he slept, raised a long-standing history of extremely violent abuse by her husband as a defense.

🏛 RULE OF LAW
Where there is evidence of battered-wife syndrome, neither an actual attack nor the threat of attack is required to justify the wife's killing of her husband in self-defense.

FACTS: Norman's (D) husband had had a long history of committing extremely violent abuse upon her. Over the years he had battered her with numerous blunt instruments, repeatedly threatened to kill her, and burnt her with cigarettes. He beat her on a daily basis. Several times Norman (D) had tried to leave, but the husband always found her and forced her to return, inflicting serious bodily harm. Finally, Norman (D) ended the matter by shooting her husband while he slept. She was charged with murder. At trial, she attempted to introduce evidence of "battered spouse syndrome" as a defense. The trial court rejected an instruction on the proffered defense. Norman (D) was convicted of manslaughter, and she appealed.

ISSUE: Where there is evidence of battered-wife syndrome, is an actual or threatened attack required to justify the wife's killing of her husband in self-defense?

HOLDING AND DECISION: (Parker, J.) No. Where there is evidence of battered-wife syndrome, an actual or threatened attack is not required to justify the wife's killing of her husband in self-defense. If a victim reasonably believes that it is necessary to kill in order to save herself from death or great bodily harm, she has raised a legitimate defense. Here, the record was replete with evidence that would have supported such a finding. That her husband was asleep when Norman (D) shot him does not preclude her from asserting self-defense. Consequently, the self-defense instruction should have been given. Reversed.

▌ ANALYSIS

The appellate court's ruling was overturned on appeal, and Norman (D) was convicted and sentenced to six years in prison, which was commuted almost immediately by the Governor. The battered spouse defense is an exception to the usual requirement that self-defense be in response to an imminent peril. Acceptance or rejection of the defense has tended to be based more on political views than legal analysis.

■══■

Quicknotes

MANSLAUGHTER The killing of another person without premeditation, deliberation or with the intent to kill or to commit a felony, which may be reasonably expected to result in death or serious bodily injury; manslaughter is characterized by reckless conduct or by some adequate provocation on the part of the actor, as determined by a subjective standard.

SELF-DEFENSE The right to protect an individual's person, family or property against attempted injury by another.

■══■

State v. Norman

State (P) v. Murdering-wife (D)

N.C. Sup. Ct., 324 N.C. 253, 378 S.E.2d 8 (1989).

NATURE OF CASE: Review of order granting new trial in homicide prosecution.

FACT SUMMARY: Norman (D), charged in the homicide of her sleeping husband, raised his habitual battery of her as a defense.

🏛 RULE OF LAW
Habitual spousal battery is not a defense to murder charges.

FACTS: Norman (D) was the victim of habitual battery by her husband, a situation of many years' duration. Norman (D) eventually shot him to death while he slept. She was charged with homicide. At trial, she sought to raise the habitual battery as a defense. The trial court rejected an instruction thereon, and Norman (D) was convicted. The court of appeals reversed, holding that the self-defense instruction should have been given. The State (P) petitioned for review.

ISSUE: Is habitual spousal battery a defense to murder charges?

HOLDING AND DECISION: (Mitchell, J.) No. Habitual spousal battery is not a defense to murder charges. An element of self-defense as a justification for homicide is imminence. One raising the defense must have been under a reasonable apprehension of imminent death or bodily injury. This requirement insures that deadly force will be used only as a means of last resort. The evidence in this case showed that no harm was "imminent" or about to happen to Norman (D) when she shot her husband. While the court is not unmindful of the plight of battered wives, it does not believe it to be good policy to permit them to take the law into their own hands based on subjective speculation regarding the probability of assaults in the future by their husbands. Reversed.

DISSENT: (Martin, J.) The proper analysis is whether the defendant had a basis for a belief that self-help was necessary to prevent probable grave harm in the future.

▶ ANALYSIS

The spousal-battery syndrome, as a defense, represents a major departure from established law regarding self-defense. As discussed by the court here, self-defense traditionally requires immediate peril. Battered-spouse syndrome and its cousin, the battered-child syndrome, almost by definition do not incorporate this element.

Quicknotes

MANSLAUGHTER The killing of another person without premeditation, deliberation or with the intent to kill or to commit a felony, which may be reasonably expected to result in death or serious bodily injury; manslaughter is characterized by reckless conduct or by some adequate provocation on the part of the actor, as determined by a subjective standard.

SELF-DEFENSE The right to protect an individual's person, family or property against attempted injury by another.

People v. Kurr

State (P) v. Manslaughter defendant (D)

Mich. Ct. App., 253 Mich. App. 317, 654 N.W.2d 651 (2002).

NATURE OF CASE: Appeal from a conviction for voluntary manslaughter.

FACT SUMMARY: When the trial court disallowed a jury instruction on "defense of others," Kurr (D), who argued that she killed her boyfriend to protect her unborn children, argued that she was deprived of her due process right to present a defense.

🏛 RULE OF LAW
A defense of others jury instruction is appropriate when a mother kills to defend her unborn child.

FACTS: Kurr (D), who was pregnant, stabbed and killed her boyfriend when the boyfriend punched her two times in the stomach after she warned him not to hit her because she was pregnant with his babies. She testified that when he came toward her a third time to attack, she stabbed and killed him. The trial court disallowed her requested jury instruction that her attempt to protect her unborn children gave rise to a "defense of others" theory of defense. Kurr (D) appealed.

ISSUE: Is a defense of others jury instruction appropriate when a mother kills to defend her unborn child?

HOLDING AND DECISION: (Meter, J.) Yes. A defense of others jury instruction is appropriate when a mother kills to defend her unborn child. Case law in Michigan allows a person to use deadly force in defense of another. This defense should also extend to the protection of a fetus, viable or nonviable, from an assault against the mother, based primarily upon the fetal protection legislation adopted by the Michigan legislature. This legislation punishes individuals who harm or kill fetuses and embryos under varying circumstances. The statute sets forth penalties for harming a fetus or embryo during an intentional assault against a pregnant woman or for causing a miscarriage or stillbirth even without malicious intent specifically toward the fetus or embryo. The plain language of these statutory provisions shows the legislature's conclusion that fetuses are worthy of protection as living entities as a matter of public policy. Indeed, one provision of the statute specifies a punishment of up to life imprisonment. This court emphasizes, however, that the defense is available solely in the context of an assault against the mother. Indeed, the legislature has not extended the protection of the criminal laws to embryos existing outside a woman's body, such as, for example, frozen embryos stored for future use. In the instant case, the failure to give a defense of others instruction deprived Kurr (D) of her due process right to present a defense. Reversed and remanded.

▶ ANALYSIS

Traditionally, the defense of others defense concept applied solely to those persons with whom the defendant had a special relationship, such as a wife or brother. However, the defense now makes no distinction between strangers and relatives with regard to its application. The *Kurr* court noted that since Michigan had not codified the defense of others theory in its criminal statutes, the court was therefore not bound by restrictive statutory definitions of the word "others." The *Kurr* court also specified that its holding did not apply to what the United States Supreme Court had held to constitute lawful abortions.

■■■

Quicknotes

DEFENSE OF OTHERS A defense to criminal liability for harm or threats made upon another in defense of someone other than oneself.

DUE PROCESS RIGHTS The constitutional mandate requiring the courts to protect and enforce individuals' rights and liberties consistent with prevailing principles of fairness and justice, and prohibiting the federal and state governments from such activities that deprive its citizens of a life, liberty or property interest.

JURY INSTRUCTIONS A communication made by the court to a jury regarding the applicable law involved in a proceeding.

VOLUNTARY MANSLAUGHTER The killing of another person without premeditation, deliberation or malice aforethought, but committed while in the "heat of passion" or upon some adequate provocation, thereby reducing the charge from murder to manslaughter.

■■■

State v. Boyett

State (P) v. Convicted murderer (D)

N.M. Sup. Ct., 144 N.M. 184, 185 P.3d 355 (2008).

NATURE OF CASE: Appeal from conviction for first-degree murder.

FACT SUMMARY: Boyett (D), convicted of murdering Rhodes (Victim) right outside his home, contended that the defense of habitation did not require the intruder to cross the habitation's threshold and was not restricted to instances when the victim was killed inside the defendant's home.

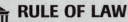 **RULE OF LAW**

Defense of habitation as a defense to murder does not require the intruder to cross the habitation's threshold and be killed by the defendant inside the home.

FACTS: Rhodes (Victim) was Boyett's (D) romantic rival; both had a romantic interest in Wilder, and both hated each other. Eventually, Boyett (D) and Wilder planned to marry. A few days before the wedding, Wilder absconded from the home she shared with Boyett (D) and spent time with Victim without telling Boyett (D). The day before the wedding, Wilder departed Victim's company to return home, but had a car accident on the way. She was able to walk back home. Shortly after Wilder arrived, Victim arrived at the house. Boyett (D) shot her in the head from around four feet away. Boyett (D) was charged with murder in the first degree. The prosecution argued that Victim had come to the house to return Wilder's car keys, Boyett (D) opened the front door, shouted at her to leave, and then immediately shot her. Boyett (D) claimed that Victim came to the house with the intent of killing him to prevent his marrying Wilder. He testified that he heard a loud banging at the front door, grabbed the gun that he kept nearby, and opened the door only to find a furious Victim on the doorstep. He shouted at Victim, telling her to get off his property, but in the process of trying to run her off, he observed her draw the gun that he knew she routinely carried. In fear for his life, he raised his revolver and shot Victim. Boyett (D) asserted that if he had not shot her, she would have fired her gun and fatally wounded him. One of Boyett's (D) defenses was that he acted lawfully, inter alia, in defense of habitation. The trial court did not permit his jury instruction related to defense of habitation, because the court concluded that it was inapplicable because Boyett (D) did not shoot Victim inside his home. The state's highest court granted review.

ISSUE: Does defense of habitation as a defense to murder require the intruder to cross the habitation's threshold and be killed by the defendant inside the home?

HOLDING AND DECISION: (Serna, J.) No. Defense of habitation as a defense to murder does not require the intruder to cross the habitation's threshold and be killed by the defendant inside the home. Entry into the defendant's home has never been a prerequisite to this defense, which requires that the defendant reasonably believes that the intruder intends to commit a felon in the defendant's home and that it is necessary to kill the intruder to prevent the felony. The defense does not apply where the victim flees from the defendant or where the victim has lawfully entered the defendant's home. In certain circumstances, however, defense of habitation may justify the occupant's use of lethal force against an intruder who is outside the home where the intruder is attempting to forcibly enter the home and commit felonious violence against the occupants. The defense is inapplicable where the intruder is attempting to enter the home to commit a non-violent felony. For these reasons, the trial court erred in excluding the defense of habitation instruction on the ground that the victim was killed outside Boyett's (D) home. However, to have been entitled to the instruction, Boyett (D) had to adduce some evidence that Victim was attempting to forcibly enter his home to commit a violent felony, but he failed to do so. There was no evidence that Victim was endeavoring by violence to enter his home or that she intended violence to persons inside. Even if Boyett (D) reasonably believed that Victim intended to commit a violent felony in his home, defense of habitation would have justified his actions only if he could show that Victim was attempting to force entry to his home. Here, however, the evidence showed only that after knocking on the door, Victim had retreated some four feet from it and was waiting for it to open. No evidence showed that, at the time she was killed, Victim was attempting to gain entry to Boyett's (D) home with the intent to commit a violent felony therein. Therefore, because there was no evidence to support Boyett's (D) theory that he killed Victim in defense of his habitation, the trial court's refusal to give the jury instruction was not error. Affirmed.

▶ **ANALYSIS**

If Boyett (D) reasonably believed that Victim was going to shoot him and then enter his home to continue the shooting, that belief would support the theories of self-defense and defense of another, but it would not support the defense of habitation because no forced entry by Victim would be involved. As this case makes clear, defense of

Continued on next page.

habitation does not justify the use of deadly force solely to protect personal property or to protect against the commission of misdemeanors.

■══■

Quicknotes

FIRST-DEGREE MURDER The willful killing of another person with deliberation and premeditation; first-degree murder also encompasses those situations in which a person is killed within the perpetration of, or attempt to perpetrate, specified felonies.

■══■

Nelson v. State

Joyrider (D) v. State (P)

Alaska Sup. Ct., 597 P.2d 977 (1979).

NATURE OF CASE: Appeal from conviction for reckless destruction of personal property and joyriding.

FACT SUMMARY: When Dale Nelson (D) was convicted of reckless destruction of personal property and joyriding when he took two state trucks to use in trying to extricate his own truck which was stuck in a marshy area off the highway, he argued that the court failed adequately to instruct on the defense of necessity.

🏛 RULE OF LAW
The defense of necessity may be raised only if the defendant's actions, although violative of the law, were necessary to prevent an even greater harm from occurring.

FACTS: Shortly after midnight, Dale Nelson (Nelson) (D) drove his four-wheel truck onto a side road off the highway where it became bogged down in a marshy area. He was afraid it might tip over, and he and two companions tried unsuccessfully for an hour to extricate it. An acquaintance came by and drove Nelson (D) and one of the companions to a state highway department yard (which had "no-trespassing" signs posted) where heavy equipment was parked. After waiting several hours for someone to come by, Nelson (D) took a dump truck as well as a front loader to use to attempt to extricate his own vehicle. These vehicles also became stuck and were considerably damaged. Nelson was tried and convicted in the district court of reckless destruction of personal property and joyriding. The superior court affirmed, and Nelson (D) appealed, arguing that the trial judge failed properly to instruct the jury on the defense of necessity.

ISSUE: May the defense of necessity be raised only if the defendant's actions, although violative of the law, were necessary to prevent an even greater harm from occurring?

HOLDING AND DECISION: (Matthews, J.) Yes. The defense of necessity may be raised only if the defendant's actions, although violative of the law, were necessary to prevent an even greater harm from occurring. The rationale of the necessity defense is not that a person, when faced with the pressure of circumstances of nature, lacks the mental element which the crime in question requires. Rather, it is because the law ought to promote the achievement of higher values at the expense of lesser crimes, and sometimes the greater good for society will be accomplished by violating the literal language of the criminal law. The instruction here given adequately describes these requirements for the jury. Nelson (D) is correct in arguing that the necessity defense is available if a person acted in the reasonable belief that an emergency existed and there were no alternatives available even if that belief was mistaken. However, even assuming that the instruction given was not worded adequately to convey these concepts, such error here would be harmless since, on the facts, Nelson (D) failed to make out a case for the necessity defense. The stuck vehicle did not constitute such a dire emergency as to warrant the dangers posed by Nelson's wrongfully trespassing and taking the truck in question, nor had Nelson (D) actually been deprived of available lawful alternatives. For example, during the time period involved, people stopped on several different occasions and offered their services in the form of physical assistance, rides, or offers to telephone state troopers or a tow truck. Nelson's (D) fears about damage to his truck roof were no justification for his appropriation of sophisticated and expensive equipment. Affirmed.

▶ ANALYSIS

Legal commentators generally agree that there are three essential elements to the defense of necessity: (1) the act charged must have been done to prevent a significant evil; (2) there must have been no adequate alternative; and (3) the harm caused must not have been disproportionate to the harm avoided. Section 3.02 of the Model Penal Code accepts the view that a principle of necessity, properly conceived, affords a general justification for conduct that would otherwise constitute an offense. It reflects the judgment that such a qualification on criminal liability, like the general requirements of culpability, is essential to the rationality and justice of the criminal law.

■=■

Quicknotes

NECESSITY DEFENSE A defense to liability for unlawful activity where the conduct is unavoidable and is justified by preventing the occurrence of a more serious harm.

■=■

United States v. Schoon

Federal government (P) v. Trespasser (D)

971 F.2d 193 (9th Cir. 1991).

NATURE OF CASE: Appeal from conviction for obstructing Internal Revenue Service activities and failing to comply with a federal officer's order.

FACT SUMMARY: Schoon (D), having occupied federal property to draw attention to U.S. policies in El Salvador, raised necessity as a defense when prosecuted for trespass.

🏛 RULE OF LAW
Necessity may not be raised as a defense to indirect civil disobedience.

FACTS: Schoon (D) occupied an Internal Revenue Service office in Tucson, Arizona with a group of people. Their purpose was to protest U.S. policy toward El Salvador. Schoon (D) and two others (D) were arrested for obstruction. At trial, they raised the defense of necessity, contending that their acts were justified by their purpose to end bloodshed in El Salvador, which they contended was caused by U.S. policy. The trial court rejected the defense. They were convicted, and they appealed.

ISSUE: May necessity be raised as a defense to indirect civil disobedience?

HOLDING AND DECISION: (Boochever, J.) No. Necessity may not be raised as a defense to indirect civil disobedience. The defense of necessity is an essentially utilitarian concept that excuses behavior that would otherwise be criminal. Essentially, if a greater good is served by disobedience to a law, the defense is permissible. A defendant raising the defense must show (1) that he was faced with a choice of evils and (2) chose the lesser evil, (3) reasonably anticipated a direct causal relationship between his conduct and the harm to be averted, and (4) had no legal alternatives to violating the law in question. Civil disobedience takes two forms: direct, where the defendant violates a law to protest it, and indirect, where he violates one law to protest another law or policy. The situation in this case presents indirect civil disobedience. In such a situation, the element of necessity as a matter of law is not present. A legislative policy cannot constitute a cognizable harm, so the first element is not met. Further, there is no provable link between the defendant's conduct and the alleged harm. Finally, a legal alternative, petitioning the applicable legislative body to change its policy, is always present. Consequently, the elements for necessity are not met in a case such as that presented here. Affirmed.

CONCURRENCE: (Fernandez, J.) Necessity is grounded not on utilitarianism alone but also on what is right and proper.

▶ ANALYSIS

The defendant's efforts to apply necessity as a defense here certainly were more along the lines of a political statement than a legal analysis. Necessity rarely applies when the individual involved is not in direct danger or at least close to a dangerous situation. An attempt to influence political policy will very rarely implicate necessity.

Quicknotes

NECESSITY DEFENSE A defense to liability for unlawful activity where the conduct is unavoidable and is justified by preventing the occurrence of a more serious harm.

TRESPASS Unlawful interference with, or damage to, the real or personal property of another.

The Queen v. Dudley and Stephens

Government (P) v. Shipwrecked crewmen (D)

Queen's Bench Division, 14 Q.B.D. 273 (1884).

NATURE OF CASE: Sentencing after a jury special verdict in a murder trial.

FACT SUMMARY: After being shipwrecked at sea with little or no food and water, Dudley (D) and Stephens (D) killed Parker, a teenage boy who was shipwrecked with them, so that they could feed on his body to survive.

🏛 RULE OF LAW
The killing of another, even though those doing the killing think it necessary to avoid death by starvation, constitutes murder and is punishable as such.

FACTS: Dudley (D), Stephens (D), Brooks, and Parker, the crew on an English yacht, were cast away in a storm on the high seas and were forced into an open boat belonging to the yacht. They had no water and only two tins of turnips. Their food was entirely consumed after twelve days. Parker, a teenager, became ill and weak. After eighteen days, Dudley (D) proposed to Stephens (D) and Brooks that they kill Parker and eat his flesh to survive, but Brooks refused to participate in their scheme. On the twentieth day, with no sign of another vessel, Dudley (D) killed Parker, and the three men fed on the body and blood of the boy for four days. On the fourth day, they were rescued by a passing vessel. The three men undoubtedly would have died of famine before being rescued, and Parker would have died before them, due to his weakened condition. After trial, the jury returned a special verdict, praying for the advice of the court because they couldn't decide if the killing of Parker constituted felony and murder.

ISSUE: Does the killing of another, even though those doing the killing think it necessary to avoid death by starvation, constitute felony and murder, and is it punishable as such?

HOLDING AND DECISION: (Lord Coleridge, C.J.) Yes. The killing of another, even though those doing the killing think it necessary to avoid death by starvation, constitutes murder and is punishable as such. The jury's special verdict said that if the court was of the opinion that the killing of Parker was felony and murder, then the jurors say that Dudley (D) and Stephens (D) were each guilty of felony and murder as alleged in the indictment. Death sentence imposed.

▶ ANALYSIS

In the *Dudley and Stephens* case, the court's death sentence was subsequently commuted by the Crown to six months' imprisonment. It might be noted that currently the Model Penal Code does not rule out the use of its choice-of-evils provision in homicide cases.

■≡■

Quicknotes

FELONY MURDER The unlawful killing of another human being while in the commission of, or attempted commission of, specified felonies.

NECESSITY DEFENSE A defense to liability for unlawful activity where the conduct is unavoidable and is justified by preventing the occurrence of a more serious harm.

■≡■

United States v. Contento-Pachon

Federal government (P) v. Drug smuggler (D)

723 F.2d 691 (9th Cir. 1984).

NATURE OF CASE: Appeal from conviction of drug running.

FACT SUMMARY: Contento-Pachon (D), who was charged with drug smuggling, sought to raise duress as a defense due to alleged threats against him by his employer if he did not follow orders.

🏛 RULE OF LAW
The duress defense contains three elements: an immediate threat of death or serious bodily injury, a well-grounded fear that the threat will be carried out, and no reasonable opportunity to escape.

FACTS: Contento-Pachon (D), a Colombian, was recruited by a drug producer to smuggle cocaine into the United States. According to Contento-Pachon (D), he initially refused, but the exporter threatened to harm his family if he refused. He did not notify authorities, he claimed, because many were "on the take" from drug producers. He attempted to smuggle the drugs into the United States and was apprehended. He was charged with drug trafficking. At trial, he claimed duress, but the court rejected the defense. He was convicted and appealed.

ISSUE: Does the duress defense involve a threat of death, a well-grounded fear that the threat will be carried out, and no opportunity to escape?

HOLDING AND DECISION: (Boochever, J.) Yes. There are three elements of duress: (1) immediate threat of death or great bodily harm; (2) a well-grounded fear that the threat will be carried out; and (3) no reasonable opportunity to escape. The district court rejected the defense, as it found the first and third elements lacking. However, "immediacy" does not mean that a threat is imminent; it only means that the threat be more than a vague, unspecified danger. A jury could have so found. Also, a jury could have found, in light of police corruption, that Contento-Pachon's (D) decision not to go to the police was reasonable. Therefore, the issue of duress should have gone to the jury. [The court agreed with the district court that necessity was inapplicable as a defense.] Reversed.

CONCURRENCE AND DISSENT: (Coyle, J.) Contrary to the majority's findings, the district court's conclusion regarding duress was adequately supported by the record.

▶ ANALYSIS

Duress and necessity are similar in effect but analytically different. Duress is considered to negate the mens rea of a crime, while necessity negates the actus reus. Also, duress is inflicted by human agents; necessity is usually caused by nonhuman events.

■=■

Quicknotes

DURESS Unlawful threats or other coercive behavior by one person that cause another to commit acts he would not otherwise do.

NECESSITY DEFENSE A defense to liability for unlawful activity where the conduct is unavoidable and is justified by preventing the occurrence of a more serious harm.

■=■

People v. Unger

State (P) v. Escaped inmate (D)

Ill. Sup. Ct., 66 Ill. 2d 333, 362 N.E.2d 319 (1977).

NATURE OF CASE: Prosecution for escape from prison.

FACT SUMMARY: Unger (D) escaped from a minimum security honor farm allegedly to avoid homosexual assaults and threats of death.

🏛 RULE OF LAW
The defenses of necessity and compulsion are available in escape cases, and the jury should be so instructed where evidence adduced at trial is sufficient to raise the defense.

FACTS: Unger (D) was repeatedly assaulted sexually and threatened with death and physical injury at a minimum security honor farm. Unger (D) left the farm and was apprehended several days later. Unger (D) alleged that his escape was not voluntary and had been caused by compulsion (the acts of others) and necessity (outside forces, e.g., natural conditions). The court refused to instruct the jury that these facts were a defense to the charge. Rather, the court instructed the jury that Unger's (D) reasons for escaping were immaterial. The appellate court reversed the conviction.

ISSUE: Are compulsion or necessity defenses to an escape charge?

HOLDING AND DECISION: (Ryan, J.) Yes. While escape situations do not fit within the traditional ambit of either compulsion or necessity defenses, they have been recognized by several jurisdictions in similar situations. Since compulsion requires an imminent threat of great bodily harm, many commentators suggest that the situation fits within the necessity defense. The prisoner is forced to choose between the lesser of two evils. We likewise find that compulsion and necessity are a defense to a charge of escape. Where the defendant raises sufficient evidence at trial, the jury should be instructed as to the availability of the defense. It is a limited defense and the jury may consider factors such as whether the defendant's fears were justified; whether the threat was imminent and sufficiently severe; whether there was time to resort to either the courts or prison officials and if this would be effective; and whether the prisoner immediately reported his escape to the police. These factors go to the weight of the defense. A jury might find the defense valid even if one or more of these factors are missing. Affirmed.

▶ ANALYSIS

Duress was recognized as a defense to escape in a situation similar to *Unger. People v. Harmon*, 53 Mich. App. 482

(1974). The traditional response by most jurisdictions is that the defense should not be available on public policy grounds. Other jurisdictions would allow the defense on a limited basis, only if certain conditions existed, which were similar to those stated by the majority in *Unger. People v. Lovercamp*, 43 Cal. App. 3rd 823 (1974).

■■■

Quicknotes

DURESS Unlawful threats or other coercive behavior by one person that causes another to commit acts he would not otherwise do.

NECESSITY DEFENSE A defense to liability for unlawful activity where the conduct is unavoidable and is justified by preventing the occurrence of a more serious harm.

■■■

People v. Anderson

State (P) v. Murderer (D)

Cal. Sup. Ct., 28 Cal. 4th 767, 50 P.3d 368 (2002).

NATURE OF CASE: Appeal from conviction for murder.

FACT SUMMARY: When Anderson (D) was charged and convicted of first-degree murder, he argued that the fact he was coerced to kill the victim constituted a viable defense.

> 🏛 **RULE OF LAW**
> Duress does not justify killing an innocent person.

FACTS: Anderson (D) was charged with kidnapping and murdering Margaret Armstrong in a children's camp. Anderson (D) and others suspected the victim of molesting two girls who resided in the camp. Anderson's (D) defense was that he was coerced to kill the victim by the father of one of the girls who told Anderson (D) he would "beat the shit out of him" if he failed to kill the victim. A jury convicted Anderson (D) of first-degree murder and kidnapping, and the intermediate appellate court affirmed. Anderson (D) appealed, arguing that duress may justify the killing of an innocent person.

ISSUE: Does duress justify killing an innocent person?

HOLDING AND DECISION: (Chin, J.) No. Duress does not justify killing an innocent person. When a defendant commits murder under duress, the resulting harm (the death of an innocent person) is at least as great as the threatened harm (the death of the defendant). When confronted with an apparent situation such as above, a person can always choose to resist. As a practical matter, death will rarely, if ever, inevitably result from a choice not to kill. The law should require people to choose to resist rather than kill an innocent person. There is no evidence that the legislature has abrogated this common law rule. Furthermore, California today is tormented by gang violence. If duress is recognized as a defense to the killing of innocents, then a street or prison gang need only create an internal reign of terror and murder can be justified, at least by the actual killer. Persons who know they can claim duress will be more likely to follow a gang order to kill instead of resisting than would those who know they must face the consequences of their acts. Accepting the duress defense for any form of murder would thus encourage killing. Absent a strong indication that the legislature intended to remove the sanctions of the criminal law from the killing of an innocent even under duress, this court will not do so. Nor can duress reduce murder to the lesser crime of manslaughter by negating malice. Affirmed.

CONCURRENCE AND DISSENT: (Kennard, J.) The legislation making duress a defense unless the crime be punishable with death, implicitly incorporates by reference other statutory provisions defining crimes and prescribing their punishments. The Model Penal Code allows the defense of duress to be asserted against all criminal charges, including murder. Even persons of reasonable firmness surely break at different points depending on the stakes that are involved. Even homicide may sometimes be the product of coercion that is truly irresistible and long and wasting pressure may break down resistance more effectively than a threat of immediate destruction. However, here, Anderson (D) himself was not threatened with death and failed to present sufficient evidence of duress, thus the conviction should be affirmed.

▶ ANALYSIS

A state legislature's decision whether to allow a duress defense to a murder charge reflects a variety of societal judgments. It has been said by some authorities that if duress is not a defense to a noncapital crime, then the law has created a situation in which one is better off breaking the law than obeying it because by committing the crime one risks only a prison sentence, while by refusing to commit the crime one risks death or very serious injury from the person imposing the duress.

■══■

Quicknotes

DURESS Unlawful threats or other coercive behavior by one person that causes another to commit acts he would not otherwise do.

■══■

United States v. Veach

Federal government (P) v. Convicted federal criminal, intoxicated at time of crimes (D)

455 F.3d 628 (6th Cir. 2006).

NATURE OF CASE: Appeal from conviction for resisting a federal law enforcement officer, 18 U.S.C. § 111(a)(1), and for threatening to assault and murder a federal law enforcement officer with intent to impede such officer in the performance of official duties, 18 U.S.C. § 115(a)(1)(B).

FACT SUMMARY: After he got into an accident, Veach (D), who was intoxicated at the time, resisted arrest and threatened federal law enforcement officers. He was convicted for resisting a federal law enforcement officer, 18 U.S.C. § 111(a)(1), and for threatening to assault and murder a federal law enforcement officer with intent to impede such officer in the performance of official duties, 18 U.S.C. § 115(a)(1)(B). He contended that the trial court erred in excluding a defense based on voluntary intoxication.

RULE OF LAW
(1) Voluntary intoxication is not a defense to the crime of resisting a federal law enforcement officer, 18 U.S.C. § 111(a)(1).(2) Voluntary intoxication is a defense to the crime of threatening to assault and murder a federal law enforcement officer with intent to impede such officer in the performance of official duties, 18 U.S.C. § 115(a)(1)(B).

FACTS: Veach's (D) automobile was involved in a collision with another vehicle in a national park. United States Park Rangers suspected that Veach (D) was intoxicated and performed various field sobriety tests and a portable breath test on him that confirmed their initial impressions. While he was being secured for transport, Veach (D) attempted to pull away from one of the officers, who fell on his knee. Additionally, while he was being transported, Veach (D) threatened the officers, saying that he would kill and decapitate them, and repeated these threats on a couple of other occasions while he was transported between a hospital and the detention center. Based on this conduct, a jury convicted Veach (D) for resisting a federal law enforcement officer, 18 U.S.C. § 111(a)(1), and for threatening to assault and murder a federal law enforcement officer with intent to impede such officer in the performance of official duties, 18 U.S.C. § 115(a)(1)(B). The trial court granted the Government's (P) motion in limine to exclude presentation of a defense of voluntary intoxication. The court of appeals granted review.

ISSUE:
(1) Is voluntary intoxication a defense to the crime of resisting a federal law enforcement officer, 18 U.S.C. § 111(a)(1)?

(2) Is voluntary intoxication a defense to the crime of threatening to assault and murder a federal law enforcement officer with intent to impede such officer in the performance of official duties, 18 U.S.C. § 115(a)(1)(B)?

HOLDING AND DECISION: (Daughtrey, J.)
(1) No. Voluntary intoxication is not a defense to the crime of resisting a federal law enforcement officer, 18 U.S.C. § 111(a)(1). Intoxication, whether voluntary or involuntary, may preclude the formation of specific-intent and thus serves to negate an essential element only of specific-intent crimes; it cannot serve as a defense to general-intent crimes. Thus the issue is whether § 111 (a)(1) is a general-intent or a specific-intent crime. Under § 111, a violator is punished solely for the forcible assault on, resistance to, opposition to, impedance of, intimidation of, or interference with a designated individual. No other intent on the defendant's part need be shown; the mere intentional performance of the prohibited act is sufficient to subject the perpetrator to federal criminal liability. Accordingly, the crime is a general-intent crime and the trial court was correct in concluding that voluntary intoxication could not serve as a viable defense thereto. Affirmed as to this issue.

(2) Yes. Voluntary intoxication is a defense to the crime of threatening to assault and murder a federal law enforcement officer with intent to impede such officer in the performance of official duties, 18 U.S.C. § 115(a)(1)(B). Unlike § 111, this provision contains language requiring specific intent. Not only must the Government (P) prove beyond a reasonable doubt that the defendant threatened certain action against a government official but also that the defendant made such a threat for the specific purpose of interfering with the performance of official duties or of retaliating for the performance of such duties. Because a defendant must possess a particular mens rea to be guilty of the crimes described in § 115, Veach (D) should have been allowed to present evidence to the jury that he was too intoxicated at the time of his arrest to form the requisite specific intent. Reversed and remanded as to this issue.

ANALYSIS

There is currently a trend to limit or altogether abolish voluntary intoxication as a defense. In the states that follow this trend, a defendant may still negate the element of intent by proving that the intoxication was involuntary.

Continued on next page.

The Model Penal Code, in § 2.08(1), provides that intoxication is a defense if it negates an element of the crime. Thus, unlike the court in *Veach*, it does not apply a specific-intent/general-intent dichotomy.

■══■

Quicknotes

INTENT   The state of mind that exists when one's purpose is to commit a criminal act.

MOTION IN LIMINE   Motion by one party brought prior to trial to exclude the potential introduction of prejudicial evidence.

SPECIFIC INTENT   The intent to commit a specific unlawful act that is a required element for criminal liability for certain crimes.

SPECIFIC INTENT CRIME   A crime that requires the intent to commit a specific unlawful act in order for criminal liability to be imposed.

VOLUNTARY INTOXICATION   The voluntary consumption of substances that the defendant knows or should know will obscure his judgment; voluntary intoxication may be considered when determining whether the defendant possessed the requisite intent.

■══■

United States v. Freeman

[Parties not identified.]

357 F.2d 606 (2d Cir. 1966).

NATURE OF CASE: [Nature of case not stated in casebook excerpt.]

FACT SUMMARY: [Fact summary not stated in casebook excerpt.]

🏛 RULE OF LAW
[Rule of law not stated in casebook excerpt.]

FACTS: [Facts not stated in casebook excerpt.]

ISSUE: [Issue not stated in casebook excerpt.]

HOLDING AND DECISION: (Kaufman, J.) [The casebook opinion excerpt consisted of a discussion of the philosophical-legal foundations for the insanity defense. The opinion stated, in essence, that criminal law exists for three purposes: retribution, deterrence, and rehabilitation. None of these goals, said the court, is advanced by imposing criminal sanctions on one unable to comprehend the character of his actions.]

▶ ANALYSIS

The insanity defense has been recognized, to some extent, since at least the mid-sixteenth century. For the most part, the defense has centered on a defendant's cognitive process. Calls to change this focus to deal more with behavior have for the most part been unsuccessful.

■■■

Quicknotes

INSANITY DEFENSE An affirmative defense to a criminal prosecution that the defendant suffered from a mental illness, thereby relieving him of liability for his conduct.

MENS REA Criminal intent.

■■■

State v. Johnson

State (P) v. Alleged criminal (D)

R.I. Sup. Ct., 121 R.I. 254, 399 A.2d 469 (1979).

NATURE OF CASE: Review of a criminal conviction.

FACT SUMMARY: Johnson (D) argued that a new standard of insanity should be adopted by the court.

🏛 RULE OF LAW
When, as a result of mental disease or defect, the defendant lacked substantial capacity to appreciate the criminality of his conduct or when, as a result of mental disease or defect, the defendant lacked substantial capacity to conform his conduct to the requirements of law, he is relieved of responsibility.

FACTS: Johnson (D) raised the defense of insanity to criminal charges. The *M'Naghten* test, *M'Naghten Case*, 8 Eng. Rep. 718 (1843), had been used in Rhode Island to determine the criminal responsibility of those who claimed they were blameless by reason of mental illness. The test's emphasis upon knowledge of right and wrong resulted in an all-or-nothing approach which had been widely criticized. The irresistible impulse test had also been the subject of widespread criticism. The *Durham* or "product" test, *Durham v. United States*, 214 F.2d 862 (1954), has been abandoned because the elusive, undefined concept of productivity gave the jury inadequate guidance. The expert witnesses, in effect, usurped the jury function. Johnson (D) argued, on appeal following his conviction, that the *M'Naghten* test should be abandoned in favor of a modernized rule.

ISSUE: When, as a result of mental disease or defect, the defendant lacked substantial capacity to appreciate the criminality of his conduct or when, as a result of mental disease or defect, the defendant lacked substantial capacity to conform his conduct to the requirements of law, is he relieved of responsibility?

HOLDING AND DECISION: (Doris, J.) Yes. When, as a result of mental disease or defect, the defendant lacked substantial capacity to appreciate the criminality of his conduct or when, as a result of mental disease or defect, the defendant lacked substantial capacity to conform his conduct to the requirements of law, he is relieved of responsibility. The Model Penal Code test of criminal responsibility represents a significant, positive improvement over earlier rules. It acknowledges that volitional, as well as cognitive impairments must be considered by the jury in its resolution of the responsibility issue.

▶ ANALYSIS

The court in this case discussed the evolution of the defense of insanity. The *M'Naghten* test focused on a defendant's knowledge of the nature, quality, and wrongfulness of his acts. The Model Penal Code uses the word "appreciate" which conveys a broader sense of understanding than simple cognition.

Quicknotes

DURHAM TEST A defense to a criminal prosecution relieving a defendant from liability if his conduct was the result of a mental disease or defect.

IRRESISTIBLE IMPULSE RULE A defense to a criminal prosecution that the defendant, due to some mental disease or defect, was unable to resist the impulse to commit the crime due to his inability to control his actions.

M'NAGHTEN RULE A defense to a criminal prosecution that the defendant was not guilty due to a mental disease or defect that rendered him incapable of knowing the nature and quality of his conduct or that such conduct was wrong.

MODEL PENAL CODE INSANITY DEFENSE A person is not liable for his criminal offenses if at the time of committing the crime(s) he suffered from a mental disease or defect and thereby lacked the substantial capacity to appreciate the wrongfulness of his actions or to conform his actions to the requirements of law.

State v. Wilson

State (P) v. Alleged-murderer (D)

Conn. Sup. Ct., 242 Conn. 605, 700 A.2d 633 (1997).

NATURE OF CASE: Appeal from murder conviction.

FACT SUMMARY: Wilson (D), who was convicted of murder after pleading insanity as an affirmative defense, contended that the trial court's refusal to instruct the jury on the moral component of the insanity defense was reversible error.

🏛 RULE OF LAW
A defendant may establish that he lacked substantial capacity to appreciate the wrongfulness of his conduct if he can prove that, at the time of the criminal act, as a result of mental disease or defect, he substantially misperceived reality and harbored a delusional belief that society, under the circumstances as the defendant honestly but mistakenly understood them, would not have morally condemned his actions.

FACTS: Wilson (D) exhibited symptoms of a mental disorder manifested by a delusional belief that a high school classmate and his father were systematically destroying his life. Wilson (D) believed that he was being poisoned and hypnotized so that others could obtain control of his thoughts. Finally, after quarreling with his friend's father, he shot him dead. Wilson (D) later turned himself in to the police and explained that he had to do it to combat an alleged mind control conspiracy. At trial, Wilson (D) raised his mental illness as an affirmative defense, but the jury rejected his claim of insanity and convicted him of murder. Wilson (D) appealed, claiming that the judge committed reversible error in refusing to give the jury an instruction that he was entitled to prevail if the evidence established that Wilson (D) believed his conduct to be morally justified.

ISSUE: May a defendant establish that he lacked substantial capacity to appreciate the wrongfulness of his conduct if he can prove that, at the time of the criminal act, as a result of mental disease or defect, he substantially misperceived reality and harbored a delusional belief that society, under the circumstances as the defendant honestly but mistakenly understood them, would not have morally condemned his actions?

HOLDING AND DECISION: (Palmer, J.) Yes. A defendant may establish that he lacked substantial capacity to appreciate the wrongfulness of his conduct if he can prove that, at the time of the criminal act, as a result of mental disease or defect, he substantially misperceived reality and harbored a delusional belief that society, under the circumstances as the defendant honestly but mistakenly understood his

actions. Under Connecticut law, lack of capacity due to mental disease or defect is an affirmative defense if the defendant lacked substantial capacity either to appreciate the wrongfulness of his conduct or to control his conduct within the requirements of the law. By choosing the term "wrongfulness" instead of "criminality," the legislature intended to import a moral element into Connecticut's insanity defense. A defendant would be able to prevail under the insanity defense if, as a result of his mental disease or defect, he sincerely believed that society would approve of his conduct if it shared his understanding of the circumstances underlying his actions. Wilson (D) presented sufficient evidence from which a jury reasonably could have found, by a preponderance of the evidence, that, due to a mental disease or defect, he misperceived reality and, in acting on the basis of that misperception, did not substantially appreciate that his actions were contrary to societal morality. The evidence presented at trial warranted an instruction defining the term "wrongfulness" in terms of societal morality consistent with our explication of that definition above. Reversed and remanded.

CONCURRENCE: (Katz, J.) The insanity defense should also apply to individuals who are mentally ill and because of that illness believe that society's rules do not apply to their actions. Such persons are not capable of appreciating the legal and social import of their acts and, therefore, should not be held criminally responsible.

DISSENT: (McDonald, J.) If Wilson (D) recognizes his conduct is both criminal and wrong in the eyes of society, as murder clearly is, public safety demands that he be held responsible for his actions. It should not be a defense that Wilson (D) believes society did not approve of his conduct only because society failed to appreciate a needed "greater social good" that would come from those same actions.

▶ ANALYSIS

Today no court in any jurisdiction applies the personal morality standard for wrongfulness. There is still a debate on moral wrongs versus legal wrongs. Some courts treat them as the same.

■=■

Quicknotes

INSANITY DEFENSE An affirmative defense to a criminal prosecution that the defendant suffered from a mental illness, thereby relieving him of liability for his conduct.

Continued on next page.

M'NAGHTEN RULE A defense to a criminal prosecution that the defendant was not guilty due to a mental disease or defect that rendered him incapable of knowing the nature and quality of his conduct or that such conduct was wrong.

MODEL PENAL CODE INSANITY DEFENSE A person is not liable for his criminal offenses if at the time of committing the crime(s) he suffered from a mental disease or defect and thereby lacked the substantial capacity to appreciate the wrongfulness of his actions or to conform his actions to the requirements of law.

■══■

Perez v. Cain

Convicted murderer (D) v. State official (P)

529 F.3d 588 (5th Cir. 2008).

NATURE OF CASE: Appeal from grant of writ of habeas corpus to convicted murderer overturning his conviction.

FACT SUMMARY: Perez (D), who shot and killed a police officer, and who was convicted of first-degree murder and sentenced to life without parole, asserted that he was not guilty by reason of insanity, as so found by numerous experts for the defense. The State (P) did not present any expert testimony as to whether he was insane.

🏛 RULE OF LAW
Where a criminal defendant has presented overwhelming expert evidence that he was insane at the time of the crime, his conviction must be overturned where the state has produced insufficient evidence through cross-examination and argument to controvert the expert evidence, so that no rational jury could have found that the defendant was sane at the time of the crime.

FACTS: Believing that he was being pursued by people who wanted to kill him, Perez (D) drove with his 12-year-old son from Texas to New Orleans, where he fatally shot and killed a police officer. According to Perez's (D) son, Perez had acted paranoid all along the drive, taking back roads, suspecting various cars of following him, and taking real or imagined actions to throw off his "pursuers." Both the son and Perez's (D) wife reported that Perez (D) had been acting unusual and edgy in the days before the drive. According to police, the son had indicated to them that Perez (D) was being pursued by gang members because he had ripped off drug dealers, although a search of Perez's (D) car revealed no drugs. The state trial court appointed doctors to examine Perez (D) to determine whether he was competent to stand trial. Over a year after the shooting, Perez (D) was determined to be a danger to himself and was transferred to a forensic facility. His treating psychiatrist at the facility testified that Perez (D) was not competent because his thoughts were disorganized and he had difficulty communicating in a manner that indicated a significant degree of mental illness, as did his auditory hallucinations and delusions. Perez's (D) condition eventually improved through the use of anti-psychotic medication, and he was eventually restored to competency, at which point he was transferred out of the facility for trial. At trial, Perez (D) pleaded not guilty by reason of insanity. In addition to presenting testimony from his wife and son, Perez's (D) defense presented expert testimony from seven psychiatric experts about his delusions, who all agreed that he suffered from severe mental illness and

delusions of paranoia and persecution. The experts were well-qualified and disinterested. All seven experts agreed that Perez (D) was not malingering, and six of them (excluding his doctor at the facility) testified that Perez's (D) mental illness prevented him from knowing right from wrong on the night of the shooting. The State (P) did not present any expert witness testimony as to Perez's (D) mental state, but instead relied on cross-examination of the defense witnesses. It also called a detective to rebut the son's and wife's testimony, on the theory that Perez (D) and his family fooled the medical experts by making up a story that Perez (D) feared someone was trying to kill him. The jury convicted Perez (D) of first-degree murder and he was sentenced to life imprisonment without parole. The state courts rejected his appeals and he then filed a petition for habeas corpus in federal court. The district court concluded that the evidence was insufficient for the jury to find that Perez (D) had failed to show that he was insane. The State (P) appealed, and the court of appeals granted review.

ISSUE: Where a criminal defendant has presented overwhelming expert evidence that he was insane at the time of the crime, must his conviction be overturned where the state has produced insufficient evidence through cross-examination and argument to controvert the expert evidence, so that no rational jury could have found that the defendant was sane at the time of the crime?

HOLDING AND DECISION: (Reavley, J.) Yes. Where a criminal defendant has presented overwhelming expert evidence that he was insane at the time of the crime, his conviction must be overturned where the state has produced insufficient evidence through cross-examination and argument to controvert the expert evidence, so that no rational jury could have found that the defendant was sane at the time of the crime. The sufficiency standard asks whether, after viewing the evidence in the light most favorable to the prosecution, any rational trier of fact could have found the essential elements of the crime beyond a reasonable doubt. Under state law, a criminal defendant is presumed sane, but this presumption may be rebutted by a preponderance of the evidence. Legal insanity is proved if the circumstances indicate that a mental disease or mental defect rendered the offender incapable of distinguishing between right and wrong with reference to the conduct in question. Therefore, the issue here is whether, viewing the evidence in the light most favorable to the State (P), any rational trier of fact could have found beyond a reasonable doubt that Perez (D) did not prove by a preponderance of

Continued on next page.

the evidence that he was insane at the time of the offense. Although the State (P) was not required to present expert evidence to contradict Perez (D) and establish that he was sane, expert opinions of insanity may not be ignored absent a reason that is objectively present for doing so. The state appellate court held that the evidence was sufficient for the jury to find Perez (D) did not show he was insane because: there was a substantial delay—from between 9 and 17 months—between the shooting and the time the experts examined Perez (D); the experts based their opinions on information provided by the wife and son, whose testimony it found was inconsistent with pretrial statements; and Perez's (D) behavior could be explained by a fear of retaliation by rebuffed drug dealers. As to the delay, the state appellate court found that notes from the hospital where Perez (D) was admitted the night of the shooting indicated he was oriented, responsive, and obeying commands. It also found that Perez's (D) doctor at the forensic facility had indicated that his condition could have been attributed in some part to his 13 months of incarceration. Thus, the state court reasoned that a rational jury could have found these facts gave a more accurate picture of Perez's (D) mental state at the time of the offense than the experts' subsequent examinations. The state court's conclusion was erroneous because the hospital notations only meant that Perez (D) was generally not unconscious and knew who he was, where he was, and what time it was. As to the facility doctor's testimony that Perez's (D) incarceration could have contributed to the condition in which he found Perez (D) when he was admitted to the facility, this did not reveal whether the doctor believed the incarceration was the sole cause of Perez's (D) condition or to the degree that it affected him. The doctor was not asked whether Perez (D) was sane at the time of the offense. Thus, the jury was given nothing from which it could infer whether Perez (D) was sane or not on the night of the shooting, and, accordingly, there was no rational basis for the jury to infer that Perez (D) was sane at the time of the shooting and became insane thereafter due to incarceration. Further, impugning the veracity of the wife's and son's testimony was insufficient to permit the jury to ignore the experts' opinion. Although the experts did receive important information from the wife and son, they did not rely solely on this information when forming their opinions, and they also formed their opinions on the basis of personal examinations and other materials. Finally, the record objectively does not indicate that Perez (D) may have been justified in his fear of pursuit by drug dealers. There was no evidence that drug dealers were in pursuit of him, no drugs were found in his car, and even though the son had told the police that he and Perez (D) were being followed by gangs, he also told police that he had told them that because that is what Perez (D) had told him, and had told the police that Perez (D) was not involved in narcotics. In other words, there simply was not basis for a rational jury to conclude that Perez (D) was being chased by drug dealers. Furthermore, the experts observed Perez (D) manifesting

psychotic behavior independently of whether anyone was pursuing him. Thus, for these reasons, Perez (D) produced overwhelming evidence that he was insane at the time of the shooting, and the State (P) failed to produce sufficient evidence to rebut this defense. Perez (D) established by a preponderance of the evidence that he was insane; the state appellate court's conclusion that a rational jury could have found otherwise was an objectively unreasonable application of federal law. Affirmed.

▶ ANALYSIS

Expert evidence may be rebutted by showing the incorrectness or inadequacy of the factual assumptions on which the opinion is based, the reasoning by which an expert progresses from his material to his conclusion, the interest or bias of the expert, inconsistencies or contradictions in his testimony as to material matters, material variations between the experts themselves, and a defendant's lack of cooperation with the expert.

■=■

Quicknotes

INSANITY DEFENSE An affirmative defense to a criminal prosecution that the defendant suffered from a mental illness, thereby relieving him of liability for his conduct.

WRIT OF HABEAS CORPUS A proceeding in which a defendant brings a writ to compel a judicial determination of whether he is lawfully being held in custody.

■=■

Clark v. Arizona

Convicted murderer (D) v. State (P)

548 U.S. 735 (2006).

NATURE OF CASE: Appeal from a murder conviction.

FACT SUMMARY: When Clark (D), an undisputed paranoid schizophrenic, was precluded from presenting diminished capacity evidence in his first-degree murder trial, he argued that his right to due process had been violated.

> 🏛 **RULE OF LAW**
> A state's prohibition of diminished capacity evidence by a criminal defendant does not violate due process.

FACTS: During a traffic stop, Clark (D) shot and killed a police officer. He was prosecuted for first-degree murder. Clark (D) did not dispute the shooting but relied on his undisputed paranoid schizophrenia at the time of the incident, denying that he had the specific intent to shoot a law enforcement officer or knowledge that he was doing so, as required by statute. The trial court ruled that Clark (D) could not rely on evidence bearing on insanity to dispute the mens rea. In other words, the court refused to allow psychiatric testimony to negate specific intent and held that Arizona did not allow evidence of a defendant's mental disorder short of insanity to negate the mens rea element of a crime. Clark (D) was convicted and the state's intermediate appellate court affirmed. The United States Supreme Court granted certiorari.

ISSUE: Does a state's prohibition of diminished capacity evidence by a criminal defendant violate due process?

HOLDING AND DECISION: (Souter, J.) No. A state's prohibition of diminished capacity evidence by a criminal defendant does not violate due process. The state restricts mental-disease evidence and capacity evidence—usually provided by experts—not observation evidence. The Constitution does not prohibit such a restriction where there is a good reason for it, as where its probative value is outweighed by other considerations. Also, if evidence may be excluded in its entirety, its consideration may be subject to limitation. Here, there are risks associated with mental illness and capacity evidence that can be hedged by channeling its consideration to the insanity issue on which the defendant has the burden of persuasion. Generally, these risks arise from the controversial nature of some categories of mental illness; the potential for mental-disease evidence to mislead; and the danger of according greater certainty to capacity evidence than experts claim for it. First, the diagnosis may hide disagreement by professionals about what constitutes a certain mental illness.

Second, there is the potential of mental-disease evidence to mislead jurors (when they are the fact finders) through the power of this kind of evidence to suggest that a defendant suffering from a recognized mental disease lacks cognitive, moral, volitional, or other capacity, when that may not be a sound conclusion at all. Even when a category of mental disease is broadly accepted and the assignment of a defendant's behavior to that category is uncontroversial, the classification may suggest something very significant about a defendant's capacity, when in fact the classification tells little or nothing about the defendant's ability to form mens rea. Finally, there are particular risks inherent in the opinions of the experts who supplement the mental disease classifications with opinions on incapacity, namely, whether the mental disease rendered a particular defendant incapable of the cognition necessary for moral judgment or mens rea or otherwise incapable of understanding the wrongfulness of the conduct charged. Unlike observational evidence, capacity evidence consists of judgments fraught with multiple perils, such as, for example, that a defendant's state of mind at the crucial moment can be elusive no matter how conscientious the enquiry, and the law's categories that set the terms of the capacity judgment are not the categories of psychology that govern the expert's professional thinking. The empirical and conceptual problems add up to a real risk that an expert's judgment in giving capacity evidence will come with an apparent authority that psychologists and psychiatrists do not claim to have. This risk, like the difficulty in assessing the significance of mental-disease evidence, supports Arizona's decision to channel such expert testimony to consideration on the insanity defense, on which the party seeking the benefit of this evidence has the burden of persuasion. Affirmed.

DISSENT: (Kennedy, J.) Clark (D) should be permitted to introduce critical and reliable evidence showing he did not have the requisite intent or knowledge to be convicted of intentionally or knowingly killing a police officer. By being able to present evidence of his condition, Clark (D) would be able to explain his conduct in a way that would bear on the effort to determine, as a factual matter, whether he knew he was killing an officer. An explanation of his condition would help the jury understand how Clark (D) processed information, i.e., his cognition, on which knowledge relies, and whether his schizophrenia impacted his cognition and, therefore, what he knew. It thus makes little sense to divorce the observation evidence in the case from an explanation that makes it comprehensible. The

Continued on next page.

Court fails to recognize the meaning of the offense element here at issue. The element of mens rea is based on a factual determination. Clark's (D) evidence of mental illness, therefore, has a direct and substantial bearing upon what he knew, or thought he knew to be the facts when he pulled the trigger. The State (P) has failed to set forth sufficient reasons to support its categorical exclusion of this evidence. First, some mental illness evidence may be reliable, so not all types of this evidence should be disallowed per se. Second, the complexities of this area do not justify taking the factual issue of a person's mental illness away from the jury when it is crucial for the defense. If jury confusion is an issue in this case, it is merely so because of the majority's conflation of the insanity defense and the question of intent. Third, while mental-illness evidence can be misleading in some cases, it is clear that in this case evidence of Clark's (D) mental illness bears directly on whether he had mens rea. The expert testimony bolstered the testimony of lay witnesses and was relevant as to whether he knew he was killing a human, let alone a police officer. The fact that state (P) and defense experts drew different conclusions about the effect of Clark's (D) mental illness on his mental state made the evidence contested, but not unreliable, irrelevant, or misleading. Finally, by shifting the burden of proof on the intent or knowledge element of the offense, the State (P) unconstitutionally relieves itself of the responsibility of proving that element beyond a reasonable doubt.

▶ ANALYSIS

In the *Clark* decision, the United States Supreme Court made clear that not every state will find it worthwhile to make the judgment Arizona has made, but the point is simply that Arizona has sensible reasons to assign the risks as it has done by channeling the evidence in the manner it has without running afoul of an accused's due process rights.

■══■

Quicknotes

CAPACITY The legal or physical ability to act or to understand the consequences of one's actions.

DIMINISHED CAPACITY A defense to criminal liability; that the perpetrator suffered from a mental incapacity at the time the crime was committed so that he did not possess the requisite mental state.

DUE PROCESS The constitutional mandate requiring the courts to protect and enforce individuals' rights and liberties consistent with prevailing principles of fairness and justice and prohibiting the federal and state governments from such activities that deprive its citizens of life, liberty, or property interest.

MENS REA Criminal intent.

■══■

In re Devon T.

State (P) v. Juvenile drug possessor (D)

Md. Ct. Spec. App., 85 Md. App. 674, 584 A.2d 1287 (1991).

NATURE OF CASE: Appeal as to the applicability of the infancy defense to a charge of juvenile delinquency.

FACT SUMMARY: After Devon T. (D), a junior high school student just under the age of 14, was arrested when he was found with twenty bags of heroin, he raised the infancy defense.

🏛 RULE OF LAW
To overcome the presumption of incapacity, the state is required to show that the juvenile, at the time of the delinquent act, knew right from wrong.

FACTS: A school security guard searched Devon (D), a junior high school student, finding 20 plastic bags containing heroin. There were no needle marks or other indications of personal use on Devon's (D) body. Devon (D) was arrested and charged with committing an act which, if committed by an adult, would have constituted the crime of possession of heroin with intent to distribute. At the time of the offense, Devon (D) was just under 14 years of age. Before the juvenile master, Devon (D) raised the infancy defense. The State (P) then had the burden of rebutting the presumption of criminal incapacity. The circuit court found that Devon (D) was delinquent. Devon (D) appealed.

ISSUE: To overcome the presumption of incapacity is the state required to show that the juvenile knew right from wrong?

HOLDING AND DECISION: (Moylan, J.) Yes. To overcome the presumption of incapacity, the state is required to show that the juvenile knew right from wrong. Where children accused of a crime are between the ages of seven and fourteen, there is a rebuttable presumption of criminal incapacity. In this case, since Devon (D) was almost 14 at the time he was found with the heroin, he would be expected to possess cognitive capacity. Also of some weight was the fact that Devon (D) was essentially at or near grade level in school. Further, the juvenile master observed firsthand Devon's (D) receiving of legal advice from his lawyer, his acknowledgment of his understanding of it, and his acting upon it. The most significant circumstance was the finding of the court that the criminal activity in which Devon (D) was engaged was not mere possession of heroin but was possession with the intent to distribute. Thus, the surrounding circumstances here were sufficient to overcome the presumption of incapacity due to infancy, and the State (P) has carried its burden of overcoming the presumption. Affirmed.

▶ ANALYSIS

As this case shows, the cognitive capacity to distinguish right from wrong in the language of *M'Naghten* is not a characteristic of the insanity defense exclusively. It has traditionally been the common denominator criterion for a whole family of defenses based upon mental incapacity—insanity, infancy, mental retardation, and involuntary intoxication. The rationale behind its use in the infancy defense is that a child is not criminally responsible unless he is capable of entertaining criminal intent—that is, distinguishing between right and wrong.

Quicknotes

INCAPACITY Lack of capacity or ability to function legally, physically or mentally.

INFANCY (DEFENSE) A defense to a criminal prosecution of a minor that the minor was incapable of criminal conduct on the basis of his age.

M'NAUGHTEN RULE A defense to a criminal prosecution that the defendant was not guilty due to a mental disease or defect that rendered him incapable of knowing the nature and quality of his conduct or that such conduct was wrong.

Latimer v. The Queen

Convicted murderer (D) v. Government (P)

Can. Sup. Ct., 1 S.C.R. 3, 193 D.L.R. (4th) 577 (2001).

NATURE OF CASE: Appeal from murder conviction.

FACT SUMMARY: When Latimer (D) was convicted of murder for killing his daughter, he argued the defense of necessity.

🏛 RULE OF LAW
The defense of necessity encompasses the three elements of an urgent situation of clear and imminent peril, lack of a reasonable legal alternative, and proportionality between the harm inflicted and the harm avoided.

FACTS: Robert Latimer's (D) 12-year-old daughter, Tracy, suffered a permanent severe form of cerebral palsy. She was quadriplegic and immobile. She had the mental capacity of a four-year-old, permanently suffered five to six seizures daily despite medication and permanently experienced a great deal of pain which could not be alleviated by medication. Medically, however, she was not terminally ill. She was subjected to a continual series of complex painful surgeries none of which would cure her condition. Tracy's condition existed from birth, and Latimer's (D) care for her "for many years was admirable." He loved her greatly and at all times participated actively in her care and nurture. Finally, just before another scheduled surgery which he was told would in fact cause her further pain and would indeed need to be followed by still additional surgeries, Latimer (D) gave Tracy a quiet death by carbon monoxide. Latimer (D) was convicted of second-degree murder and appealed, arguing that the trial judge improperly refused to permit the jury to consider the defense of necessity.

ISSUE: Must the defense of necessity encompass the three elements of an urgent situation of clear and imminent peril, lack of a reasonable legal alternative, and proportionality between the harm inflicted and the harm avoided?

HOLDING AND DECISION: (By the Court) Yes. The defense of necessity encompasses the three elements of an urgent situation of clear and imminent peril, lack of a reasonable legal alternative, and proportionality between the harm inflicted and the harm avoided. Here, there was no "air of reality" to the three requirements of necessity. The first requirement of imminent peril was not met because Latimer (D) was not dealing with an emergency but with an obstinate and long-standing state of affairs. Tracy's proposed surgery did not pose an imminent threat to her life, nor did her medical condition. Secondly, Latimer (D) had at least one reasonable legal alternative to killing his daughter: he could have struggled on. As to

proportionality, it is difficult at the conceptual level, to imagine a circumstance in which the proportionality argument could be met for a homicide. Even assuming a proportionality argument could be applied here, the harm inflicted in this case (ending Tracy's life) was immeasurably more serious than the pain resulting from Tracy's operation which Latimer (D) sought to avoid. Killing a person to relieve suffering produced by a medically manageable physical or mental condition is not a proportionate response to the harm represented by the non-life-threatening suffering resulting from that condition. Appeal dismissed.

▶ ANALYSIS

In the United States, there is a division of viewpoints as to whether the proportionality requirement could ever be met for a homicide. Several jurisdictions deny the necessity defense in murder cases. Nevertheless, the American Penal Code proposes that the defense of necessity should be available for homicide.

■=■

Quicknotes

NECESSITY DEFENSE A defense to liability for unlawful activity where the conduct is unavoidable and is justified by preventing the occurrence of a more serious harm.

■=■

Robinson v. California

Drug addict (D) v. State (P)

370 U.S. 660 (1962).

NATURE OF CASE: Review of drug-related conviction for drug addiction.

FACT SUMMARY: Robinson (D) was convicted under a California statute criminalizing drug addiction and argued that imprisonment for the crime constituted cruel and unusual punishment.

🏛 RULE OF LAW
A state may not criminalize drug addiction.

FACTS: Robinson (D) was prosecuted under a state law criminalizing drug addiction. He was convicted. The conviction was affirmed on appeal. Robinson (D) appealed, contending that the law inflicted cruel and unusual punishment in violation of the Eighth and Fourteenth Amendments. The United States Supreme Court granted review.

ISSUE: May a state criminalize drug addiction?

HOLDING AND DECISION: (Stewart, J.) No. A state may not criminalize drug addiction. A state has broad powers to proscribe the importation, use, sale, or possession of controlled substances. However, the medical consensus is that addiction is an illness. A state may not, consistent with the Eighth Amendment, make it a criminal offense to be mentally ill or to suffer from a disease. Criminalizing drug addiction is no different. Consequently, the statute is unconstitutional. Reversed.

CONCURRENCE: (Douglas, J.) A prosecution based on status, when civil proceedings would do as well or better, is inconsistent with the Eighth Amendment.

CONCURRENCE: (Harlan, J.) Since addiction alone cannot reasonably be thought to amount to more than a propensity to use drugs, the law authorizes criminal punishment for the mere desire to commit a criminal act.

DISSENT: (White, J.) The statute punishes not an illness but repeated use of drugs, which constitutes repeated violations of the law.

▶ ANALYSIS

The Court has long tended to look askance at "status" crimes. The criminal law exists, the court has said, to punish behavior. When a certain status is prohibited, such as vagrancy or addiction, serious Eighth Amendment concerns are raised.

Quicknotes

ACTUS REUS The unlawful act that gives rise to criminal liability, as distinguished from the required mental state.

CRUEL AND UNUSUAL PUNISHMENT Punishment that is excessive or disproportionate to the offense committed and which is prohibited by the Eighth Amendment to the United States Constitution.

Powell v. Texas

Chronic alcoholic (D) v. State (P)

392 U.S. 514 (1968).

NATURE OF CASE: Appeal from conviction for public drunkenness.

FACT SUMMARY: Powell (D), a chronic alcoholic, was found to have a condition beyond his control which resulted in his being intoxicated in public, an act for which he was arrested.

RULE OF LAW
In light of current medical knowledge, it appears that chronic alcoholics in general do not suffer from such an irresistible compulsion to drink and to get drunk in public, that they are utterly unable to control their performance of either or both of these acts, and thus cannot be deterred at all from public intoxication.

FACTS: Powell (D), a chronic alcoholic, was found guilty of being drunk in public. It was argued that his appearance in public was not of his own volition, and that to punish him for his illness would be cruel and unusual in violation of the Eighth Amendment as applied to the states by the Fourteenth Amendment. The medical profession has not firmly determined whether alcoholism is an illness, is physically addicting, or merely psychologically habituating.

ISSUE: Is alcoholism a condition of such an involuntary nature that to punish an appearance in public while intoxicated would be cruel and unusual?

HOLDING AND DECISION: (Marshall, J.) No. There is widespread argument in the medical profession over whether alcoholism is a disease. A disease is anything the medical profession determines it to be. Facilities for treating indigent alcoholics are woefully lacking. At least a short time in jail permits the alcoholic to sober up. Generally, commission to an institution is for the time it takes to cure, while time in jail for drunkenness is usually limited. Powell (D) was not convicted for being a chronic alcoholic, but for being drunk in public. He is not within the ambit of *Robinson v. California*, 370 U.S. 660 (1962), which holds that a conviction for being of the status of a drug addict alone is cruel and unusual. Here, the conviction protects public safety and health. *Robinson* says a person may be punished only for committing some act which society has an interest in preventing. Affirmed.

CONCURRENCE: (Black, J.) "The States should (not) be held constitutionally required to make the inquiry as to what part of a defendant's personality is responsible for his actions and to excuse anyone whose action was, in some complex, psychological sense, the result of a 'compulsion.'"

CONCURRENCE: (White, J.) If it cannot be a crime to have an irresistible urge to use narcotics, it should not be a crime to yield to that compulsion. But here, there is nothing in the record to show that the chronic alcoholic has a compulsion to drink in public.

DISSENT: (Fortas, J.) "Alcoholism is caused and maintained by something other than the moral fault of the alcoholic, something that, to a greater or lesser extent . . . cannot be controlled by him." Thus, to punish the alcoholic would be cruel and unusual punishment.

▶ ANALYSIS

It would appear, at least according to Justice White, that once one proves his compulsion, he cannot be protected from conviction for failing to take precautions against it. For example, an epileptic may not be punished for his illness, unless he drives a vehicle. Yet the dissent, while stipulating that the statute did not punish the mere status of alcoholism, feels that the accused was punished for a condition he was helpless to avoid. Is the majority then taking the pragmatic way out? Recognizing the lack of adequate care facilities for indigent chronic alcoholics, it would seem that the Court would rather have the public drunk spend a night in jail to dry out than be committed for an unspecified term to an inadequate institution until deemed "cured."

Quicknotes

ACTUS REUS The unlawful act, that gives rise to criminal liability, as distinguished from the required mental state.

INVOLUNTARY INTOXICATION A defense to criminal liability for an unlawful act committed when the defendant involuntarily consumed substances rendering him incapable of understanding the nature of his acts.

IRRESISTIBLE IMPULSE RULE A defense to a criminal prosecution that the defendant, due to some mental disease or defect, was unable to resist the impulse to commit the crime due to his inability to control his actions.

State v. Kargar

State (P) v. Alleged-sexual molester (D)

Me. Sup. Jud. Ct., 679 A.2d 81 (1996).

NATURE OF CASE: Appeal from a criminal conviction for gross sexual assault.

FACT SUMMARY: Kargar (D), an Afghani refugee, was convicted of sexual assault after being seen kissing his infant son's penis, a common practice among Afghani people.

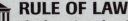

RULE OF LAW

The focus in a de minimis determination is on whether the admittedly criminal conduct was envisioned by the legislature when it defined the crime.

FACTS: Kargar (D) was arrested after a neighbor saw him kissing his infant son's penis. Kargar (D) moved for a dismissal pursuant to the de minimis statute. Following the presentations of witnesses at a de minimis hearing, the court denied Kargar's (D) motion and found him guilty of two counts of gross sexual assault. Kargar (D) appealed, claiming that the court erred as a matter of law because it found culture, lack of harm, and his innocent state of mind irrelevant to its de minimis analysis.

ISSUE: Is the focus in a de minimis determination on whether the admittedly criminal conduct was envisioned by the legislature when it defined the crime?

HOLDING AND DECISION: (Dana, J.) Yes. The focus in a de minimis determination is on whether the admittedly criminal conduct was envisioned by the legislature when it defined the crime. The de minimis statute requires an individual, case-specific analysis. The trial court was required to consider the possibility that the result of a conviction in this case could not have been anticipated by the legislature when it defined the crime of gross sexual assault. All of the evidence presented at the de minimis hearing supports the conclusion that there was nothing "sexual" about Kargar's (D) conduct. Although the court responded to a call for leniency by imposing an entirely suspended sentence, the two convictions expose Kargar (D) to severe consequences, including his required registration as a sex offender and the possibility of deportation. Since the legislature did not envision the extenuating circumstances present in this case, in order to avoid an injustice, the de minimis analysis requires that Kargar's (D) convictions be vacated.

▶ ANALYSIS

In jurisdictions where there is no de minimis statute, the prosecutor's discretion or judge's leniency would be the only hope for such a defendant to avoid conviction. The cultural defense is part of the movement for a greater understanding of multiculturalism. Multiculturalism should not, however, be used to undermine progress in protecting the rights of minorities, women, and children.

■══■

Quicknotes

DE MINIMIS STATUTE Provides that the court may dismiss a prosecution if it finds the defendant's conduct was within a customary tolerance, or did not actually cause or threaten the harm sought to be prevented by the law defining the crime.

■══■

Inchoate Offenses

Quick Reference Rules of Law

People v. Gentry

State (P) v. Boyfriend (D)

Ill. App. Ct., 157 Ill. App. 3d 899, 510 N.E.2d 963 (1987).

NATURE OF CASE: Appeal from a conviction for attempted murder.

FACT SUMMARY: When Gentry's (D) girlfriend was severely burned after he spilled gasoline on her during a drunken argument, Gentry (D) was charged with the crime of attempted murder.

RULE OF LAW
A finding of specific intent to kill is a necessary element of the crime of attempted murder.

FACTS: Gentry (D) and his girlfriend, Ruby Hill, were drinking one afternoon in the apartment they shared. When they began to argue, Gentry (D) spilled gasoline on Hill, which ignited when she went near the kitchen stove. Gentry (D), was able to smother the flames with a coat, but only after Hill had been severely burned. Gentry (D) was charged with attempted murder. Gentry (D) objected to the trial court's instruction to the jury, which stated that a person commits murder when he kills with intent to kill or do harm or with knowledge that his conduct creates a strong probability of death or great bodily harm. He argued that attempted murder required a showing of specific intent to kill. Gentry (D) was convicted of the charge and appealed.

ISSUE: Is a finding of specific intent to kill a necessary element of the crime of attempted murder?

HOLDING AND DECISION: (Linn, J.) Yes. A finding of specific intent to kill is a necessary element of the crime of attempted murder. The State (P) would read the attempt instruction as requiring a showing of any of the alternative mental states sufficient for a conviction of murder, making no distinction between the mental state required to prove murder and the mental state required to prove attempted murder. The State's (P) analysis and conclusion are erroneous. Intent to do bodily harm, or knowledge that the consequences of an act may result in death or great bodily harm, is not enough for a charge of attempted murder. Thus, the jury was misinstructed in this case. Gentry's (D) conviction and sentence are reversed, and the case is remanded for a new trial before a properly instructed jury.

ANALYSIS

The Illinois legislature manifested a desire to treat intent and knowledge as distinct mental states when imposing criminal liability for conduct. Knowledge is not intent, as defined by the state statutes, and a jury instruction should reflect this distinction. Accordingly, in a prosecution for attempted murder, which requires a specific intent, any incompatible elements must be omitted from the jury instructions.

Quicknotes

ATTEMPT An intent combined with an act falling short of the thing intended.

KNOWINGLY Intentionally; willfully; an act that is committed with knowledge as to its probable consequences.

SPECIFIC INTENT The intent to commit a specific unlawful act which is a required element for criminal liability for certain crimes.

Bruce v. State

Shooter (D) v. State (P)

Md. Ct. App., 317 Md. 642, 566 A.2d 103 (1989).

NATURE OF CASE: Appeal from a conviction for attempted first-degree felony murder.

FACT SUMMARY: After Bruce (D) shot the owner of a shoe store in the stomach during the course of a robbery attempt, a jury found Bruce (D) guilty of attempted first-degree felony murder, among other charges.

🏛 RULE OF LAW
Because a criminal attempt requires specific intent and a conviction for felony murder does not require a specific intent to kill, attempted felony murder is not a crime in Maryland.

FACTS: Bruce (D) and two other men went into a shoe store. Bruce (D), masked and armed with a handgun, ordered the owner to open the cash register. Upon finding the register empty, Bruce (D) aimed the gun at the owner's face and threatened to kill him. When the owner ducked down and moved forward, banging into Bruce (D), Bruce (D) shot him in the stomach. The owner recovered after hospitalization. A jury found Bruce (D) guilty of attempted first-degree felony murder. Bruce (D) appealed, contending that "attempted felony murder" was not a crime in Maryland.

ISSUE: Is attempted felony murder a crime in Maryland?

HOLDING AND DECISION: (Murphy, C.J.) No. Because a criminal attempt requires specific intent and a conviction for felony murder does not require a specific intent to kill, attempted felony murder is not a crime in Maryland. All murder committed in the perpetration of, or attempt to perpetrate, certain designated felonies, including robbery, is murder in the first degree. To secure a conviction for first-degree murder under the felony murder doctrine, the State (P) is merely required to prove a specific intent to commit the underlying felony, and that death occurred in the perpetration or attempt to perpetrate the felony. It is not necessary to prove a specific intent to kill or to demonstrate the existence of willfulness, deliberation, or premeditation. Because a conviction for felony murder requires no specific intent to kill, it follows that because a criminal attempt is a specific-intent crime, attempted felony murder is not a crime in Maryland. Reversed.

▌ANALYSIS

Most states have agreed with *Bruce* that no such crime as attempted felony murder exists, but the state of Florida, in *Amlotte v. State*, 456 So.2d 448 (1984), held otherwise. It found that an individual who commits a specific overt act during the commission of a felony, which could, but does not, cause the death of another, will have committed the crime of attempted felony murder. On the issue of felony murder in general, the Model Penal Code adopts a rebuttable presumption approach, whereby recklessness and indifference are presumed if the killing occurs during one of a number of specified felonies. See Model Penal Code § 210.2.

Quicknotes

ATTEMPT An intent combined with an act falling short of the thing intended.

FELONY MURDER The unlawful killing of another human being while in the commission of, or attempted commission of, specified felonies.

SPECIFIC INTENT The intent to commit a specific unlawful act which is a required element for criminal liability for certain crimes.

United States v. Mandujano

Federal government (P) v. Criminal defendant (D)

499 F.2d 370 (5th Cir. 1974).

NATURE OF CASE: [Nature of case not stated in casebook excerpt.]

FACT SUMMARY: [Fact summary not stated in casebook excerpt.]

🏛 RULE OF LAW
There must be some appreciable fragment of the crime committed for an act to qualify as an "attempt."

FACTS: [Facts not stated in casebook excerpt.]

ISSUE: Must there be some appreciable fragment of the crime committed for an act to qualify as an "attempt"?

HOLDING AND DECISION: (Rives, J.) Yes. There must be some appreciable fragment of the crime committed for an act to qualify as an "attempt." Apparently there is no legislative history indicating exactly what Congress meant when it used the word "attempt." The courts in many jurisdictions have tried to elaborate on the distinction between mere preparation and attempt. In *Mims v. United States*, 375 F.2d 135 (5th Cir. 1967), this court noted that the question of a satisfactory standard for telling where preparations end and attempt begins had not been decided. However, the test from *People v. Buffum*, 40 Cal. 2d 709 (Cal. 1953), has frequently been approved. That test states that preparation alone is not enough. There must be some appreciable fragment of the crime committed. It must be in such progress that it will be consummated unless interrupted by circumstances independent of the will of the attempter, and the act must not be equivocal in nature.

▶ ANALYSIS

Comment to the Model Penal Code has catalogued a number of formulations for determining when preparation for a crime becomes an attempt. Under the physical proximity doctrine, the overt act required for an attempt must be proximate to the completed crime. In the dangerous proximity doctrine, the nearer the act to the crime, the stronger is the case for calling the act an attempt. The indispensable element test emphasizes any indispensable aspect of the criminal endeavor over which the actor has not yet acquired control. Under the probable desistance test, conduct constitutes an attempt if it will result in the crime intended without interruption from an outside source. The abnormal step approach denotes that an attempt is a step toward crime which goes beyond the point where the normal citizen would desist. Finally, under the unequivocality test, an attempt is committed when the actor's conduct manifests intent to commit a crime.

Quicknotes

ACTUS REUS The unlawful act, that gives rise to criminal liability, as distinguished from the required mental state.

ATTEMPT An intent combined with an act falling short of the thing intended.

OVERT ACT An open act evidencing an intention to commit a crime.

Commonwealth v. Peaslee

State (P) v. Individual indicted for alleged arson (D)

Mass. Sup. Jud. Ct., 177 Mass. 267, 59 N.E. 55 (1901).

NATURE OF CASE: Appeal from indictment for attempted arson.

FACT SUMMARY: Peaslee (D) arranged certain combustibles in order to burn down a building but never went through with his plan.

🏛 RULE OF LAW
A defendant cannot be convicted of criminal attempt where he has taken preparatory steps to fulfilling a crime, but changes his mind before committing the last act necessary to effect the crime.

FACTS: Peaslee (D) constructed and arranged certain combustibles in a building, in order to set it on fire. The materials were made ready to be lit, and if lit, would have set fire to the building. (Peaslee (D) wished to get the insurance proceeds.) The plan required that a candle, which was on a shelf six feet away, be placed on a piece of wood in a pan of turpentine and lit. Peaslee (D) solicited a man in his employment to go to the building and do the actual lighting. This offer was refused, however. Later, Peaslee (D) and the man drove toward the building with the intent to light the materials. When they were within a quarter of a mile from their destination, however, Peaslee (D) changed his mind and drove away. This was the nearest he ever came to accomplishing the intended arson. Peaslee (D) was indicted for attempted arson.

ISSUE: Can a defendant be convicted of criminal attempt where he has taken preparatory steps to fulfilling a crime, but changes his mind before committing the last act necessary to effect the crime?

HOLDING AND DECISION: (Holmes, C.J.) No. A defendant cannot be convicted of criminal attempt where he has taken preparatory steps to fulfilling a crime, but changes his mind before committing the last act necessary to effect the crime. In attempt cases, the question is whether the defendant came near enough to accomplishing the substantive crime, so the issue is one of degree. Usually there is attempt where either the final action is completed but the crime is averted through some circumstance unknown to the defendant, or where the final action is thwarted by outside forces (e.g., the police intervene at the last moment). However, when the defendant has taken only first steps toward achieving a crime, there is still the chance that the would-be criminal can change his mind. Therefore, strictly speaking, those first steps cannot be called attempt, i.e., preparation is not attempt. Nevertheless, when preparation comes very close to accomplishing the intended criminal result, the mere intent to complete the crime renders the crime so probable that a criminal attempt may be found to exist. Again, this is primarily a question of degree and weighing of facts. Here, the defendant did not have the "present intent to set the fire." To be able to convict the defendant of attempted arson, without any help from anyone else, it would have to be shown that he had "a present intent to accomplish the crime without much delay, and to have had this intent at a time and place where he was able to carry it out." On the pleadings, this has not been shown. If the defendant were to be convicted of soliciting arson, he might be so convicted under the facts of this case, but the indictment failed to plead solicitation as the last act necessary to effectuate the crime. If it had, the outcome might be different, i.e., the defendant could have been convicted. The conviction cannot stand on the pleadings as they are. Exceptions sustained.

▶ ANALYSIS

Because an attempt is, in general, a specific-intent crime, the fact that a defendant in an attempt case has the opportunity to change his mind before taking the last step necessary to effectuate the crime—as in this case—directly bears on the question of whether the defendant had the requisite present intent to commit the crime. Justice Holmes makes clear that the acts must be accompanied by a "present intent," and that the defendant "must be shown to have had a present intent to accomplish the crime without much delay, and to have had this intent at a time and place where he was able to carry it out." The example he uses to illustrate this principle is that if the defendant had been trying to light the materials and was thwarted by the police, he could have been convicted of attempt, because he had the present intent to complete the last step necessary to accomplish the crime.

■▬■

Quicknotes

ARSON The unlawful burning of a building or structure.

ATTEMPT An intent combined with an act falling short of the thing intended.

■▬■

People v. Rizzo

State (P) v. Attempted-robber (D)

N.Y. Ct. App., 246 N.Y. 334, 158 N.E. 888 (1927).

NATURE OF CASE: Appeal from conviction for attempt to commit robbery in the first degree.

FACT SUMMARY: Rizzo (D) and three others set out with the intention to commit a robbery but they were arrested before they found the person they intended to rob.

🏛 RULE OF LAW
An attempt to commit a crime requires an act "tending," but failing, to effect its commission, which encompasses only those acts which are so near to the accomplishment of the crime that in all reasonable probability the crime itself would have been committed but for timely interference.

FACTS: Rizzo (D) and three others set out in a car to rob one Charles Rao of a payroll he was to carry from the bank for the United Lathing Company. Rizzo's (D) job was to point out Rao to the others. In fact, the police were following the four as they rode around looking for Rao. They were arrested at the site of one of the buildings being constructed by United Lathing as they were canvassing the buildings looking for Rao. Neither Rao nor another man, who was supposed to carry a payroll, was at the building at the time of the arrest. Rizzo (D) appealed his conviction for attempt to commit robbery in the first degree, asserting that his conduct had not been sufficient to constitute an "attempt."

ISSUE: To be guilty of an "attempt" to commit a crime, must one engage in acts which are so near to the accomplishment of the crime that in all reasonable probability the crime itself would have been committed but for timely interference?

HOLDING AND DECISION: (Crane, J.) Yes. An act, done with intent to commit a crime, and tending, but failing, to effect its commission, is "an attempt to commit that crime." However, the line is drawn between acts which are remote and those which are proximate and near to the consummation. That is, the law considers those acts "tending" to the commission of the crime to be the ones which are so near to its accomplishment that, in all reasonable probability, the crime itself would have been committed but for timely interference. Here, the defendants had not even found or seen the man they intended to rob. Their acts were not so near to the result that the danger of success was very great. Thus, no "attempt" was made to commit the crime. Reversed. New trial granted.

▶ ANALYSIS

It is interesting that the Model Penal Code provision dealing with criminal attempt lists certain acts that shall not be insufficient as a matter of law to constitute an "attempt." The list includes lying in wait, searching for, or following, the contemplated victim of the crime, and reconnoitering the place contemplated for the commission of the crime.

∎══∎

Quicknotes

ATTEMPT An intent combined with an act falling short of the thing intended.

ROBBERY The unlawful taking of property from the person of another through the use of force or fear.

∎══∎

People v. Miller

State (P) v. Attempted-murderer (D)

Cal. Sup. Ct., 2 Cal. 2d 527, 42 P.2d 308 (1935).

NATURE OF CASE: Appeal from attempted murder conviction.

FACT SUMMARY: When Miller (D) was prosecuted for attempted murder for threatening to kill Jeans and then confronting him with a loaded rifle although not pointing the rifle at him, he argued that such acts fell short of an attempt.

🏛 RULE OF LAW
The crime of attempt requires evidence of a direct act, however slight, toward commission of the intended crime.

FACTS: Early on the day in question, Miller (D), under the influence of liquor and in the presence of others, threatened to kill Albert Jeans. Later in the day, Miller (D) entered the field in which Jeans was working, carrying a .22-caliber rifle. Miller (D) walked in a direct line toward Jeans. He stopped and appeared to be loading his rifle. At no time did he lift the rifle as though to take aim. Jeans fled. Another person took the rifle from Miller (D). The rifle was found to be loaded. Miller (D) was found guilty of attempt to commit murder and appealed, arguing that his acts fell short of constituting an attempt.

ISSUE: Does the crime of attempt require evidence of a direct act, however slight, toward commission of the intended crime?

HOLDING AND DECISION: (Shenk, J.) Yes. The crime of attempt requires evidence of a direct act, however slight, toward commission of the intended crime. The reason for requiring evidence of a direct act toward commission of the intended crime is that in the majority of cases up to that time the conduct of the defendant, consisting merely of acts of preparation, has never ceased to be equivocal. This is necessarily so, irrespective of the declared intent. It is that quality of being equivocal that must be lacking before the act becomes one which may be said to be a commencement of the commission of the crime, or an overt act, or before any fragment of the crime itself has been committed. As long as the equivocal quality remains, no one can say with certainty what the intent of the defendant is. Here, up to the moment the gun was taken from Miller (D), no one could say with certainty whether he had come into the field to carry out his threat to kill Jeans or merely to demand his arrest by the constable. Reversed.

▶ ANALYSIS

Under the strictest version of the unequivocality standard, an act does not constitute an attempt unless the specific criminal goal of the actor is evident from their conduct, without considering any statement which the actor may have made before, during, or after the incident regarding the actor's state of mind.

■■■

Quicknotes

ATTEMPT An effort or try, combined with the act falling short of the goal intended.

ATTEMPTED MURDER An intent to commit murder plus an action taken toward commission of the crime, falling short of completion.

■■■

State v. Reeves

State (P) v. Attempted-murderers (D)

Tenn. Sup. Ct., 916 S.W.2d 909 (1996).

NATURE OF CASE: Appeal from conviction for attempt to commit second-degree murder.

FACT SUMMARY: Two girls (D) made a plan to kill their homeroom teacher with rat poison.

🏛 RULE OF LAW
When an actor possesses materials to be used in the commission of a crime, at or near the scene of the crime, and where the possession of those materials can serve no lawful purpose under the circumstances, the jury is entitled, but not required, to find that the actor has taken a substantial step toward the commission of the crime if such action is strongly corroborative of the actor's overall criminal purpose.

FACTS: Reeves and Coffman (D), two 12-year-old students, made a plan to kill their homeroom teacher, Geiger, with rat poison. They communicated their plan to several other students, who relayed the information until it reached the principal. When Geiger entered her classroom, she observed Reeves and Coffman (D) leaning over her desk and a purse lying next to her coffee. Rat poison was found in Coffman's (D) purse. The two were found delinquent by the juvenile court and appealed. A jury found the girls (D) guilty of attempt to commit second-degree murder and Reeves appealed. The court of appeals affirmed, and Reeves (D) applied to this court for permission to appeal.

ISSUE: When an actor possesses materials to be used in the commission of a crime, at or near the scene of the crime, and where the possession of those materials can serve no lawful purpose under the circumstances, is the jury entitled, but not required, to find that the actor has taken a substantial step toward the commission of the crime if such action is strongly corroborative of the actor's overall criminal purpose?

HOLDING AND DECISION: (Drowota, J.) Yes. When an actor possesses materials to be used in the commission of a crime, at or near the scene of the crime, and where the possession of those materials can serve no lawful purpose under the circumstances, the jury is entitled, but not required, to find that the actor has taken a substantial step toward the commission of the crime if such action is strongly corroborative of the actor's overall criminal purpose. Prior to the adoption of Tenn. Code Ann. § 39-12-101, the rule followed was that set forth in *Dupuy v. State*, 204 Tenn. 624 (1959), which distinguished "mere preparation" from the "act itself," finding no liability for the former. Such a rule endangers the public and undermines the objective of attempt law; it must be abandoned. Affirmed.

CONCURRENCE AND DISSENT: (Birch, J.) I concur in the majority's statement of the rule to be applied in deciding whether a criminal attempt has occurred. I dissent in its application to this case since the "entire course of action" of the girls (D) was not "strongly corroborative" of intent to commit second-degree murder and that the evidence was insufficient as a matter of law.

▶ ANALYSIS

Prior to this case, in order to make out a case of criminal attempt the following elements had to be shown: (1) an intent to commit a specific crime; (2) an overt act toward its commission; and (3) failure to consummate the crime.

■▬■

Quicknotes

ATTEMPT An intent combined with an act falling short of the thing intended.

CRIMINAL ATTEMPT An intent to commit a criminal offense plus an action taken toward commission of the crime.

OVERT ACT An open act evidencing an intention to commit a crime.

SECOND-DEGREE MURDER The unlawful killing of another person, without premeditation, and characterized by either intent to kill or by a reckless disregard for human life.

SUBSTANTIAL STEP In reference to the crime of attempt, the undertaking of an action or omission that constitutes a substantial step in a general scheme to commit a crime.

■▬■

People v. Thousand

State (P) v. Attempted-obscenity violator (D)

Mich. Sup. Ct., 465 Mich. 149, 631 N.W.2d 694 (2001).

NATURE OF CASE: State's appeal of trial court's granting of defense motion to quash information.

FACT SUMMARY: When Thousand (D) was charged with attempted distribution of obscene material to a minor (over the Internet), he argued that since the young girl with whom he thought he was communicating was in actuality an undercover sheriff, it would have been legally impossible to have committed the offense.

RULE OF LAW
The defense of impossibility is not available to a charge of attempt.

FACTS: A deputy sheriff assigned to the Internet Crimes Bureau, posing as a minor (a 14-year-old girl named "Bekka") on the Internet, entered a "chat room" and engaged in a series of conversations with Thousand (D) (a 23-year-old male) which were sexually explicit. Thousand (D) made repeated lewd invitations to "Bekka" to engage in various sexual acts, despite various indications of her young age. The two planned to meet. When Thousand (D) arrived at the meeting, he was arrested and charged with attempted distribution of obscene material to a minor. Thousand (D) moved to quash the information, arguing that, because the existence of a child victim was an element of the offense, the evidence was legally insufficient to support the charge. The circuit court agreed and dismissed the case, holding that it was legally impossible for Thousand (D) to have committed the charged offense. The court of appeals affirmed the dismissal, and the state appealed.

ISSUE: Is the defense of impossibility available to a charge of attempt?

HOLDING AND DECISION: (Young, J.) No. The defense of impossibility is not available to a charge of attempt. This court is unable to discern from the words of the attempt statute any legislative intent that the concept of "impossibility" provides any impediment to charging a defendant with, or convicting him of, an attempted crime, notwithstanding any factual mistake—regarding either the attendant circumstances or the legal status of some factor relevant thereto—that the defendant may harbor. The attempt statute carves out no exception for those who, possessing the requisite intent to commit an offense prohibited by law and taking action toward the commission of that offense, have, as here, acted under an extrinsic misconception. It is unquestioned in the instant case that Thousand (D) could not be convicted of the crime of distributing obscene material to a minor (since the "vic-

tim" was not in fact a minor but a police officer). Instead, Thousand (D) is charged with the distinct offense of attempt, which requires only that the prosecution prove intention to commit an offense prohibited by law, coupled with conduct toward the commission of that offense. The notion it would be "impossible" for Thousand (D) to have committed the completed offense is simply irrelevant to the analysis. Dismissal of the charges is reversed.

DISSENT: (Kelly, J.) There is ample evidence that the doctrine of legal impossibility has been adopted in Michigan. Furthermore, it does not follow from the fact that the statutes do not expressly incorporate the concept of impossibility that the defense is inapplicable. Because impossibility is a viable defense, the dismissal of the charges should here be affirmed.

ANALYSIS

As made clear in the *Thousand* decision, in deciding guilt on a charge of attempt, the trier of fact must examine the unique circumstances of the particular case and determine whether the prosecution has proven that the defendant possessed the requisite specific intent and that he engaged in some act "toward the commission" of the intended offense. It should be noted that the Model Penal Code eliminates the defense of impossibility to a charge of attempt.

Quicknotes

ATTEMPT An effort or try, combined with the act falling short of the goal intended.

Commonwealth v. McCloskey

State (P) v. Inmate convicted of attempted prison breach (D)

Pa. Super. Ct., 234 Pa. Super. 577, 341 A.2d 500 (1975).

NATURE OF CASE: Appeal from conviction for attempted prison breach.

FACT SUMMARY: McCloskey (D), a prison inmate, argued that by voluntarily abandoning his plan to escape from prison and then telling a guard of his abandonment, he should be exonerated from the charge of attempted prison breach.

🏛 RULE OF LAW
A person who voluntarily abandons a criminal offense exonerates himself from criminal responsibility.

FACTS: McCloskey (D), a prison inmate, voluntarily approached Larson (a prison guard) and told Larson that he had planned to make a prison breach the night before, "but I changed my mind because I thought of my family, and I got scared of the consequences." McCloskey (D) had previously scaled an internal prison wall and placed items of civilian clothing into a laundry bag before he changed his mind, went back to work at his prison job, and then told the guard about his planned escape and how he had changed his mind. McCloskey (D) was found guilty of attempted prison breach and appealed, contending that the evidence showed that he had voluntarily abandoned the crime.

ISSUE: Does a person who voluntarily abandons a criminal offense exonerate himself from criminal responsibility?

HOLDING AND DECISION: (Hoffman, J.) Yes. A person who voluntarily abandons a criminal offense exonerates himself from criminal responsibility. Here, the evidence indicates that McCloskey (D) scaled a fence within the prison walls that led to the recreation yard and then to the prison wall. The Commonwealth's (P) evidence supports McCloskey's (D) claim that he went only as far as the yard before giving up his plan to escape. Thus he was still within the prison and still only contemplating a prison breach, but not yet attempting the act. He was, therefore, in a position to abandon the criminal offense voluntarily, thereby exonerating himself from criminal responsibility for the crime of attempted prison breach. Sentence is vacated and McCloskey (D) is ordered discharged.

CONCURRENCE: (Cercone, J.) McCloskey's (D) voluntary abandonment of his escape plan is a sufficient defense to the crime of attempted prison breach, but not the fact that he went only as far as the yard before giving up his plan to escape.

▶ ANALYSIS

Sound reasons of public policy underscore the recognition of voluntary abandonment as an affirmative defense. As explained by the drafters of the Model Penal Code, the defense of complete and permanent abandonment should be allowed because voluntary abandonment negates the conclusion that the accused continues to be dangerous. Furthermore, the knowledge that voluntary abandonment exonerates a person from criminal liability provides a motive to desist prior to the completion of the crime.

■■■

Quicknotes

ATTEMPT An effort or try, combined with the act falling short of the goal intended.

■■■

United States v. Alkhabaz

Federal government (P) v. Alleged-threatener (D)

104 F.3d 1492 (6th Cir. 1997).

NATURE OF CASE: Government's (P) appeal of judgment of district court quashing an indictment.

FACT SUMMARY: When Alkhabaz (D) was charged with violation of a federal statute which prohibits interstate communications containing threats to kidnap or injure another person, he argued that his sadistic e-mails and Internet stories did not constitute "threats" within the meaning of the statute.

> ### 🏛 RULE OF LAW
> Communication objectively indicating a serious expression of intention to inflict bodily harm does not constitute a threat unless the communication is conveyed to further some goal through intimidation.

FACTS: Abraham Alkhabaz (D) and others exchanged e-mail messages over the Internet, the content of which expressed a sexual interest in violence against women and girls, and also posted an Internet story describing torture, rape, and murder of a young woman who shared the name of one of the sender's university classmates. This act triggered notification to the university authorities. The e-mailers were charged with violation of a federal statute which prohibits interstate communications containing threats to kidnap or injure another person. The federal district court granted Alkhabaz's (D) motion to quash the indictment, and the government appealed.

ISSUE: Does a communication objectively indicating a serious expression of intention to inflict bodily harm constitute a threat only if the communication is conveyed to further some goal through intimidation?

HOLDING AND DECISION: (Martin, Jr., C.J.) Yes. Communication objectively indicating a serious expression of intention to inflict bodily harm does not constitute a threat unless the communication is conveyed to further some goal through intimidation. The government must allege and prove three elements to support a conviction under the instant statute: (1) a transmission in interstate commerce; (2) a communication containing a threat; and (3) the threat must be to injure or kidnap the person of another. Here, the first and third elements cannot be seriously challenged. However, as to the second element (whether there is a "threat"), it is necessary to consider precisely what type of conduct Congress intended to prohibit. At their core, threats are tools employed when one wishes to have some effect, or achieve some goal, through intimidation. This is true regardless whether the goal is highly reprehensible or seemingly innocuous. To achieve the intent of Congress, to constitute a communica-

tion containing a "threat," the communication must be such that a reasonable person would take the statement as a serious expression of an intention to inflict bodily harm (the mens rea), and would perceive such expression as being communicated to effect some change or achieve some goal through intimidation (the actus reus). Applying this test, the communications in this case do not constitute a threat since no reasonable person would perceive the communications as being conveyed to effect some change or achieve some goal through intimidation. Quite the opposite, the communicators apparently sent the e-mail messages to each other in an attempt to foster a friendship based on shared sexual fantasies. Affirmed.

DISSENT: (Krupansky, J.) The statutory language is simple, clear, concise, and unambiguous. The plain, expressed statutory language commands only that the alleged communication must contain "any threat" to kidnap or physically injure "any person," made for "any reason" or no reason. The statute by its terms does not confine the scope of criminalized communications to those directed to identified-individuals and intended to effect some particular change or goal.

▶ ANALYSIS

In *Alkhabaz*, the court notes that it is one of the most fundamental postulates of the criminal justice system that conviction can result only from a violation of clearly defined standards of conduct. Indeed, the law does not punish bad purpose standing alone, but rather requires that mens rea accompany the actus reas specifically proscribed by statute.

■═■

Quicknotes

ACTUS REUS The unlawful act, that gives rise to criminal liability, as distinguished from the required mental state.

MENS REA Criminal intent.

■═■

State v. Mann

State (P) v. Criminal defendant (D)

N.C. Sup. Ct., 317 N.C. 164, 345 S.E.2d 365 (1986).

NATURE OF CASE: [Nature of case not stated in casebook excerpt.]

FACT SUMMARY: [Fact summary not stated in casebook excerpt.]

🏛 RULE OF LAW
Solicitation involves the asking, enticing, inducing, or counseling of another to commit a crime.

FACTS: [Facts not stated in casebook excerpt.]

ISSUE: Does solicitation involve the asking, enticing, inducing, or counseling of another to commit a crime?

HOLDING AND DECISION: (Martin, J.) Yes. Solicitation involves the asking, enticing, inducing, or counseling of another to commit a crime. The solicitor conceives the criminal idea and furthers its commission via another person by suggesting to, inducing, or manipulating that person. A solicitor, however, may be more dangerous and more culpable than a conspirator since a conspirator may merely passively agree to a criminal scheme, while the solicitor plans, schemes, and incites the solicitation, then hides behind the conspirator.

▶ ANALYSIS

This heavily edited excerpt is apparently included only to illustrate the general principles of criminal solicitation. Once the crime that was the goal of the solicitation has either been committed or attempted, the solicitation merges into the underlying crime. The solicitor is then guilty of either the crime committed or attempted under the principles of complicity.

■■■

Quicknotes

MERGER DOCTRINE A rule of law whereby, if a defendant committed a single criminal act that constitutes two separate offenses, the lesser-included offense merges into the higher offense; the defendant may only be charged with the higher offense.

SOLICITATION Contact initiated by an attorney for the purpose of obtaining employment.

■■■

State v. Cotton

State (P) v. Child molester (D)

N.M. Ct. App., 109 N.M. 769, 790 P.2d 1050 (1990).

NATURE OF CASE: Appeal from a conviction for criminal solicitation.

FACT SUMMARY: When Cotton (D) wrote to ask his wife to prevent her 14-year-old daughter from testifying at his trial for sexually molesting her, he was convicted of criminal solicitation, although his wife never received the letters.

🏛 RULE OF LAW
The offense of solicitation requires some form of actual communication from the defendant to the person intended to be solicited.

FACTS: After Cotton (D), his wife, children, and a stepdaughter moved to New Mexico, his wife and children returned to Indiana. Later, Cotton's (D) 14-year-old stepdaughter moved back to New Mexico to live with him. Cotton (D) was subsequently arrested for multiple counts of criminal sexual penetration of a minor. While awaiting trial, he wrote two letters to his wife, asking her to get his stepdaughter to return to Indiana so that she would be unable to testify against him. Neither letter was ever mailed. Unknown to Cotton (D), his cellmate had removed the letters and given them to law enforcement authorities. Cotton (D) contended that the evidence did not support the charges of solicitation since his wife had never received the letters. Cotton (D) was convicted on two counts of criminal solicitation. This appeal followed.

ISSUE: Does the offense of solicitation require some form of actual communication from the defendant to the person to be solicited?

HOLDING AND DECISION: (Donnelly, J.) Yes. The offense of solicitation requires some form of actual communication from the defendant to the person to be solicited. A person is guilty of criminal solicitation if he solicits, commands, requests, induces, employs, or otherwise attempts to promote or facilitate another person to engage in conduct constituting a felony. New Mexico's criminal solicitation statute significantly omits the section of the Model Penal Code declaring that an uncommunicated solicitation to commit a crime may constitute criminal solicitation. This omission indicates an implicit legislative intent that the offense of solicitation requires some form of actual communication of a defendant to either an intermediary or the person intended to be solicited, indicating the subject matter of the solicitation. Since Cotton's (D) messages were never communicated to his wife, Cotton's (D) convictions for solicitation are reversed and the case remanded.

▶ ANALYSIS

The ALI, Model Criminal Code, § 5.02(2) provides in pertinent part: "It is immaterial that the actor fails to communicate with the person he solicits to commit a crime if his conduct was designed to effect such communication." According to LaFave & Scott, *Substantive Criminal Law* § 6.1 (1986), even where the solicitor's letter is intercepted before it reaches the addressee, the act is nonetheless criminal, although it may be that the solicitor must be prosecuted for an attempt to solicit on such facts. The court here implied that Cotton (D) should have, in fact, been charged with attempted solicitation.

■■■

Quicknotes

ATTEMPT An intent combined with an act falling short of the thing intended.

INCHOATE Impartial or incomplete.

SOLICITATION Contact initiated by an attorney for the purpose of obtaining employment.

■■■

People v. Carter

State (P) v. Conspirator (D)

Mich. Sup. Ct., 415 Mich. 558, 330 N.W.2d 314 (1982).

NATURE OF CASE: [Nature of case not stated in casebook excerpt.]

FACT SUMMARY: [Fact summary not stated in casebook excerpt.]

🏛 RULE OF LAW
Criminal conspiracy is defined as "a partnership in criminal purposes," a mutual agreement or understanding, express or implied, between two or more persons to commit a criminal act or to accomplish a legal act by unlawful means.

FACTS: [Facts not stated in casebook excerpt.]

ISSUE: Is conspiracy a mutual agreement or understanding between two persons to commit a criminal act or to accomplish a legal act by unlawful means?

HOLDING AND DECISION: (Moody, Jr., J.) Yes. Criminal conspiracy is defined as "a partnership in criminal purposes," a mutual agreement or understanding, express or implied, between two or more persons to commit a criminal act or to accomplish a legal act by unlawful means. Conspiracy is a crime that is separate and distinct from the substantive crime that is its object. The gist of the offense of conspiracy lies in the unlawful agreement. The crime is complete upon formation of the agreement. The guilt or innocence of a conspirator does not depend upon the accomplishment of the goals of the conspiracy. More importantly, a conviction of conspiracy does not merge with a conviction of the completed offense. Thus, a defendant may be convicted and punished for both the conspiracy and the substantive crime.

▶ ANALYSIS

While the offense of conspiracy has its origins in the common law, it is now specifically proscribed by statute, which sets forth the penalties for its commission. The criminalization of conspiracy has been justified by the assumption that collective criminal agreement is a greater threat to the public than individual action. Concerted action increases the chance that a complex crime will be successfully committed while decreasing the chance that the individual involved will back out.

■■■

Quicknotes

CONSPIRACY Concerted action by two or more persons to accomplish some unlawful purpose.

INCHOATE Impartial or incomplete.

■■■

Pinkerton v. United States

Brothers (D) v. Federal government (P)

328 U.S. 640 (1946).

NATURE OF CASE: Appeal from conviction for conspiracy to violate the Internal Revenue Code.

FACT SUMMARY: Walter (D) and Daniel Pinkerton (D), brothers who live a short distance apart, were convicted of various substantive violations of the Internal Revenue Code and conspiracy to violate same.

🏛 RULE OF LAW
As long as a conspiracy continues, the overt act of one partner may be the act of all without any new agreement specifically directed to that act.

FACTS: Walter (D) and his brother, Daniel Pinkerton (D), were convicted of various substantive violations of the Internal Revenue Code and conspiracy to violate same. They lived a short distance apart on Daniel's (D) farm and were apparently involved in unlawful dealings in whiskey. Daniel (D) contended that as only Walter (D) committed the substantive offenses, he could not be held to the conspiracy even though the substantive offenses were committed in furtherance of the conspiracy.

ISSUE: In addition to evidence that the offense was, in fact, committed in furtherance of the conspiracy, is evidence of direct participation in commission of the substantive offense or other evidence from which participation might fairly be inferred necessary?

HOLDING AND DECISION: (Douglas, J.) No. Here there was a continuous conspiracy with no evidence that Daniel (D) had withdrawn from it. As long as a conspiracy continues, the conspirators act for each other in carrying it forward. An overt act of one partner may be the act of all without any new agreement specifically directed to that act. Criminal intent to do the act is found in the formation of the conspiracy. The conspiracy contemplated the very act committed. Affirmed.

DISSENT: (Rutledge, J.) There was no evidence that Daniel (D) counseled, advised, or had knowledge of the particular acts or offenses. Simply finding them to be general partners in a crime is a dangerous precedent.

▶ *ANALYSIS*

It is possible that the approach taken here had in mind the development of modern organized crime. Anyone who professed his allegiance to the criminal acts of another might be held to conspiracy. Questions also arise as to punishment of one who has withdrawn from the conspiracy. The test for abandonment of a conspiracy is generally whether the abandoning conspirator has brought home to his fellow conspirators that he is quitting. Even if not a defense, a withdrawal may start the statute of limitations to run at that point, prevent his being held for crimes committed after his withdrawal, or prevent admission of evidence against him of acts or declarations his former co-conspirators did or said after his withdrawal.

Quicknotes

CONSPIRACY Concerted action by two or more persons to accomplish some unlawful purpose.

OVERT ACT An open act evidencing an intention to commit a crime.

WITHDRAWAL The removal of cash or other assets from the location in which it is held.

People v. Swain

Government (P) v. Alleged-criminal conspirator (D)

Cal. Sup. Ct., 12 Cal. 4th 593, 909 P.2d 994 (1996).

NATURE OF CASE: Review of a criminal conspiracy conviction.

FACT SUMMARY: Swain (D) was found guilty of conspiring to murder a young boy in a drive-by shooting.

🏛 RULE OF LAW
A conviction of conspiracy to commit murder requires a finding of intent to kill, and cannot be based on a theory of implied malice.

FACTS: Swain (D) was a passenger in a van during a drive-by shooting. He admitted firing shots from the van, but claimed he fired in self-defense. He was found to be not guilty of murder, but guilty of conspiracy. The jury made a finding that the target offense of the conspiracy was murder in the second degree. California law recognizes three theories of second-degree murder: unpremeditated murder with express malice, implied malice murder, and second-degree felony murder. The jury in this case was instructed on the elements of murder, including principles of implied malice second-degree murder. The court of appeals concluded that it could find no authority supportive of the proposition that the crime of conspiracy to commit murder in the second degree must be accompanied by an intent to kill (i.e., express malice). Swain (D) appealed, claiming that conviction of conspiracy to commit murder necessarily required proof of express, not implied, malice, the functional equivalent of intent to kill.

ISSUE: Does a conviction of conspiracy to commit murder require a finding of intent to kill?

HOLDING AND DECISION: (Baxter, J.) Yes. A conviction of conspiracy to commit murder requires a finding of intent to kill, and cannot be based on a theory of implied malice. The element of malice aforethought in implied malice murder cases is derived or implied, in part through hindsight, so to speak, from proof of the specific intent to do some act dangerous to human life and the circumstance that a killing has resulted therefrom. Due to the nature of implied malice murder, it would be illogical to conclude one can be guilty of conspiring to commit murder where the requisite element of malice is implied. Conspiracy is an inchoate crime that is fixed as of the time of agreement to commit the crime and commission of a crime could never be established, or deemed complete, unless and until a killing actually occurred. Reversed.

▶ ANALYSIS

The elements of conspiracy are agreement, specific intent, two or more persons, unlawful object or means, and an overt act. The prosecution must show that the conspirators intended to agree but also that they intended to commit the elements of the offense. This would be at odds with an implied malice element for a murder charge.

Quicknotes

CRIMINAL INTENT An intention to carry out a criminal offense.

INCHOATE Impartial or incomplete.

MALICE The intention to commit an unlawful act without justification or excuse.

MURDER Unlawful killing of another person either with deliberation and premeditation or by conduct demonstrating a reckless disregard for human life.

People v. Lauria

State (P) v. Supplier to prostitutes (D)

Cal. Ct. App., 251 Cal. App. 2d 471, 59 Cal. Rptr. 628 (1967).

NATURE OF CASE: Action for conspiracy to further prostitution.

FACT SUMMARY: Lauria (D) knew that some of his answering service customers were prostitutes who used his service for business purposes.

🏛 RULE OF LAW
The intent of a supplier (who knows of the criminal use to which his goods are put) to participate in the criminal activity may be inferred from circumstances showing that he has a stake in the criminal venture or by the aggravated nature of the crime itself.

FACTS: Lauria (D) and three people who used his answering service were arrested for prostitution. Lauria (D) knew that one of the people was a prostitute. He said he did not arbitrarily tell the police about prostitutes who used his service for business purposes.

ISSUE: Does a supplier necessarily become a part of a conspiracy to further an illegal venture by furnishing goods or services which he knows are to be used for criminal purposes, where the crime involved is a misdemeanor?

HOLDING AND DECISION: (Fleming, J.) No. Both the knowledge of the illegal use of the goods or services and the intent to further that use are necessary to support a conviction for conspiracy. Intent may be inferred from circumstances of the sale which show that the supplier had acquired a special interest in the activity. Or a supplier may be liable on the basis of knowledge alone where he furnishes goods which he knows will be used to commit a serious crime. However, this does not apply to misdemeanors. Here, Lauria (D) was not shown to have a stake in the venture and he is charged with a misdemeanor. Hence, he could not be charged with conspiracy to further prostitution. Affirmed.

▶ ANALYSIS

In *U.S. v. Falcone*, 311 U.S. 205 (1940), the sellers of large quantities of sugar, yeast, and cans were absolved from participation in a moonlighting conspiracy. In *Direct Sales Co. v. U.S.*, 319 U.S. 703 (1943), a wholesale drug company was convicted of conspiracy to violate the narcotic laws by selling large quantities of drugs to a physician who was supplying them to addicts. The Court distinguished these two leading cases on the basis of the character of the goods. The restricted character of the goods in *Direct Sales* showed that the defendant knew of their illegal use

and had taken the step from knowledge to intent and agreement.

Quicknotes

CONSPIRACY Concerted action by two or more persons to accomplish some unlawful purpose.

CRIMINAL INTENT An intention to carry out a criminal offense.

MISDEMEANOR Any offense that does not constitute a felony, which is generally less severe and for which a lesser punishment is imposed.

Commonwealth v. Azim

State/municipality (P) v. Driver (D)

Pa. Super. Ct., 313 Pa. Super. 310, 459 A.2d 1244 (1983).

NATURE OF CASE: Appeal from a conviction for simple assault, robbery, and conspiracy.

FACT SUMMARY: After Azim (D) drove the car in which the two men who beat, robbed, and choked the victim were riding, he was convicted of simple assault, robbery, and conspiracy.

🏛 RULE OF LAW
Once a conspiracy is established and upheld, a member of the conspiracy is also guilty of the criminal acts of his co-conspirators.

FACTS: Azim (D) drove a car in which James (D) and Robinson (D) were passengers. Azim (D) sat at the wheel with the engine running, the lights on, and the car doors open, while James (D) and Robinson (D) got out of the car and assaulted the victim, taking his wallet. He then drove James (D) and Robinson (D) from the scene. All three were arrested and charged with simple assault, robbery, and conspiracy. Azim (D) argued that because his conspiracy conviction was not supported by sufficient evidence against him, the charges of assault and robbery must also fail. Azim (D) was convicted as charged. Azim (D) appealed, seeking dismissal of all the charges brought against him.

ISSUE: Once a conspiracy is established and upheld, is a member of the conspiracy also guilty of the criminal acts of his co-conspirators?

HOLDING AND DECISION: (Per curiam) Yes. Once a conspiracy is established and upheld, a member of the conspiracy is also guilty of the criminal acts of his co-conspirators. Among the circumstances relevant to proving conspiracy are association with alleged conspirators, knowledge of the commission of the crime, presence at the scene of the crime, and, at times, participation in the object of the conspiracy. Conspiracy to commit burglary has been found where a defendant drove codefendants to the scene of a crime and later picked them up. Thus, there is no merit in Azim's (D) claim that he was merely a hired driver, with no knowledge of his passengers' criminal activity. A rational fact finder could find, beyond a reasonable doubt, that Azim (D) conspired with his passengers to commit assault and robbery. Affirmed.

▶ ANALYSIS

By its very nature, the crime of conspiracy can often only be proven by circumstantial evidence. Although a conspiracy cannot be based upon mere suspicion or conjecture, a conspiracy may be inferred by showing the relationship, conduct, or circumstances of the parties and overt acts on the part of the co-conspirators. See *Commonwealth v. Carter*, 272 Pa. Super. 411 (1979).

Quicknotes

CIRCUMSTANTIAL EVIDENCE Evidence that, though not directly observed, supports the inference of principal facts.

CONSPIRACY Concerted action by two or more persons to accomplish some unlawful purpose.

OVERT ACT An open act evidencing an intention to commit a crime.

Commonwealth v. Cook

Municipality (P) v. Rape conspirator (D)

Mass. App. Ct., 10 Mass. App. 668, 411 N.E.2d 1326 (1980).

NATURE OF CASE: Appeal from a conviction of conspiracy to commit rape.

FACT SUMMARY: After Cook's (D) brother raped a 17-year-old victim, Cook (D) was convicted of conspiracy to commit rape and as an accessory to rape.

🏛 **RULE OF LAW**
Two or more persons who seek by some concerted action to accomplish a criminal act may be punished for a conspiracy.

FACTS: When the 17-year-old victim went to see her boyfriend, he was not at home. As she approached a platform area in the apartment projects which was apparently used as a common meeting point for informal socializing, Cook (D) and his brother, Maurice, invited the victim to socialize with them. After Maurice suggested that they walk to a nearby convenience store for cigarettes, they followed a path through a wooded area, where the victim slipped and fell. Maurice jumped on her, forcibly raping her. The brothers were arrested. Maurice was indicted for rape, and Cook (D) was charged with conspiracy and as an accessory to rape. Cook (D) was convicted. This appeal followed.

ISSUE: May two or more persons who seek by some concerted action to accomplish a criminal act be punished for a conspiracy?

HOLDING AND DECISION: (Greaney, J.) Yes. Two or more persons who seek by some concerted action to accomplish a criminal act may be punished for a conspiracy. It is essential to a conviction for conspiracy to prove the existence of an unlawful agreement. It must also be shown that a defendant was aware of the objective of the alleged conspiracy. Proof of a conspiracy may rest entirely or mainly on circumstantial evidence, but an acquittal must be ordered if any essential element of the crime is left to surmise, conjecture, or guesswork. Under those principles, the events up to the time the victim fell were not sufficient to establish a criminal agreement. The purpose for leaving the socializing area was innocuous and was suggested by Maurice, not Cook (D). The fact that Cook (D) may have aided and abetted the crime does not establish a conspiracy, particularly where the evidence shows that Maurice and Cook (D) did not engage in any prior planning. Reversed.

▶ **ANALYSIS**

Accomplice and conspiratorial liability are not synonymous. One can be an accomplice, aiding in the commission of a substantive offense, without necessarily conspiring to commit it. The holdings which separate the two types of criminal activity do so because of fundamental distinctions between them. Accomplice liability does not include the necessity of establishing the agreement or consensus which is the hallmark of a conspiracy.

■━■

Quicknotes

ACCOMPLICE An individual who knowingly, purposefully or voluntarily combines with the main actor in the commission or attempted commission of a criminal offense.

AID AND ABETTING Assistance given in order to facilitate the commission of a criminal act.

CONSPIRACY Concerted action by two or more persons to accomplish some unlawful purpose.

■━■

People v. Foster

State (P) v. Robber (D)

Ill. Sup. Ct., 99 Ill. 2d 48, 457 N.E.2d 405 (1983).

NATURE OF CASE: Appeal from a conviction for conspiracy to commit robbery.

FACT SUMMARY: After Ragsdale was approached by Foster (D) about robbing an elderly man, Ragsdale feigned agreement with the plan in order to gain additional information and then informed the police of the planned robbery.

🏛 RULE OF LAW

A person commits conspiracy when, with intent that an offense be committed, he agrees with another to the commission of that offense.

FACTS: Foster (D) approached Ragsdale in a bar, asking him if he was interested in making some money by robbing an elderly man who kept many valuables in his possession. When he realized that Foster (D) was serious, Ragsdale tried to gather additional information by feigning agreement to the plan. Ragsdale told Foster (D) he would not be ready until he found someone else to help them. Ragsdale then informed the police of the planned robbery. When Foster (D) and Ragsdale arrived at the intended robbery victim's residence, the police met them there and arrested them. After a jury trial, Foster (D) was convicted of conspiracy to commit robbery. The appellate court, determining that the conspiracy statute required actual agreement between at least two persons to support a conspiracy conviction, reversed Foster's (D) conviction. The State (P) appealed.

ISSUE: Does a person commit conspiracy when, with intent that an offense be committed, he agrees with another to the commission of that offense?

HOLDING AND DECISION: (Underwood, J.) Yes. A person commits conspiracy when, with intent that an offense be committed, he agrees with another to the commission of that offense. Since the statute is presently worded in terms of "a person," the State (P) urges that only one person need intend to agree to the commission of an offense. However, the committee comments to the state statute simply do not address this unilateral/bilateral issue. It is doubtful that the drafters could have intended such a profound change in the law of conspiracy without mentioning it in their comments. Moreover, Illinois has a solicitation statute that embraces virtually every situation in which one may be convicted of conspiracy under the unilateral theory, and the penalties for solicitation and conspiracy are substantially similar. There would appear to have been little need for the legislature to adopt the unilateral theory of conspiracy in light of the existence of the solicitation statute. Thus, the rule encompasses the bilateral theory of conspiracy. The evidence is not sufficient in this case to sustain conviction. Affirmed.

▶ ANALYSIS

Ill. Rev. Stat. 1981, Ch. 38, Par. 8-2 previously contained the language "If two or more persons conspire or agree together." The State (P) reasoned that the drafters would not have deleted the words "two or more persons" if they had intended to retain the bilateral theory. The court, however, was mindful of the rule of construction which requires that statutory ambiguities be resolved in favor of criminal defendants.

■═■

Quicknotes

CONSPIRACY Concerted action by two or more persons to accomplish some unlawful purpose.

ROBBERY The unlawful taking of property from the person of another through the use of force or fear.

SOLICITATION Contact initiated by an attorney for the purpose of obtaining employment.

■═■

Kilgore v. State

Murder conspirator (D) v. State (P)

Ga. Sup. Ct., 251 Ga. 291, 305 S.E.2d 82 (1983).

NATURE OF CASE: Appeal from a conviction for murder.

FACT SUMMARY: After Kilgore (D) and another person killed the victim, Roger Norman, at the behest of Norman's brother-in-law, Kilgore (D) was convicted for Norman's murder and given a life sentence.

🏛 RULE OF LAW
To have a conspiracy, there must be an agreement between two or more persons to commit a crime.

FACTS: Three attempts were made on the life of Roger Norman. The first unsuccessful attempt was carried out by Oldaker and Benton at the behest of Tom Carden, Norman's brother-in-law. The second unsuccessful attempt was carried out by Kilgore (D) and Berry, also at Carden's behest. Kilgore (D) successfully carried out the third attempt with Price. The two shot Norman in the head, killing him, while he was driving to his home in Alabama. At trial, the State (P) introduced evidence of a conspiracy to kill Norman in order to help prove Kilgore (D) guilty of murder. Kilgore (D) objected to testimony by Oldaker that Benton told him that Tom Carden ordered the hit. Kilgore (D) argued that he and Benton never conspired to kill Norman, and thus Benton's statement was inadmissible hearsay. The State (P) countered that hearsay statements by one conspirator are admissible against all conspirators. Kilgore (D) appealed.

ISSUE: To have a conspiracy, must there be an agreement between two or more persons to commit a crime?

HOLDING AND DECISION: (Bell, J.) Yes. To have a conspiracy, there must be an agreement between two or more persons to commit a crime. The hearsay testimony in this case was only admissible if Oldaker, Benton, and Kilgore (D) were co-conspirators. Under the facts of the case, Kilgore (D) was not a co-conspirator of Benton and Oldaker. Here, there was no community of interests between Benton and Oldaker on the one hand and Kilgore (D) on the other. The success of Benton's and Oldaker's attempt to kill Norman was not dependent in any way on Kilgore (D), nor was the success of Kilgore's (D) attempt to kill Norman aided by Oldaker and Benton. In addition, Benton and Oldaker had no reason to know of Kilgore (D), nor had he any reason to know of them. Thus, they were not co-conspirators. Consequently, Oldaker's testimony was inadmissible hearsay.

▶ ANALYSIS

The court noted that if any conspiracy existed here, it was of the "wheel" type, where there is usually a "hub," or common source of the conspiracy, who deals individually with different persons, "spokes," who do not know each other. It is more difficult to infer an agreement in this type of conspiracy. In contrast, a "chain" conspiracy of the type involved in drug trafficking is characterized by "links" of personnel, all dependent on the success of the whole enterprise. Courts tend to treat such links as co-conspirators despite a lack of communication among them.

■■■

Quicknotes

CONSPIRACY Concerted action by two or more persons to accomplish some unlawful purpose.

HEARSAY An out-of-court statement made by a person other than the witness testifying at trial that is offered in order to prove the truth of the matter asserted.

PREJUDICIAL ERROR An error that affects the outcome of a trial, the judgment of which may be reversed, establishing a basis for a new trial.

■■■

Braverman v. United States

Liquor conspirator (D) v. Federal government (P)

317 U.S. 49 (1942).

NATURE OF CASE: Appeal after conviction for conspiracy.

FACT SUMMARY: Although it was proved that Braverman (D) and others had made a single agreement to violate several laws, they were each charged with several conspiracies.

 RULE OF LAW
When co-conspirators make one agreement, even to violate several laws, they can be convicted of only one conspiracy.

FACTS: Braverman (D) and others collaborated in the illicit manufacture, transportation, and distribution of liquor in violation of several Internal Revenue laws. They were charged and convicted on several counts. Each count charged a conspiracy to violate a different law.

ISSUE: Can co-conspirators who conspire to violate several laws be convicted of a conspiracy as to each law violated?

HOLDING AND DECISION: (Stone, C.J.) No. Whether the object of a single agreement is to commit one or many crimes, it is the agreement which constitutes the conspiracy. The one agreement cannot be taken to be several agreements and, hence, several conspiracies because its object is the violation of several statutes rather than one. The single agreement is the prohibited conspiracy, and however diverse its objects, it violates only one section of the criminal code. Hence, only one penalty can be imposed. The convictions in this case must be reversed because more than one penalty was imposed for the single agreement.

ANALYSIS

Braverman has been criticized on the ground that an agreement to commit several crimes should be treated in the same way as an attempt to commit several crimes. In his writings, Professor LaFave says that this objection is not convincing for two reasons. The first is that conspiracy, unlike attempt, is defined in terms of agreement. The second is that conspiracy, in contrast to attempt, reaches farther back into preparatory conduct. *Braverman* has also been criticized as tending to place a premium on foresight in crime.

Quicknotes

ATTEMPT An intent combined with an act falling short of the thing intended.

CONSPIRACY Concerted action by two or more persons to accomplish some unlawful purpose.

Iannelli v. United States

Gambling conspirator (D) v. Federal government (P)

420 U.S. 770 (1975).

NATURE OF CASE: Appeal from court of appeals affirmation of convictions for conspiracy to violate and violation of a federal gambling statute.

FACT SUMMARY: In holding that the convictions of Iannelli (D) and others were proper, the court of appeals affirmed the trial court's convictions for both conspiracy to violate and violation of a federal statute making certain gambling activities by five or more persons illegal. It found inapplicable the rule precluding conviction for conspiracy when the substantive offense related thereto is, by definition, nonunilateral, and requires the participation of all those who were in fact involved (Wharton's Rule).

🏛 RULE OF LAW

According to Wharton's Rule, one cannot be convicted for conspiracy if there has been a conviction for the substantive crime which is its target if that crime, by definition, requires the participation of two or more persons and the participation of all those who were actually participants, therein. This rule functions as an aid to determining legislative intent, and in the face of evidence of contrary intent, it will not be applicable.

FACTS: 18 U.S.C. § 1955 makes it a crime for five or more persons to conduct, finance, manage, supervise, direct, or own a gambling business prohibited by state law. Iannelli (D) and a group of others totaling more than five, having been convicted of both conspiracy to violate and actual violation of this law, appealed a decision of the trial court that Wharton's Rule was inapplicable. Wharton's Rule, which makes conviction of both the conspiracy and the substantive offense connected therewith improper in certain instances, was not applicable, the court reasoned, because of the "third-party exception." It arises when the conspiracy involves the cooperation of a greater number of persons than is, by definition, required for the commission of the substantive crime. This exception was properly applied, according to the court of appeals in its review of the convictions, because the conspiracy involved more than the five persons required to commit the substantive offense. Citing interpretations by other circuits that the third-party exception to Wharton's Rule was inapplicable because § 1955 also covers gambling activities involving more than five people, Iannelli (D) appealed again.

ISSUE: Does Wharton's Rule preclude the legislature from punishing for both the conspiracy and the substantive crime which is its target?

HOLDING AND DECISION: (Powell, J.) No. Wharton's Rule is simply a presumption of legislative intent which is inapplicable where there is evidence that the legislature intended to punish both the substantive crime and the underlying conspiracy. It rests not on principles of double jeopardy but on the judicial presumption that, absent some expression, there is no intent to punish both the conspiracy and the substantive offense (of a certain type) unless that intent is somehow manifested. The classic examples of Wharton's Rule offenses—adultery, incest, bigamy, dueling—point up the essential character that give rise to the inference the judiciary made. Unlike the case at bar, those offenses were ones where the harm is restricted to those involved, the parties to the agreement are the only ones participating in the commission of the substantive offense, and the agreement connected with the substantive offense is unlikely to pose those threats to society that the conspiracy laws were designed to avert (the generation of additional agreements for other criminal endeavors, etc.). We find Congress's pointed avoidance of reference to conspiracy or agreement in § 1955, in light of the numerous references to conspiracies in the Organized Crime Control Act, to be significant and an indication that it chose not to explicitly foreclose the possibility of prosecuting conspiracy offenses under § 371 by merging them into prosecutions under § 1955. This intent is controlling; therefore, the convictions are affirmed.

▶ ANALYSIS

The rationale underlying the Wharton Rule is that there is no justification for punishing the conspiracy because of its own inherent dangers when the substantive offense it is connected with itself entails an agreement. There is, in such a case, no added threat or harm from the agreement because that harm is inherent in the substantive crime. Thus, the courts formulated this rule and either required the conspiracy indictment to be dismissed before trial or charged the jury that a conviction for the substantive offense necessarily precluded conviction for the conspiracy.

■■■

Quicknotes

CONSPIRACY Concerted action by two or more persons to accomplish some unlawful purpose.

DOUBLE JEOPARDY A prohibition against a second prosecution for the same offense after an acquittal or

Continued on next page.

conviction for that offense in a prior proceeding or against multiple punishments for the same offense.

WHARTON RULE The rule that two persons cannot be prosecuted for a conspiracy if the nature of the crime is such that it requires two persons for its commission.

■═■

Gebardi v. United States

Immoral travelers (D) v. Federal government (P)

287 U.S. 112 (1932).

NATURE OF CASE: Appeal from a conviction for conspiracy to transport a woman across state lines for sexual purposes.

FACT SUMMARY: After Gebardi (D) transported his girlfriend (D) across state lines in order to have sexual intercourse with her, they were both indicted for conspiring together to transport her across state lines for an immoral purpose, a violation of the Mann Act.

🏛 RULE OF LAW
A woman who consents to be transported across state lines for an immoral purpose does not violate the Mann Act, nor may she be convicted of a conspiracy with the man to violate it.

FACTS: Before Gebardi (D) and his wife (D) were married, he arranged to transport her to another state for the purpose of engaging in sexual intercourse with her. They engaged in illicit sexual relations in the course of a number of such journeys. Gebardi (D) purchased the railway tickets for both of them for at least one journey, and in each instance, she voluntarily consented to go on the journey for the specified immoral purpose. They were indicted for conspiring together to transport her across state lines for an immoral purpose, in violation of the Mann Act. There was no evidence showing that any other person had conspired. They were both convicted and appealed.

ISSUE: May a woman who consents to be transported across state lines for an immoral purpose violate the Mann Act as a subject of the transportation or as a conspirator?

HOLDING AND DECISION: (Stone, J.) No. A woman who consents to be transported across state lines for an immoral purpose does not violate the Mann Act as a subject of the transportation or as a conspirator. The Mann Act penalizes a person who knowingly transports or causes to be transported or aids or assists in obtaining transportation for any woman or girl, in interstate or foreign commerce, for the purpose of prostitution or debauchery or for any other immoral purpose. For a woman to fall within the ban of the statute, she must, at the least, "aid or assist" someone else in transporting, or in procuring transportation for, herself. Such aid or assistance must be more than mere agreement. On the evidence presented, Mrs. Gebardi (D) has not violated the Mann Act and is not guilty of a conspiracy to do so. As there is no proof that Gebardi (D) conspired with anyone else to bring about the transportation, the convictions must be reversed.

▶ ANALYSIS

In the failure of the Mann Act to condemn the woman's participation through mere consent, the Court saw evidence of an affirmative legislative policy to leave her acquiescence, unpunished. The statute does not impose any penalty upon the woman who consents to her own transportation. Instead, the penalties are clearly directed against the transporter. Under the Model Penal Code, § 2.06, a person cannot be an accomplice in an offense committed by another if she is the victim of that offense.

Quicknotes

CONSENT A voluntary and willful agreement by an individual possessing sufficient mental capacity to undertake an action suggested by another.

CONSPIRACY Concerted action by two or more persons to accomplish some unlawful purpose.

WHARTON RULE The rule that two persons cannot be prosecuted for a conspiracy if the nature of the crime is such that it requires two persons for its commission.

People v. Sconce

State (P) v. Withdrawing conspirator (D)

Cal. Ct. App., 228 Cal. App. 3d 693 (1991).

NATURE OF CASE: Appeal from the setting aside of a charge of conspiracy to commit murder.

FACT SUMMARY: After Sconce (D) conspired to have Estephan killed, he called it off, and the trial court later set aside the People's (P) charge of conspiracy to commit murder because it found Sconce (D) had effectively withdrawn from the conspiracy.

🏛 RULE OF LAW
Withdrawal from a conspiracy requires an affirmative and bona fide rejection or repudiation of the conspiracy, communicated to the co-conspirators.

FACTS: Sconce (D) met with Garcia, offering him $10,000 to kill Estephan. Garcia was supposed to find someone to do the killing or to do it himself. After Garcia engaged an ex-convict, Dutton, to do the killing, they went to inspect the area around the victim's house. The decision was made to plant a bomb under Estephan's car. About three weeks after Sconce's (D) initial conversation with Garcia, Sconce (D) called it off. The People (P) filed an information charging Sconce (D) with conspiracy to commit murder. Prior to trial, the trial court set the information aside because it found that Sconce (D) had effectively withdrawn from the conspiracy. The People (P) appealed.

ISSUE: Does withdrawal from a conspiracy require an affirmative and bona fide rejection or repudiation of the conspiracy, communicated to the co-conspirators?

HOLDING AND DECISION: (Klein, J.) Yes. Withdrawal from a conspiracy requires an affirmative and bona fide rejection or repudiation of the conspiracy, communicated to the co-conspirators. Under California law, withdrawal is a complete defense to conspiracy only if accomplished before the commission of an overt act. However, withdrawal avoids liability only for the target offense or for any subsequent act committed by a co-conspirator in pursuance of the common plan. In regard to the conspiracy itself, the individual's change of mind is ineffective. He cannot undo that which he has already done. Thus, even if it is assumed that Sconce (D) effectively withdrew from the conspiracy, the withdrawal does not relate back to the criminal formation of the unlawful combination, i.e., the conspiracy, which is complete upon the commission of an overt act. Reversed.

▶ ANALYSIS

The Model Penal Code recognizes the defense of renunciation, using the following language: "It is an affirmative defense that the actor, after conspiring to commit a crime, thwarted the success of the conspiracy, under circumstances manifesting a complete and voluntary renunciation of his criminal purpose." The defense of renunciation, however, is not the same as withdrawal. Renunciation is not available as a defense in California.

Quicknotes

CONSPIRACY Concerted action by two or more persons to accomplish some unlawful purpose.

OVERT ACT An open act evidencing an intention to commit a crime.

WITHDRAWAL The removal of cash or other assets from the location in which it is held.

CHAPTER 11

Liability for the Conduct of Another

Quick Reference Rules of Law

State v. Ward

State (P) v. Accomplice to crime (D)

Md. Ct. App., 284 Md. 189, 396 A.2d 1041 (1978).

NATURE OF CASE: [Nature of case not stated in casebook excerpt.]

FACT SUMMARY: [Fact summary not stated in casebook excerpt.]

⚖ RULE OF LAW
An accessory cannot be tried before a principal and cannot be convicted of a higher crime than the principal.

FACTS: [Facts not stated in casebook excerpt.]

ISSUE: May an accessory be tried before or convicted of a higher crime than the principal?

HOLDING AND DECISION: (Orth, J.) No. An accessory may not be tried before or convicted of a higher crime than the principal. In the field of felony, the common law divided guilty parties into principals and accessories. Principals came to be classified as in the first degree (perpetrators) or in the second degree (abettors), and accessories as before the fact (inciters) or after the fact (criminal protectors). At the common law, the principal in the second degree may be tried and convicted prior to the trial of the principal in the first degree or even after the latter has been tried and acquitted. Furthermore, a principal in the second degree may be convicted of a higher crime or a lower crime than the principal in the first degree. With respect to accessories, however, the common law took a different path. An accessory cannot be tried, without his consent, before the principal and cannot be convicted of a higher crime than his principal.

▶ ANALYSIS

The common law of England developed the doctrine of accessoryship applicable to felonies. Maryland is one of the few, if not the only state, which has retained this doctrine in virtually the same form as it existed at the time of William Blackstone in the 18th century, and it represents the law of Maryland at the present time. The majority of states, however, no longer draw a distinction between principals and accessories after the fact.

■■■

Quicknotes

ACCESSORY An individual who combines with the main actor in the commission or attempted commission of a criminal offense, either before or after its performance.

ACCOMPLICE An individual who knowingly, purposefully or voluntarily combines with the main actor in the commission or attempted commission of a criminal offense.

PRINCIPAL An individual who commits a crime or induces another to commit a crime.

■■■

State v. Hoselton

State (P) v. Friend of thieves (D)

W. Va. Sup. Ct. App., 179 W. Va. 645, 371 S.E.2d 366 (1988).

NATURE OF CASE: Appeal from a conviction for entering, without breaking, a vessel, with intent to commit larceny.

FACT SUMMARY: After Hoselton (D) and his friends entered a barge, his friends stole certain items from the storage unit, but Hoselton (D) did not participate in the theft.

 RULE OF LAW
To convict a person as an aider and abettor, and thus a principal in the second degree, the prosecution must demonstrate that he or she shared the criminal intent of the principal in the first degree.

FACTS: While Hoselton (D), who was 18, was with several of his friends, his friends entered a barge, stealing tools and other items. Hoselton (D) stood on the end of the barge because he did not want to go down into the storage unit. From where he was standing, he could not see what his friends were doing, but he admitted he knew they were committing a crime. Hoselton (D) did not assist the others in placing the goods in their automobile. He was then immediately driven home. None of the stolen items, or profits on their resale, was given to Hoselton (D). When asked by the police if he was keeping a lookout, Hoselton (D) said: "You could say that. I just didn't want to go down in there." Hoselton (D) contended that the evidence was insufficient to support a conviction for entering with intent to commit larceny. He was tried and convicted. This appeal followed.

ISSUE: To convict a person as an aider and abettor, and thus a principal in the second degree, must the prosecution demonstrate that he or she shared the criminal intent of the principal in the first degree?

HOLDING AND DECISION: (Per curiam) Yes. To convict a person as an aider and abettor, and thus a principal in the second degree, the prosecution must demonstrate that he or she shared the criminal intent of the principal in the first degree. In this case, the State (P) contends that the evidence is sufficient to establish that Hoselton (D) was a lookout. However, a lookout is one who keeps watch by prearrangement and thereby participates in the offenses charged. In both his voluntary statement and during his trial testimony, Hoselton (D) stated that he had no prior knowledge of his friends' intentions to steal anything from the barge. His response that "you could say" he was a lookout, standing completely alone, does not establish him as an aider and abettor. Thus,

the State (P) did not prove that Hoselton (D) was a lookout. Reversed.

ANALYSIS

The court notes that it has consistently held that lookouts are aiders and abettors, principals in the second degree. An aider and abettor must in some sort associate himself with the venture, must participate in it as something that he wishes to bring about, and must seek by his action to make it succeed. Therefore, if the evidence shows that an accused acted as a lookout, it has established the requisite act and mental state to support a conviction of aiding and abetting.

━━━

Quicknotes

ACCOMPLICE LIABILITY Liability of an individual who knowingly, purposefully, or voluntarily combines with the main actor in the commission or attempted commission of a criminal offense.

PRINCIPAL IN THE FIRST DEGREE An individual who commits a crime.

PRINCIPAL IN THE SECOND DEGREE An individual who is either physically or constructively present at the scene of a crime and who facilitates another in the commission of that crime.

━━━

Riley v. State

Assault convict (D) v. State (P)

Alaska Ct. App., 60 P.3d 204 (2002).

NATURE OF CASE: Appeal from conviction for first-degree assault.

FACT SUMMARY: Richard Riley (D) argued that the court erred by instructing the jury that Riley's (D) culpability was the same regardless whether he were found to be a principal or an accomplice.

🏛 RULE OF LAW
The mental state of acting with sufficient recklessness to give rise to first-degree assault is the same whether the defendant is charged as a principal or an accomplice.

FACTS: After Richard Riley (D) and Edward Portalla opened fire on an unsuspecting crowd of young people, seriously wounding two persons, the two shooters were indicted on two counts of first-degree assault (recklessly causing serious physical injury by means of a dangerous instrument). The ballistics analysis did not reveal which of the two men's weapons had fired the wounding shots. The jurors were instructed that, as to each count of the first-degree assault, they should decide whether Riley (D) acted as a "principal" (by firing the wounding shot) or, if they could not decide beyond a reasonable doubt which man fired the shots, they should decide whether Riley (D) acted as an "accomplice" (by aiding or abetting Portalla to fire the wounding shot). The jurors found Riley (D) guilty as an accomplice in the wounding of both victims. Riley (D) appealed, arguing that the instruction erred in telling the jury that Riley's (D) culpability would be the same regardless whether he were found as a principal or an accomplice.

ISSUE: Is the mental state of acting with sufficient recklessness to give rise to first-degree assault the same whether the defendant is charged as a principal or an accomplice?

HOLDING AND DECISION: (Mannheimer, J.) Yes. The mental state of acting with sufficient recklessness to give rise to first-degree assault is the same whether the defendant is charged as a principal or an accomplice. With regard to the results of a defendant's conduct, the State (P) must prove that an accomplice had whatever culpable mental state is required for the underlying crime. Here, Riley (D) could properly be convicted of statutory first-degree assault either upon proof that he personally shot a firearm into the crowd or (alternatively) upon proof that, acting with intent to promote or facilitate Portalla's act of shooting into the crowd, Riley (D) solicited, encouraged, or assisted Portalla to do so. These are alternative ways of proving that Riley (D) was accountable for the conduct that inflicted the injuries. The State (P) was also obliged to prove that Riley (D) acted with the culpable mental state specified by the first-degree assault statute. But regardless whether Riley (D) acted as a principal or an accomplice, the applicable culpable mental state remained the same: recklessness as to the possibility that this conduct would cause serious physical injury. Affirmed.

▶ ANALYSIS

The standard interpretation of the statutory phrase "intent to promote or facilitate the commission of the offense" is that it requires proof of the accomplice's intent to promote or facilitate another person's conduct that constitutes the actus reus of the offense.

Quicknotes

ACCOMPLICE An individual who knowingly, purposefully or voluntarily combines with the main actor in the commission, or attempted commission, of a criminal offense.

State v. Linscott

State (P) v. Robbery participant (D)

Me. Sup. Jud. Ct., 520 A.2d 1067 (1987).

NATURE OF CASE: Appeal from a conviction for murder and robbery.

FACT SUMMARY: When an intended robbery victim was killed during the robbery in which Linscott (D) participated with three other men, Linscott (D) was convicted of robbery and, on a theory of accomplice liability, of murder.

> ## 🏛 RULE OF LAW
> An accessory is liable for any criminal act that was the natural or probable consequence of the crime that he advised or commanded, although such consequence may not have been intended by him.

FACTS: Linscott (D) and three other men decided to rob a reputed cocaine dealer, Grenier, at his house. One of the men, Fuller, had a sawed-off shotgun. It was decided that Linscott (D) would break the living room picture window then Fuller would merely show the shotgun to Grenier. After Linscott (D) broke the window, Fuller immediately fired a shot, hitting Grenier in the chest. Fuller removed money from Grenier's pants pocket. At a jury-waived trial, Linscott (D) testified that he had no knowledge of any reputation for violence that Fuller may have had and that he had no intention of causing anyone's death during the robbery. The trial justice found Linscott (D) guilty of robbery and, on a theory of accomplice liability, of murder. Linscott (D) appealed, contending that the State's (P) accomplice liability statute violated his right to due process because he lacked the requisite intent to commit murder. This appeal followed.

ISSUE: Is an accessory liable for any criminal act that was the natural or probable consequence of the crime that he advised or commanded, although such consequence may not have been intended by him?

HOLDING AND DECISION: (Scolnik, J.) Yes. An accessory is liable for any criminal act that was the natural or probable consequence of the crime that he advised or commanded, although such consequence may not have been intended by him. The "foreseeable consequence" rule merely carries over the objective standards of accomplice liability as used in the common law. Thus, a rule allowing for a murder conviction under a theory of accomplice liability based upon an objective standard is appropriate, despite the absence of evidence that a defendant possessed the culpable subjective mental state that constitutes an element of the crime of murder. Furthermore, the grading scheme, for sentencing purposes, is not fundamentally unfair or disproportionate. There is no con-stitutional defect in this statutory provision or any fundamental unfairness in its operation. Affirmed.

▶ ANALYSIS

One court has set out a four-part test to determine whether a defendant may be convicted as an aider and abettor. First, the jury must determine the crime originally contemplated and committed by the perpetrator. Next, it must decide whether the defendant knew of the perpetrator's intent and intended to facilitate the crime. Then, it must determine whether additional crimes other than those contemplated occurred and, if so, whether they were reasonably foreseeable consequences of the original crimes. See *People v. Woods*, 8 Cal. App. 4th 1570 (1992).

■☰■

Quicknotes

ACCESSORY An individual who combines with the main actor in the commission or attempted commission of a criminal offense, either before or after its performance.

ACCOMPLICE LIABILITY Liability of an individual who knowingly, purposefully, or voluntarily combines with the main actor in the commission or attempted commission of a criminal offense.

■☰■

State v. V.T.

State (P) v. Convicted accomplice to theft (D)

Utah Ct. App., 2000 Utah Ct. App. 189, 5 P.3d 1234 (2000).

NATURE OF CASE: Appeal from theft conviction in juvenile court.

FACT SUMMARY: V.T. (D) contended that there was insufficient evidence to support the adjudication that he was an accomplice in the theft from his relative's apartment of a camcorder.

▥ RULE OF LAW
▥ Passive behavior in the presence of a crime and friendship with the crime's perpetrators alone does not support accomplice liability.

FACTS: V.T. (D) and his friends Moose and Joey stayed at V.T.'s (D) relative's apartment overnight. The next day, the relative discovered that her guns had been stolen and later discovered that her camcorder had been stolen. The camcorder was recovered at a pawn shop and contained a videotape showing Moose calling a friend, in V.T.'s (D) presence, discussing the camcorder's pawning. V.T. (D) never gestured or spoke during this footage. V.T. (D) was tried in juvenile court under an accomplice theory and was convicted of theft of the camcorder (the court found insufficient evidence to support theft of a firearm charges). V.T. (D) appealed, contending that there was insufficient evidence to support the adjudication that he was an accomplice in the camcorder's theft, and the state's intermediate appellate court granted review.

ISSUE: Can passive behavior in the presence of a crime and friendship with the crime's perpetrators alone, support accomplice liability?

HOLDING AND DECISION: (Orme, J.) No. Passive behavior in the presence of a crime and friendship with the crime's perpetrators alone does not support accomplice liability. The defendant must take an affirmative action that instigates, incites, emboldens, or helps other in committing the crime for there to be "encouragement" that supports accomplice liability. Mere presence, or even prior knowledge, does not make one an accomplice. Accordingly, the evidence here did not support the juvenile's court's conclusion that V.T. (D) was an accomplice to the camcorder theft, since no evidence was produced indicating that V.T. (D) had encouraged, solicited, requested, commanded, or intentionally aided the other two boys in the theft. Reversed.

▌ ANALYSIS

Presence alone may give rise to accomplice liability where the presence—as in the case of a lookout—is designed to encourage the perpetrator or otherwise facilitates the crime. In such instances, the presence of the defendant is equated to aiding and abetting the crime.

■═■

Quicknotes

ACCOMPLICE LIABILITY Liability of an individual who knowingly, purposefully or voluntarily combines with the main actor in the commission, or attempted commission, of a criminal offense.

■═■

Wilcox v. Jeffery

Concert attendee (D) v. Court (P)

King's Bench Division, 1 All. E.R. 464 (1951).

NATURE OF CASE: Appeal from a conviction for aiding and abetting an unlawful act.

FACT SUMMARY: After Wilcox (D) attended and reviewed a concert played in London by Coleman Hawkins, an American saxophonist who had been given leave to land in England provided he did not work while there, Wilcox (D) was convicted of aiding and abetting Hawkins in the commission of an illegal act.

🏛 RULE OF LAW
A person, who through his actions encourages an illegal act, is guilty of aiding and abetting that illegal act.

FACTS: Coleman Hawkins, a celebrated American saxophonist, came to the United Kingdom at the invitation of a jazz club. Hawkins was granted leave to land with the condition that he take no employment paid or unpaid while in the United Kingdom. However, Hawkins played a concert at the club. Wilcox (D) attended that concert as a spectator in order to review the concert for the periodical he owned. He paid for his own ticket and wrote a laudatory description, fully illustrated, of the concert. Wilcox (D) was charged with aiding and abetting Hawkins, in contravention of the Aliens Order, by encouraging him through attendance at the concert. Wilcox (D) was convicted as charged. This appeal followed.

ISSUE: Is a person, who through his actions encourages an illegal act, guilty of aiding and abetting that illegal act?

HOLDING AND DECISION: (Lord Goddard, C. J.) Yes. A person, who through his actions encourages an illegal act, is guilty of aiding and abetting that illegal act. An immigration officer giving leave to an alien to land in the United Kingdom may attach such conditions as he may think fit to the grant of leave to land. It was an illegal act for Hawkins to play the concert, and Wilcox (D) knew it. If he had gone to protest on behalf of the musicians' union or booed, there might have been some evidence that he was not aiding and abetting. However, it seems clear in this case that Wilcox (D) was there, not only to approve and encourage what was done but to take advantage of it by getting "copy" for his paper. In those circumstances there was evidence on which the magistrate could find that Wilcox (D) aided and abetted Hawkins. Thus, the appeal fails. Affirmed.

at the scene of the crime is necessary to make one accountable as an accomplice, presence plus little else (e.g., psychological encouragement) may be enough. The degree of influence over the principal is immaterial. A causal link, in the sense that the crime would not have occurred "but for" the assistance, is not required. This no-causation rule is partially due to the difficulty of proving causation in the accomplice context.

Quicknotes

ACCESSORY An individual who combines with the main actor in the commission or attempted commission of a criminal offense, either before or after its performance.

ACCOMPLICE LIABILITY Liability of an individual who knowingly, purposefully, or voluntarily combines with the main actor in the commission or attempted commission of a criminal offense.

PRINCIPAL A person or entity who authorizes another (the agent) to act on its behalf and subject to its authority to the extent that the principal may be held liable for the actions of the agent.

▶ ANALYSIS

This case is an example of "peripheral" assistance. Although some degree of aid in addition to mere presence

State v. Helmenstein

State (P) v. Burglary accomplice (D)

N.D. Sup. Ct., 163 N.W.2d 85 (1968).

NATURE OF CASE: Appeal from a conviction for burglary.

FACT SUMMARY: After Helmenstein (D) and some of his friends burglarized a grocery store, five of the friends, all accomplices, testified against Helmenstein (D).

🏛 RULE OF LAW
A conviction may be based on the testimony of an accomplice only if his testimony is corroborated by other evidence connecting the defendant to the offense.

FACTS: Two groups of young people met in a park. After sitting around drinking beer, someone suggested that they break into a grocery store in a nearby town. They all agreed on the idea. Three people, including Helmenstein (D), broke into the store, stealing beer, cigarettes, candy, and bananas. Then they all agreed on what story they would tell if any of them should be questioned. After Helmenstein (D) was arrested and charged with burglary of a grocery store, five members of the group testified against him. The store owner testified as to the value of the merchandise stolen, but his testimony in no way connected Helmenstein (D) to the offense. The trial court found Helmenstein (D) guilty as charged. Helmenstein (D) appealed, arguing that his friends' statements, without more, were inadmissible.

ISSUE: May a conviction be based upon the testimony of an accomplice if his testimony is corroborated by other evidence connecting the defendant to the offense?

HOLDING AND DECISION: (Strutz, J.) Yes. A conviction may be based upon the testimony of an accomplice only if his testimony is corroborated by other evidence as connecting the defendant to the offense. The corroboration is not sufficient if it merely shows the commission of the offense or the circumstances thereof. Here, all five of the people who testified against Helmenstein (D) were clearly accomplices in the commission of the offense. The record shows that the burglary in this case was the result of a plan in which each of the parties had a part, that each of them encouraged and countenanced the offense, and that each of them thus was involved in its commission. Because there is no evidence, other than that of persons who also are accomplices, connecting Helmenstein (D) with the commission of the offense, the evidence against him is insufficient to sustain the judgment of conviction. Reversed.

▶ ANALYSIS

Accomplices have a special incentive to fabricate testimony since they are often granted immunity based on their willingness to testify. Moreover, it is in their own interest to shift the blame to others and downplay their own role in the crime.

■■■

Quicknotes

ACCOMPLICE LIABILITY Liability of an individual who knowingly, purposefully, or voluntarily combines with the main actor in the commission or attempted commission of a criminal offense.

■■■

People v. Genoa

State (P) v. Cocaine purchaser (D)

Mich. Ct. App., 188 Mich. App. 461, 470 N.W.2d 447 (1991).

NATURE OF CASE: Appeal from the dismissal of a charge of attempted possession with intent to deliver an illegal drug.

FACT SUMMARY: Genoa (D) was arrested after he agreed to finance the purchase of a kilogram of cocaine when he was approached by an undercover policeman.

🏛 RULE OF LAW
While the conviction of the principal is not necessary to a conviction of an accessory, it must be proven that the underlying crime was committed by someone and that the defendant either committed or aided and abetted the commission of that crime.

FACTS: Genoa (D) was approached by an undercover agent of the Michigan State Police, who proposed that Genoa (D) help finance the purchase of a kilogram of cocaine. The police agent claimed he would then sell the cocaine, repaying Genoa (D) the initial investment plus a profit. Genoa (D) accepted the proposal and returned with the money. The police agent turned the money over to the Michigan State Police, and Genoa (D) was subsequently charged with attempted possession with intent to deliver cocaine. The trial court dismissed the charge against Genoa (D) on the ground that because the police agent never intended to commit the contemplated crime and, indeed, never did commit it, Genoa (D), though he believed he was giving money for an illegal enterprise, financed nothing. The prosecution appealed.

ISSUE: While the conviction of the principal is not necessary to a conviction of an accessory, must it be proven that the underlying crime was committed by someone and that the defendant either committed or aided and abetted the commission of that crime?

HOLDING AND DECISION: (Shepherd, J.) Yes. While the conviction of the principal is not necessary to a conviction of an accessory, it must be proven that the underlying crime was committed by someone and that the defendant either committed or aided and abetted the commission of that crime. The only theory by which Genoa (D) could be prosecuted was that he attempted to aid and abet the crime of possession with intent to deliver cocaine. He certainly could not be shown to have attempted to constructively possess the cocaine himself since he was only helping to finance the proposed venture. Thus, in the case at bar, it is clear that the underlying crime was never committed by anyone. The absence of this element made it legally impossible for Genoa (D) to have committed any offense. Affirmed.

▶ ANALYSIS

While Michigan law does not distinguish between principals and accessories for purposes of culpability, certain elements must be established to show someone aided and abetted the commission of a crime. Those elements are that the underlying crime was committed, the defendant performed acts or gave encouragement, and the defendant intended the commission of the crime when giving aid or encouragement. The court noted that the inability to charge or prosecute Genoa (D) resulted from a gap in legislation.

∎═∎

Quicknotes

ACCESSORY An individual who combines with the main actor in the commission or attempted commission of a criminal offense, either before or after its performance.

ACCOMPLICE LIABILITY Liability of an individual who knowingly, purposefully or voluntarily combines with the main actor in the commission or attempted commission of a criminal offense.

PRINCIPAL A person or entity who authorizes another (the agent) to act on its behalf and subject to its authority to the extent that the principal may be held liable for the actions of the agent.

∎═∎

Bailey v. Commonwealth

Radio agitator (D) v. Municipality (P)

Va. Sup. Ct., 229 Va. 258, 329 S.E.2d 37 (1985).

NATURE OF CASE: Appeal from a conviction for involuntary manslaughter.

FACT SUMMARY: When Bailey (D) purposely agitated Murdock, then told him to get his handgun and wait outside on his porch for Bailey (D) to come over and injure or kill him, Murdock was shot by the police after Bailey (D) called them to report a man on Murdock's porch waving a gun around.

🏛 RULE OF LAW
One who effects a criminal act through an innocent or unwitting agent is a principal in the first degree.

FACTS: Bailey (D) and Murdock, both highly intoxicated, had an extended and vituperative conversation over their citizens band radios. Bailey (D) knew that Murdock had a problem with vision, that he was intoxicated, that he had a handgun, and that he was easily agitated. Bailey (D) purposely made statements to Murdock to anger him, persistently demanding that Murdock arm himself with his handgun and wait on his front porch for Bailey (D) to come and injure or kill him. Bailey (D) then made two anonymous calls to the police, reporting a man at Murdock's address waving a gun around. When the police arrived, they told Murdock to leave the gun alone and walk down the stairs. Murdock reached for the gun, stood up, advanced in the officer's direction, and opened fire. The fire was returned, and Murdock died from a gunshot wound in the chest. Before he died, Murdock said he didn't know they were the police. Bailey (D) was convicted of involuntary manslaughter, and he appealed.

ISSUE: Is one who effects a criminal act through an innocent or unwitting agent a principal in the first degree?

HOLDING AND DECISION: (Carrico, C.J.) Yes. One who effects a criminal act through an innocent or unwitting agent is a principal in the first degree. Bailey (D) orchestrated a scenario whose finale was bound to include harmful consequences to Murdock, either in the form of his arrest or his injury or death. It is clear that Bailey's (D) purpose in calling the police was to induce them to go to Murdock's home and unwittingly create the appearance that Bailey (D) himself had arrived to carry out the threats he had made over the radio. Bailey (D) undertook to cause Murdock harm and used the police to accomplish that purpose. From a legal standpoint, it is clear that the police officers who went to Murdock's home and confronted him were Bailey's (D) innocent or unwitting agents. Affirmed.

► ANALYSIS

Bailey (D) maintained that either Murdock's own reckless and criminal conduct in opening fire upon the police or the officers' return fire constituted an independent, intervening cause absolving Bailey (D) of guilt. However, an intervening act which is reasonably foreseeable cannot be relied upon as breaking the chain of causal connection between an act of negligence and subsequent injury. The jury determined that the consequences of Bailey's (D) reckless conduct could reasonably have been foreseen.

■=■

Quicknotes

INTERVENING CAUSE A cause, not anticipated by the initial actor, which is sufficient to break the chain of causation and relieve him of liability.

INVOLUNTARY MANSLAUGHTER The killing of another person without premeditation or deliberation or with the intent to kill or to commit a felony, which may be reasonably expected to result in death or serious bodily injury; involuntary manslaughter is characterized by reckless conduct in the commission of a lawful act, or by the commission of an unlawful act that is not a felony, but which leads to the killing of another.

PRINCIPAL A person or entity who authorizes another (the agent) to act on its behalf and subject to its authority to the extent that the principal may be held liable for the actions of the agent.

■=■

United States v. Lopez

Federal government (P) v. Prison inmate (D)

662 F. Supp. 1083 (N.D. Cal. 1987).

NATURE OF CASE: Motion in limine for an order barring the presentation of evidence on the defense of necessity or duress.

FACT SUMMARY: When Lopez (D) claimed that her life was unlawfully threatened by federal prison authorities, her boyfriend, McIntosh (D), helped her to escape by landing a helicopter on the prison grounds and was subsequently charged with aiding and abetting Lopez's (D) escape.

🏛 RULE OF LAW
An aider and abettor may not be held liable absent proof that a criminal offense has been committed by a principal.

FACTS: After federal prison authorities had allegedly unlawfully threatened Lopez's (D) life, her boyfriend, McIntosh (D), helped her escape by landing a helicopter on the prison grounds. They were both apprehended and prosecuted for prison escape, among other offenses. In response to their stated intention to raise a defense of necessity/duress due to the threats against Lopez (D), the Government (P) filed a motion in limine, seeking to bar the presentation of such evidence. McIntosh (D) requested that a jury instruction be given to the effect that if the jury found Lopez (D) not guilty of escape because she acted under necessity/duress, then the jury must also find McIntosh (D) not guilty of aiding and abetting her alleged escape.

ISSUE: May an aider and abettor, be held liable absent proof that a criminal offense has been committed by a principal?

HOLDING AND DECISION: (Lynch, J.) No. An aider and abettor may not be held liable absent proof that a criminal offense has been committed by a principal. The classification of a defense as a justification or an excuse has an important effect on the liability of one who aids and abets the act. A third party has the right to assist an actor in a justified act. In contrast, excuses are always personal to the actor. The defense of necessity is categorized as a justification. Here, the defense asserted by Lopez (D) most nearly resembles necessity. Accordingly, if the jury finds Lopez (D) not guilty of escape by reason of her necessity defense, her criminal act will be justified. Therefore, no criminal offense will have been committed by a principal. Since a third party has the right to assist an actor in a justified act, McIntosh (D) is entitled to his requested jury instruction.

▶ ANALYSIS

Justification defenses are those providing that although the act was committed, it was not wrongful. When a defense is categorized as an excuse, however, the result is that although the act is wrongful, the actor will not be held accountable. The court noted that Lopez (D) did not claim that the alleged threats overwhelmed her will so that her inability to make the "correct" choice should be excused. Instead, Lopez (D) claimed that she made the correct choice; thus, her act was one which was justified.

Quicknotes

ACCESSORY An individual who combines with the main actor in the commission or attempted commission of a criminal offense, either before or after its performance.

DURESS Unlawful threats or other coercive behavior by one person, that causes another to commit acts that he would not otherwise do.

NECESSITY DEFENSE A defense to liability for unlawful activity where the conduct is unavoidable and is justified by preventing the occurrence of a more serious harm.

PRINCIPAL A person or entity who authorizes another (the agent) to act on its behalf and subject to its authority to the extent that the principal may be held liable for the actions of the agent.

People v. McCoy

State (P) v. Murderer (D)

Cal. Sup. Ct., 25 Cal. 4th 1111, 24 P.3d 1210 (2001).

NATURE OF CASE: State's appeal from reversal of a murder conviction.

FACT SUMMARY: Lakey argued that, as an aider and abettor, he could not be found guilty of a greater crime than the actual perpetrator.

RULE OF LAW
An aider and abettor may be guilty of a greater homicide-related offense than the actual perpetrator committed.

FACTS: McCoy and Lakey were tried together and convicted of first-degree murder arising out of a drive-by shooting. McCoy shot to death the victim, but claimed self-defense. Although the jury rejected the defense, the court of appeal reversed McCoy's conviction on the grounds the trial judge had misinstructed the jury on the theory of imperfect (unreasonable) self-defense. The appellate court stated that if the jury had accepted this defense, McCoy would have been guilty only of voluntary manslaughter. The court of appeals also reversed Lakey's (D) murder conviction on the ground that an aider and abettor cannot be convicted of an offense greater than that of which the actual perpetrator is convicted where both persons are tried in the same trial on the same evidence. The state appealed.

ISSUE: May an aider and abettor be guilty of a greater homicide-related offense than the actual perpetrator committed?

HOLDING AND DECISION: (Chin, J.) Yes. An aider and abettor may be guilty of a greater homicide-related offense than the actual perpetrator committed. Although the mental state required of an aider and abettor is different from the mental state necessary for conviction of the actual perpetrator, the difference does not, however, mean that the mental state of an aider and abettor is less culpable than that of the actual perpetrator. On the contrary, outside of the natural and probable consequences doctrine, an aider and abettor's mental state must be at least that required of the direct perpetrator. Thus, when a person, with the mental state necessary for an aider and abettor, helps or induces another to kill, that person's guilt is determined by the combined acts of all the participants, as well as that person's own mens rea. If that person's mens rea is more culpable than another's, that person's guilt may be greater even if the other might be deemed the actual perpetrator. This court, however, expresses no view on whether or how these principles apply outside the homicide context. Reversed.

ANALYSIS

Many commentators have concluded that there is no conceptual obstacle to convicting a secondary party of a more serious offense than is proved against the primary party. As they reason, once it is proved that the principal has caused an actus reas, the liability of each of the secondary parties should be assessed according to his own mens rea.

Quicknotes

ACTUS REUS The unlawful act, that gives rise to criminal liability, as distinguished from the required mental state.

JURY INSTRUCTIONS A communication made by the court to a jury regarding the applicable law involved in a proceeding.

MENS REA Criminal intent.

SELF-DEFENSE The right to protect an individual's person, family or property against attempted injury by another.

In re Meagan R.

Government (P) v. Alleged-burglar (D)

Cal. App. 4th Dist., 42 Cal. App. 4th 17 (1996).

NATURE OF CASE: Appeal from judgment entered on juvenile court true findings of burglary.

FACT SUMMARY: Meagan R. (D) challenged a burglary finding predicated upon a finding that she entered a residence with the intent to aid and abet her own statutory rape.

🏛 RULE OF LAW
When the legislature has imposed criminal penalties to protect a specific class of individuals, it can hardly have meant that a member of that very class should be punishable either as an aider or abettor or as a co-conspirator.

FACTS: Rodriguez broke into his ex-girlfriend's home, with the assistance of 14-year-old Meagan R. (D), in order for the two to have sexual intercourse in violation of the state rape statute. Meagan R. (D) was prosecuted for burglary on a finding that she had entered a residence with the intent to aid and abet her own statutory rape. Meagan R. (D) appealed, alleging that she was a member of the protected class.

ISSUE: When the legislature has imposed criminal penalties to protect a specific class of individuals, can it have meant that a member of that very class should be punishable either as an aider or abettor or as a co-conspirator?

HOLDING AND DECISION: (Work, J.) No. When the legislature has imposed criminal penalties to protect a specific class of individuals, it can hardly have meant that a member of that very class should be punishable either as an aider or abettor or as a co-conspirator. An aider and abettor must have criminal intent in order to be convicted of a criminal offense. Where the legislature has established a rule that in crimes which necessarily involve the joint action of two or more persons, and where no punishment at all is provided for the conduct of one of the participants, the party whose participation is not denounced by statute cannot be charged with criminal conduct on either a conspiracy or aiding and abetting theory. Meagan R. (D) was the protected victim under a statutory provision designed to criminalize the exploitation of children, rather than to penalize the children themselves. Meagan R. (D), as the victim of the statutory rape, cannot be prosecuted on that charge, regardless whether her culpability is predicated upon being a co-conspirator, an aider and abettor, or an accomplice, given her legislatively protected status. Reversed.

▶ ANALYSIS

The court below had relied on the statutory rape to serve as the predicate felony in a true finding she had committed burglary. Burglary is defined as the breaking and entering of a dwelling house of another in the nighttime with the intent to commit a felony within. Rape could not be used as the felony here.

■═■

Quicknotes

BURGLARY Unlawful entry of a building at night with the intent to commit a felony therein.

FELONY A criminal offense of greater seriousness than a misdemeanor; felonies are generally defined pursuant to statute as any crime that is punishable by death or by a term of imprisonment exceeding one year.

STATUTORY RAPE Unlawful sexual intercourse by a man with a woman, either consensual or nonconsensual, under an age specified by statute.

■═■

State v. Formella

State (P) v. Convicted accomplice to theft (D)

N.H. Sup. Ct., 158 N.H. 114, 960 A.2d 722 (2008).

NATURE OF CASE: Appeal from conviction of theft as an accomplice.

FACT SUMMARY: Formella (D), who initially served as a lookout for others who stole exams but then decided that participating in the crime was wrong and stopped serving as a lookout before the crime was committed, contended that he could not be convicted of theft as an accomplice since he had withdrawn in time from the crime.

RULE OF LAW
An individual can be held criminally liable as an accomplice where the individual terminates his complicity prior to the commission of the offense but does not wholly deprive the complicity of its effectiveness.

FACTS: Formella (D), a high school student, and his friends were asked by a group of other students to serve as lookouts while the group stole mathematics exams from within the high school. Formella (D) and his friends agreed, and, on their way to their lockers, looked around to "confirm or dispel" whether anyone was there. After getting their books from their lockers, Formella (D) and his friends decided that serving as lookouts was wrong, and they left the school building. The other group succeeded in stealing the exams. Formella (D), who admitted his involvement in the theft, was convicted of theft based on criminal liability for the conduct of another, as an accomplice. Formella (D) appealed, contending that the trial court had erred in failing to make findings of fact relative to the timing of his withdrawal from the theft and the completion of the theft since the accomplice liability statute provides that a person is not an accomplice if he "terminates his complicity prior to the commission of the offense and wholly deprives it of effectiveness in the commission of the offense or gives timely warning to the law enforcement authorities or otherwise makes proper effort to prevent the commission of the offense." The state's highest court granted review.

ISSUE: Can an individual be held criminally liable as an accomplice where the individual terminates his complicity prior to the commission of the offense but does not wholly deprive the complicity of its effectiveness?

HOLDING AND DECISION: (Galway, J.) Yes. An individual can be held criminally liable as an accomplice where the individual terminates his complicity prior to the commission of the offense but does not wholly deprive the complicity of its effectiveness. It is undisputed that Formella (D) became an accomplice when he agreed to

serve as a lookout. The issue, therefore, is whether his later acts terminated his accomplice liability. Formella (D) neither timely warned the police, nor otherwise made a "proper effort" to prevent the offense. The question, therefore, is whether his termination "wholly deprived his complicity of effectiveness." The accomplice statute does not define what is required for a person to wholly deprive his complicity of effectiveness. The State (P) argues that there must be an overt act aimed at undermining the prior complicity, and Formella (D) argues no such act is required. The statute is ambiguous as to this requirement, and the legislative intent must be determined. The Model Penal Code, on which the statute is based, indicates that to deprive complicity such as is involved here of effectiveness, the withdrawing participant must not only withdraw from the commission of the offense, but also must communicate his disapproval to the principals sufficiently in advance of the commission of the crime to allow them time to reconsider as well. Here, even though Formella (D) timely withdrew before the commission of the theft, he nonetheless did not wholly deprive his complicity of its effectiveness because he made no affirmative act, such as communicating his withdrawal to the principals, which would give them a chance to reconsider committing the offense. Instead, the principals remained unaware of his withdrawal. While it is true that Formella (D) no longer served as an effective lookout after he withdrew, he did nothing to counter the effect of his prior complicity. His agreeing to serve as a lookout encouraged the principals to engage in the offense, and it was this encouragement that needed to be undone or undermined. Because there was no evidence that Formella (D) had wholly deprived his complicity of its effectiveness, it was not error for the trial court to refuse to make findings on the timing of the offense because such findings would not have altered the result. Affirmed.

ANALYSIS

As this case demonstrates, a mere change of heart, flight from the crime scene, apprehension by the police, or an uncommunicated decision not to carry out his part of the scheme will not suffice to relieve a withdrawing accomplice of criminal liability. However, as the case also notes, while the terminating accomplice does not actually have to prevent the crime from occurring, he must take some affirmative action that communicates disapproval to the principals in time for them to consider changing course.

Continued on next page.

Quicknotes

ACCOMPLICE An individual who knowingly, purposefully or voluntarily combines with the main actor in the commission, or attempted commission, of a criminal offense.

ACCOMPLICE LIABILITY Liability of an individual who knowingly, purposefully, or voluntarily combines with the main actor in the commission, or attempted commission, of a criminal offense.

COMPLICITY The act of conspiring to, or participating in, the commission of an unlawful act.

THEFT The illegal taking of another's property with the intent to deprive the owner thereof.

■═■

Commonwealth v. Koczwara

State (P) v. Tavern owner (D)

Pa. Sup. Ct., 397 Pa. 575, 155 A.2d 825 (1959).

NATURE OF CASE: Appeal from a conviction for violations of the state's liquor code.

FACT SUMMARY: After employees in Koczwara's (D) tavern, without Koczwara's (D) knowledge, served beer to minors who were unaccompanied and unsupervised by their parents or other guardians, Koczwara (D) was tried and convicted for violations of the state's Liquor Code.

🏛 RULE OF LAW
Courts may impose vicarious absolute liability for the acts of another, but a sentence of imprisonment may not be imposed vicariously.

FACTS: Koczwara (D) was the licensee and operator of a tavern. He was charged with allowing unsupervised minors to frequent the tavern and with the sale of beer to those minors, in violation of the state's Liquor Code. At trial, there was no evidence that Koczwara (D) was present on any one of the occasions testified to by the witnesses or that he had any personal knowledge of the sales to those minors or to other persons on the premises. The jury returned a verdict of guilty. Because of a prior conviction for violations of the Code, the trial judge imposed not only a fine on Koczwara (D) but sentenced him to three months in prison. Koczwara (D) appealed.

ISSUE: May courts impose vicarious absolute liability for the acts of another?

HOLDING AND DECISION: (Cohen, J.) Yes. Courts may impose vicarious absolute liability for the acts of another. It is unlawful to permit minors, unaccompanied by parents, guardians, or other supervisors, to frequent a tavern, and it is unlawful to permit beer to be sold to minors. Nowhere in the applicable subsections of the Code is there any language that would require the prohibited acts to have been done either knowingly, willfully, or intentionally. The intent of the legislature in enacting the Code was not only to eliminate the common law requirement of a mens rea but also to place a very high degree of responsibility upon the holder of a liquor license to make certain that neither he nor anyone in his employ commits any of the prohibited acts upon the licensed premises. However, liability for all true crimes, wherein an offense carries with it a jail sentence, must be based exclusively upon personal causation. Even a licensee who is meticulously careful in the choice of his employees cannot supervise every single act of the subordinates. A man's liberty cannot rest on so frail a reed as whether his employee will commit a mistake in judgment. Thus, the fine is left intact, but the imprisonment is invalid.

DISSENT: (Musmanno, J.) The majority of this court sustains the conviction of a person for acts admittedly not committed by him, not performed in his presence, not accomplished at his direction, and not even done within his knowledge. If the majority cannot sanction the incarceration of a person for acts of which he had no knowledge, how can it sanction the imposition of a fine?

▌ ANALYSIS

At common law, any attempt to invoke the doctrine of respondeat superior in a criminal case would have run afoul of deeply ingrained notions of criminal jurisprudence that guilt must be personal and individual. The regulatory statute applicable in the instant case was passed under the Commonwealth's (P) police power. While an employer in almost all cases is not criminally responsible for the unlawful acts of his employees unless he consents to, approves, or participates in such acts, courts all over the nation have struggled for years in applying this rule within the framework of controlling the sale of intoxicating liquor.

■═■

Quicknotes

INCHOATE Impartial or incomplete.

VICARIOUS LIABILITY The imputed liability of one party for the unlawful acts of another.

■═■

State v. Christy Pontiac-GMC, Inc.

State (P) v. Minnesota corporation (D)

Minn. Sup. Ct., 354 N.W.2d 17 (1984).

NATURE OF CASE: Appeal from a conviction of a corporation for theft by swindle and aggravated forgery.

FACT SUMMARY: After an employee of Christy Pontiac-GMC, Inc. (Christy Pontiac) (D) forged the signatures of two customers on rebate applications, Christy Pontiac (D) was charged and convicted of theft by swindle and aggravated forgery.

🏛 RULE OF LAW
A corporation may be held criminally liable for a specific-intent crime.

FACTS: Christy Pontiac-GMC, Inc. (Christy Pontiac) (D), a Minnesota corporation, was solely owned by James Christy (D), its president and director. Christy Pontiac (D) made two car sales after a rebate offer from GM had expired. Both customers were told that the salesman would still try to get the rebate for them. Hesli (D), a salesman and fleet manager, forged the signatures of both customers on the rebate applications, and the purchase order forms were backdated to put them within the time frame of the rebate offers. When the purchasers learned of the forged rebate applications, they complained to Christy (D). Charges were filed against Hesli (D), Christy (D), and Christy Pontiac (D). In a separate trial, Hesli (D) was found guilty of theft for the second forgery and was given a misdemeanor disposition. An indictment against Christy (D) was dismissed. Christy Pontiac (D), the corporation, was convicted as charged. This appeal followed.

ISSUE: May a corporation be held criminally liable for a specific-intent crime?

HOLDING AND DECISION: (Simonett, J.) Yes. A corporation may be held liable for a specific-intent crime. Therefore, a corporation may be prosecuted and convicted for the crimes of theft and forgery. Criminal guilt, however, requires that the agent act in furtherance of the corporation's business interests. Moreover, it must be shown that corporate management authorized, tolerated, or ratified the criminal activity. Here, since Christy Pontiac (D) got the GM rebate money, Hesli (D) was acting in furtherance of the corporation's business interests. Hesli (D) himself had middle-management responsibilities for cash rebate applications. Swandy, a corporate officer, signed the backdated retail buyer's order form for the first sale. Christy (D), the president, attempted to negotiate a settlement with the second purchaser. The evidence thus establishes that the theft by swindle and the forgeries constituted the acts of the corporation. Affirmed.

▶ ANALYSIS

The Model Penal Code provides that a corporation may be convicted of an offense if the conduct is performed by an agent of the corporation acting on behalf of the corporation within the scope of his employment. See Model Penal Code 2.07(1). The conduct need not actually benefit the corporation to impart liability. However, if the agent acts only to further his own interests—for example, is embezzling funds from the corporation—such an act is not considered to be "on behalf of the corporation."

Quicknotes

AGENT An individual who has the authority to act on behalf of another.

SPECIFIC INTENT The intent to commit a specific unlawful act which is a required element for criminal liability for certain crimes.

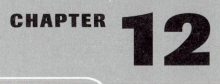
Quick Reference Rules of Law

Lee v. State

Bailee (D) v. State (P)

Md. Ct. Spec. App., 59 Md. App. 28, 474 A.2d 537 (1984).

NATURE OF CASE: [Nature of case not stated in casebook excerpt.]

FACT SUMMARY: [Fact summary not stated in casebook excerpt.]

> 🏛 **RULE OF LAW**
> Common law larceny has been broadened to include misappropriation of property by a bailee, who is a person who has control over the property with the owner's consent.

FACTS: [Facts not stated in casebook excerpt.]

ISSUE: Has common law larceny been broadened to include misappropriation of property by a bailee?

HOLDING AND DECISION: (Bell, J.) Yes. Common law larceny has been broadened to include misappropriation of property by a bailee. Larceny at common law was defined as the trespassory taking and carrying away of personal property of another with intent to steal the property. The requirement of a "trespassory taking" made larceny an offense against possession. The focus of the offense was on the physical aspect of taking and obtaining possession. Thus, a person such as a bailee, who had rightfully obtained possession of property from its owner, could not be guilty of larceny, even if he used the property in a manner inconsistent with the owner's expectations. Because of this narrow interpretation of larceny, the courts gradually broadened the offense by manipulating the concept of possession to embrace misappropriation by a person who, with the consent of the owner, already had physical control over the property.

▶ ANALYSIS

The criminal law has played a historical role in protecting property. However, history of the theft-related offenses of larceny, embezzlement, obtaining by false pretenses, and other closely related theft offenses commenced with the common law courts' concern for crimes of violence and for protecting society against breaches of peace. The application of the concept was then expanded by writ of trespass to cover all taking of another's property from his possession without his consent, even though no force was used. This latter misconduct was punished as larceny.

Quicknotes

BAILMENT The delivery of property to be held in trust and which is designated for a particular purpose, following the satisfaction of which the property is either to be returned or disposed of as specified.

LARCENY The illegal taking of another's property with the intent to deprive the owner thereof.

TRESPASS Unlawful interference with, or damage to, the real or personal property of another.

Rex v. Chisser

Government (P) v. Cravat thief (D)

Court of King's Bench, T. Raym. 275, 83 Eng. Rep. 142 (1678).

NATURE OF CASE: Prosecution for the theft of two cr[a]vats.

FACT SUMMARY: After Chisser (D) entered a shop, asked to see two cr[a]vats, and was told the price, he gave the owner an amount less than half of what was asked and then ran out of the shop with the cravats.

🏛 RULE OF LAW
The taking of goods away from a shop, without the owner's permission and without full payment, constitutes a felony.

FACTS: Chisser (D) came into Charteris's shop asking to see two cr[a]vats. She gave him the cr[a]vats to look at. After asking and being told the price, Chisser (D) offered to pay less than half that amount and then ran out of the shop, taking the cr[a]vats with him. The question was whether or not such action constituted a felony.

ISSUE: Does the taking of goods away from a shop, without the owner's permission and without full payment, constitute a felony?

HOLDING AND DECISION: [Judge not stated in casebook excerpt.] Yes. The taking of goods away from a shop, without the owner's permission and without full payment, constitutes a felony. Although the goods were delivered to Chisser (D) by the owner, they were not out of her possession by such delivery. They would not be until the full contract price had been paid. When Chisser (D) ran away with the goods, it was as if he had taken them, without having them handed to him, and run away with them. Thus, Chisser's (D) act constitutes a felony.

▶ ANALYSIS

Although the case does not explicitly use the terms, Chisser (D) had "physical" possession of the cravats, while the shop owner retained "constructive" possession. Drawing a distinction between the two allowed the common law to expand the law of larceny, which previously had given immunity from prosecution to anyone receiving possession of an object. Although a bailee receives both physical and constructive possession of a bale, he does not possess its contents. Thus, a dishonest bailee who "breaks bulk," or pilfers from a bale, commits larceny.

■==■

Quicknotes

ASPORTATION A carrying away of someone else's property.

LARCENY The illegal taking of another's property with the intent to deprive the owner, thereof.

■==■

United States v. Mafnas

Federal government (P) v. Armored-car employee (D)

701 F.2d 83 (9th Cir. 1983).

NATURE OF CASE: Appeal from a conviction for stealing money from two federally insured banks in violation of federal law.

FACT SUMMARY: After Mafnas (D), an armored car service employee, on three different occasions took money from money bags being delivered, he was convicted of three counts of stealing money from the banks for whom the money was being delivered.

🏛 RULE OF LAW
If a person receives property with instructions to deliver it to the owner, that person only acquires custody, and any subsequent decision to keep the property constitutes larceny.

FACTS: The Guam Armored Car Service (Service) employed Mafnas (D). The Bank of Hawaii and the Bank of America hired Service to deliver bags of money. On three occasions, Mafnas (D) opened the bags and removed money. As a result, he was charged with three counts of violating a federal law that makes it a crime to steal money belonging to any bank. Mafnas (D) argued that he had lawful possession of the bags, with the consent of the banks, when he took the money. He essentially claimed that he was a bailee and that the contract between the banks and Service resulted in Service's having lawful possession and not mere custody over the bags. Mafnas (D) was convicted as charged and appealed.

ISSUE: If a person receives property with instructions to deliver it to the owner, does that person acquire only custody of the property?

HOLDING AND DECISION: (Per curiam) Yes. If a person receives property with instructions to deliver it to the owner, that person acquires only custody of the property. Taking, with intent to steal, any money belonging to a bank constitutes a crime. The law distinguishes between possession and custody. The district court concluded that Mafnas (D) was given temporary custody only when asked to deliver the money bags. Mafnas's (D) later decision to take the money was larceny because it was beyond the consent of the owner, who retained constructive possession until Mafnas's (D) task was completed. Moreover, under the common law, a bailee who breaks open the bale and takes a portion or all of its contents is guilty of larceny because his taking is trespassory and is from the constructive possession of another. Either way, Mafnas (D) has committed the common crime of larceny, replete with trespassory taking. Affirmed.

▶ ANALYSIS

Case law is clear that since what was taken was property belonging to the banks, it was property or money "in the care, custody, control, management, or possession of any bank" within the meaning of the federal rule, notwithstanding the fact that it may have been in the physical possession of an armored car service serving as a bailee for hire. The court's analysis referred to *Wharton's Criminal Law*, Vol. 3, 346–357 (C. Torcia, 14th ed. 1980) and *United States v. Pruitt*, 446 F.2d 513 (6th Cir. 1971). Pruitt, who was employed by a bank as a messenger, staged a fake robbery with another person, with whom Pruitt split the money which he was delivering for the bank. The Sixth Circuit found that Pruitt's wrongful conversion constituted larceny.

Quicknotes

BAILEE Person holding property in trust for another party.

CONVERSION The act of depriving an owner of his property without permission or justification.

LARCENY The illegal taking of another's property with the intent to deprive the owner thereof.

Topolewski v. State

Meat thief (D) v. State (P)

Wis. Sup. Ct., 130 Wis. 244, 109 N.W. 1037 (1906).

NATURE OF CASE: Appeal from conviction for larceny.

FACT SUMMARY: Topolewski (D) stole meat with the aid of a bogus accomplice who provided Topolewski (D) with the meat in order for the police to capture him.

🏛 RULE OF LAW
When the owner of property aids in the commission of the offense of larceny of such property, then the accused is not guilty of that crime.

FACTS: Dolan, an employee of a meat packing company, owed Topolewski (D) some money. As payment, Topolewski (D) arranged for Dolan to place some meat on a company loading platform so that Topolewski (D) could put it on his wagon and drive away. Dolan informed the company of the plan. He was told to feign cooperation. The company instructed its loading platform manager, Klotz, not only to put the meat on the platform but also that a man would come and take it away. Klotz was not told about the impending theft. Klotz inferred that Topolewski (D) was that man and that it was proper to deliver the meat to him. Klotz did not assist Topolewski (D) in the loading of the meat, but he did allow the meat to be taken and did help arrange the wagon. Klotz also took an order from Topolewski (D) for the dispensation of a separate barrel of meat. From a conviction for larceny, Topolewski (D) appealed.

ISSUE: Does consent to a taking of property negate the element of trespassory taking in the crime of larceny?

HOLDING AND DECISION: (Marshall, J.) Yes. There can be no larceny without a trespass. Trespass is lacking where one allows his property to be taken or delivered to a person intending to commit larceny, regardless of the guilty purpose of the accused. Where the setting of a trap to catch a suspected thief goes no further than to afford an opportunity to carry out a criminal purpose, the deception so practiced is not sufficient, itself, to excuse the would-be criminal. But the deception must not amount to consent in the taking. Here, Klotz, the agent of the company, actually permitted the accused to take the meat as per his instructions from the company. In effect, meat was given to the accused by the company. A mere guilty purpose is not sufficient for conviction when one of the essential elements of the crime of larceny is missing. Since taking of the meat here was not a trespassory taking, conviction is reversed.

▶ ANALYSIS

It would seem that under these facts there would be no way for the company to set a trap to catch the accused. Once the company was informed of the plan by Dolan, they could not allow anyone to place the meat on the platform for the accused to take it away. Any placing of the meat on the platform knowing that the accused would steal it amounts to a consent to the taking. Trespass means that the accused's action at the time he takes possession must be wrongful as against some other person's lawful possession. The company here consented to the accused taking possession and, therefore, the taking was not trespassory.

■==■

Quicknotes

CONSENT A voluntary and willful agreement by an individual possessing sufficient mental capacity to undertake an action suggested by another.

LARCENY The illegal taking of another's property with the intent to deprive the owner thereof.

TRESPASS Unlawful interference with, or damage to, the real or personal property of another.

■==■

Rex v. Pear

Government (P) v. Horse seller (D)

Central Criminal Ct., 1 Leach 212, 168 Eng. Rep. 208 (1779).

NATURE OF CASE: Prosecution for the selling of another's property.

FACT SUMMARY: After Pear (D) hired a horse from a livery stable, saying that he would return it the same day, he sold the horse instead. A jury found that Pear (D) had no intention of returning the horse when he rented it.

🏛 RULE OF LAW
If a horse is leased for a particular portion of time and after that time is expired the hiring party sells the horse, converting the money to his own use, it is felony because there is then no privity of contract between the parties.

FACTS: Pear (D) rented a horse from Finch, owner of a livery stable, ostensibly to ride to the County of Surry and back on the same day. He did not go to Surry, however, but sold the horse. In addition, Pear (D) had given Finch a false home address. The jury found that Pear (D) had hired the horse with a fraudulent view and intention of selling it immediately. The question was then referred to the judges as to whether the conversion was a mere breach of trust or whether it was felonious.

ISSUE: If a horse is leased for a particular portion of time and after that time is expired the hiring party sells the horse, converting the money to his own use, is it felony since there is then no privity of contract between the parties?

HOLDING AND DECISION: (Baron Perryn, J.) Yes. If a horse is leased for a particular portion of time and after that time is expired the hiring party sells the horse, converting the money to his own use, it is felony because there is then no privity of contract between the parties. The majority of the judges thought that the question of Pear's (D) original intent in hiring the horse had been properly left to the jury. They agreed that Pear's (D) view in hiring the horse was fraudulent and that Finch's parting with the horse had not changed the nature of the possession, which remained unaltered at the time of the conversion. Thus, Pear (D) was guilty of felony.

▶ *ANALYSIS*

Larceny through the use of fraud is usually termed as "larceny by trick." Larceny by trick is distinguished from larceny by false pretenses. Under the former, one fraudu-

lently obtains possession of personal property, while under the latter, one uses deceit to obtain title to the property.

■═■

Quicknotes

CONVERSION The act of depriving an owner of his property without permission or justification.

PRIVITY OF CONTRACT A relationship, between the parties to a contract, which is required in order to bring an action for breach.

TRESPASS Unlawful interference with, or damage to, the real or personal property of another.

■═■

Brooks v. State

Workman (D) v. State (P)

Ohio Sup. Ct., 35 Ohio St. 46 (1878).

NATURE OF CASE: Prosecution for larceny.

FACT SUMMARY: Brooks (D), a workman, found a $200 roll of bank bills in the street which Newton had lost the month before and of which Newton published notice. Brooks (D), unknowing of such notice, concealed his find from his fellow workmen and kept the money.

🏛 RULE OF LAW
When a person finds goods that have been actually lost, and takes possession with intent to appropriate them to his own use, really believing, at the time, or having good ground to believe, that the owner can be found, it is larceny.

FACTS: Newton lost a roll of $200 worth of bank bills, notice of which was published by him in a newspaper. Brooks (D), a workman, found the lost money in the street about a month later. While there was no evidence as to whether he had seen the notice or knew of Newton's loss, it was shown that Brooks (D) "took pains" to hide his find from the fellow workmen whom he was with at the time. Brooks was convicted of larceny.

ISSUE: Did Brooks's (D) actions indicate a reasonable belief that the owner could be found at the time he took the lost money, thus making the taking larcenous?

HOLDING AND DECISION: (White, J.) Yes. While the finder may have reasonable grounds for believing the owner can be found, he is not required to make a diligent search for the owner. He does not have to know or have reason to know the particular person who owns the lost property. Even so, the taking will be a larceny if, at the time he finds it, the finder has reasonable grounds to believe, from the nature of the property or the circumstances under which it is found, that the owner can be found by dealing openly and not hiding the fact that he has found lost property (and had the intent to keep it at the time he took it into his possession). Refusal for a new trial affirmed.

DISSENT: (Okey, J.) The evidence fails to show that Brooks (D) had any information of a loss previous to the finding of the bills. There was no mark on the money to indicate the owner, nor was there anything in the attending circumstances pointing to one owner more than another. In violating a moral obligation, Brooks (D) should not incur criminal liability.

▶ ANALYSIS

This case raises the problem determining whether a "clue" exists as to ownership of the lost property. While no marking was present to indicate ownership and the circumstances would not appear to indicate ownership, the value of the lost property can act as a clue. Obviously, the higher the value, the greater indication there is of a clue. As $200 bank rolls are not often lost, open dealing with the find might have led to location of the owner. It is conceivable a fellow workman might have read the notice or have heard of the loss or knew someone else who knew the owner.

■■■

Quicknotes

LARCENY The illegal taking of another's property with the intent to deprive the owner thereof.

■■■

Lund v. Commonwealth

Graduate student (D) v. State (P)

Va. Sup. Ct., 217 Va. 688, 232 S.E.2d 745 (1977).

NATURE OF CASE: Appeal from a conviction for grand larceny by false pretense.

FACT SUMMARY: After Lund (D) used the computers in the university's computer center without authorization while working on his doctoral dissertation, he was tried and convicted for grand larceny.

🏛 RULE OF LAW
Labor and services and the unauthorized use of a computer cannot be construed as subjects of larceny.

FACTS: Lund (D) was a graduate student and a doctoral candidate. His faculty adviser neglected to arrange for Lund's (D) use of computer time, so Lund (D) used the computer without obtaining the proper authorization. Costs for computer time were allocated to the various departments. Lund (D) came under surveillance after various departments complained about unauthorized charges. He admitted unauthorized use of computer time, giving the investigator keys for access boxes assigned to other persons, which he said another student had given to him. Lund (D) testified that he did not think he was doing anything wrong. Four faculty members testified in Lund's (D) behalf, agreeing he would have been assigned computer time if properly requested. Lund (D) was convicted of grand larceny by false pretense. This appeal followed.

ISSUE: Can labor and services and the unauthorized use of a computer be construed as subjects of larceny?

HOLDING AND DECISION: (I'Anson, C.J.) No. Labor and services and the unauthorized use of a computer cannot be construed as subjects of larceny. Grand larceny is a taking from the person of another money or other thing of value of $5 or more or the taking not from the person of another goods and chattels of the value of $100 or more. Here, there was no evidence the keys and computer cards were stolen or that they had a market value of $100 or more. The phrase "goods and chattels" cannot be interpreted to include computer time and services. The Commonwealth (P) argues, additionally, that Lund (D) obtained the computer printouts by false pretense. However, the director of the computer center stated that the printouts had no more value than scrap paper. Hence, the evidence was insufficient for a conviction. Reversed.

▶ ANALYSIS

At common law, larceny is the taking and carrying away of the goods and chattels of another with intent to deprive the owner of the possession thereof permanently. At common law, labor or services could not be the subject of the crime of false pretense because neither time nor services may be taken and carried away. The Lund court noted that, while some jurisdictions have amended their criminal codes specifically to make it a crime to obtain labor or services by means of false pretense, there was no such provision in Virginia's statutes.

Quicknotes

CHATTEL An item of personal property.

FALSE PRETENSES The unlawful obtaining of money or property from another with intent to defraud and with the utilization of false representations.

LARCENY The illegal taking of another's property with the intent to deprive the owner thereof.

People v. Brown

State (P) v. Bicycle thief (D)

Cal. Sup. Ct., 105 Cal. 66, 38 P. 518 (1894).

NATURE OF CASE: Appeal from a conviction for burglary committed upon entering a house with intent to commit grand larceny.

FACT SUMMARY: After Brown (D) took a bicycle from the place where he was staying, he was convicted of burglary with the intent to commit grand larceny, even though he testified that he intended to return the bicycle that same evening.

RULE OF LAW

A person commits larceny when he takes the property of another with the intent to permanently deprive the owner of his property.

FACTS: Brown (D), a teenager, took a bicycle from the place where he was staying and working for his board. He hid the bicycle and himself in the brush, intending to take the bicycle back that evening. Brown (D) was discovered before he could return the bicycle and was charged with the crime of burglary, alleged to have been committed by entering the house with the intent to commit grand larceny. The instruction given by the trial judge concluded that the law of larceny did not require the intent to permanently deprive an owner of his property. Brown (D) was convicted as charged, and he appealed.

ISSUE: Does a person commit larceny when he takes the property of another with the intent to permanently deprive the owner of his property?

HOLDING AND DECISION: (Garoutte, J.) Yes. A person commits larceny when he takes the property of another with the intent to permanently deprive the owner of his property. If Brown's (D) story is true, he is not guilty of larceny in taking the bicycle. Yet, under the erroneous instructions of the court, his own words convicted him. The court told the jury that larceny may be committed, even though it was only the intent of the party taking the property to deprive the owner of it temporarily. If Brown (D) did not intend to permanently deprive the owner of the bicycle, there is no felonious intent, and his acts constitute a trespass only. Reversed.

ANALYSIS

The court noted that the authorities form an unbroken line to the effect that the felonious intent for larceny must be to deprive the owner of the property permanently. The felonious intent of the party taking need not necessarily be an intention to convert the property for his personal use. Still, it must in all cases be intent to wholly and permanently deprive the owner of his property. A trespass, which the court of appeals said Brown's (D) act did constitute, involves the taking of another's property without his consent or without any justification for a nonconsensual taking.

Quicknotes

CONVERSION The act of depriving an owner of his property without permission or justification.

LARCENY The illegal taking of another's property with the intent to deprive the owner thereof.

People v. Davis

State (P) v. Alleged thief (D)

Cal. Sup. Ct., 19 Cal. 4th 301, 965 P.2d 1165 (1998).

NATURE OF CASE: Review of petty theft conviction.

FACT SUMMARY: Davis (D) attempted to "return" and get a refund on a shirt which he had just taken from another department in the same store.

🏛 RULE OF LAW
The general rule is that the intent to steal required for conviction of larceny is intent to deprive the owner permanently of possession of the property.

FACTS: Davis (D) entered a Mervyn's department store, took a shirt from the men's department, and then went to the women's department, claiming that he had bought the shirt for his father, that it did not fit, and that he wanted to return it. The store security agent had been watching the whole time and told the sales clerk to issue a credit voucher, which she did. Davis (D) then signed it under a false name. The store security agent then detained him and charged him with the crime of petty theft. Davis (D) was convicted and appealed, contending that the elements of trespass and intent to steal were lacking. The court of appeal affirmed and the state supreme court granted review.

ISSUE: Is the general rule that the intent to steal required for conviction of larceny is intent to deprive the owner permanently of possession of the property?

HOLDING AND DECISION: (Mosk, J.) Yes. The general rule is that the intent to steal required for conviction of larceny is intent to deprive the owner permanently of possession of the property. But the general rule is flexible. When the defendant intends to sell the property back to the owner, when he intends to claim a reward for "finding" the property, or when the defendant intends to return the property to the owner for a refund, as in this case, the requisite intent to steal may be found. Davis's (D) intent to claim ownership of the shirt and to return it to Mervyn's only on condition that the store pay him a "refund" constitutes an intent to permanently deprive Mervyn's of the shirt within the meaning of the law of larceny. Because Mervyn's cannot be deemed to have consented to Davis's (D) taking possession of the shirt with the intent to steal it, Davis's (D) conduct also constituted a trespassory taking within the meaning of the law of larceny. Affirmed.

▶ ANALYSIS

The elements of theft by larceny are the taking possession of the personal property of another by means of trespass,

with intent to steal the property, and the carrying away of the property. Davis (D) took possession of the shirt owned by Mervyn's and moved it sufficiently to satisfy the asportation requirement.

■══■

Quicknotes

ASPORTATION A carrying away of someone else's property.

INTENT The state of mind that exists when one's purpose is to commit a criminal act.

LARCENY The illegal taking of another's property with the intent to deprive the owner thereof.

POSSESSION The holding of property with the right of disposition.

■══■

Rex v. Bazeley

Government (P) v. Bank teller (D)

Central Criminal Ct., 2 Leach 835, 168 Eng. Rep. 517 (1799).

NATURE OF CASE: Prosecution for tortious conversion by an employee.

FACT SUMMARY: After Bazeley (D), a bank teller, pocketed a banknote that he had received for deposit, he was charged with tortiously converting it to his own use.

RULE OF LAW
Where an employer has only a right or title to possess property but no absolute or even qualified possession of it, an employee cannot be said to have tortiously taken it from the employer's possession with a felonious intent to steal it.

FACTS: Bazeley (D), employed as a teller by Esdaile (P) and Hammett (P) in their bank, put a banknote in his pocket which he had received for deposit. He later converted it to his own use. Bazeley's (D) employers (P) prosecuted the case. Bazeley's (D) counsel argued that his employers (P) could not have had constructive possession of the banknote when Bazeley (D) was charged with having tortiously converted it to his own use. Even if they had possession of the note, Bazeley (D) could not be said to have tortiously taken it with a felonious intention to steal it. Moreover, the relationship of the parties makes this transaction merely a breach of trust.

ISSUE: Where an employer has only a right or title to possess property but no absolute or even qualified possession of it, can an employee be said to have tortiously taken it from the employer's possession with a felonious intent to steal it?

HOLDING AND DECISION: [Judge not stated in casebook excerpt.] No. Where an employer has only a right or title to possess property but no absolute or even qualified possession of it, an employee cannot be said to have tortiously taken it from the employer's possession with a felonious intent to steal it. The employers (P) here had only a right or title to possess the note and not the absolute or even qualified possession of it. It was never in their custody or under their control. Thus, at the time of the supposed conversion, the note was legally in Bazeley's (D) possession. Furthermore, there was no evidence whatever to show that any felonious intent to steal existed in Bazeley's (D) mind when the note came to his hands. Moreover, the capacity in which Bazeley (D) acted in the banking house makes this a breach of trust, which is not, either by the common law or an act of Parliament, felony.

ANALYSIS

Because no opinion was ever publicly delivered in this case, Bazeley (D) was included in the Secretary of State's letter as a proper object for a pardon. As a consequence of this case Statute 39 Geo. III. c. 85 passed, entitled, "An Act to protect Masters and others against Embezzlement, by their Clerks or Servants." The Act made such embezzlement a felony. By enacting embezzlement statutes, most jurisdictions in the United States have criminalized the conversion of property occurring in the absence of trespass.

Quicknotes

EMBEZZLEMENT The fraudulent appropriation of property lawfully in one's possession.

POSSESSION The holding of property with the right of disposition.

TITLE The right of possession over property.

People v. Ingram

State (P) v. Alleged thief (D)

Cal. Ct. App., 76 Cal. Rptr. 2d 553 (1998).

NATURE OF CASE: [Nature of case not stated in casebook excerpt.]

FACT SUMMARY: [Fact summary not stated in casebook excerpt.]

🏛 RULE OF LAW
The distinction between larceny and obtaining money or property by false pretenses turns on a question of title.

FACTS: [Facts not stated in casebook excerpt.]

ISSUE: Does the distinction between larceny and obtaining money or property by false pretenses turn on a question of title?

HOLDING AND DECISION: (Haller, J.) Yes. The distinction between larceny and obtaining money or property by false pretenses turns on a question of title. The defendant who obtains property by larceny does not obtain title, while the defendant who obtains property by false pretenses does obtain title.

▶ ANALYSIS

This is an excerpt from a case where the court distinguished common law larceny from the statutory offense of theft by false pretenses. Petition for review by the state supreme court was granted for this case. Further action was deferred pending disposition of a related issue in another case not relevant to the excerpt presented here.

■═■

Quicknotes

FALSE PRETENSES The unlawful obtaining of money or property from another with intent to defraud and with the utilization of false representations.

LARCENY The illegal taking of another's property with the intent to deprive the owner thereof.

POSSESSION The holding of property with the right of disposition.

TITLE The right of possession over property.

■═■

People v. Whight

State (P) v. Alleged thief (D)

Cal. Ct. App., 36 Cal. App. 4th 1143 (1995).

NATURE OF CASE: Appeal from a criminal conviction for grand theft by false pretense.

FACT SUMMARY: Whight (D) continued using an ATM card after his checking account had been closed by the bank.

🏛 RULE OF LAW
To support a conviction of theft for obtaining property by false pretenses, it must be shown that the defendant made a false pretense or representation, that the representation was made with intent to defraud the owner of his property, and that the owner was in fact defrauded in that he parted with his property in reliance upon the representation.

FACTS: Whight's (D) checking account had been closed by his bank but he was still able to use his ATM card at Safeway stores to obtain over $19,000 in cash. Safeway's practice was to verify the ATM cards through the use of a computer system operated by Wells Fargo Bank, which would report a code to the supermarket approving or disapproving the proposed transaction. When no link up with the customer's bank was possible, Wells Fargo was reporting a "stand in" code and Safeway would approve the transaction. At the time of his arrest, Whight (D) admitted knowing his checking account was closed. Whight (D) was convicted of grand theft by false pretenses and appealed, claiming that Safeway relied on the code issued by Wells Fargo, rather than on his representations, in approving the requests for money.

ISSUE: To support a conviction of theft for obtaining property by false pretenses, must it be shown that the defendant made a false pretense or representation, that the representation was made with intent to defraud the owner of his property, and that the owner was in fact defrauded in that he parted with his property in reliance upon the representation?

HOLDING AND DECISION: (Sparks, J.) Yes. To support a conviction of theft for obtaining property by false pretenses, it must be shown that the defendant made a false pretense or representation, that the representation was made with intent to defraud the owner of his property, and that the owner was in fact defrauded in that he parted with his property in reliance upon the representation. The false pretense may consist in any act, word, symbol, or token calculated and intended to deceive. It may be express or implied from words or conduct. Thus, when Whight (D) proffered his ATM card, he impliedly represented, falsely, that it was valid. The causal chain of reliance is not broken merely because the victim undertakes some investigation. The false pretense need not be the sole inducing cause. The computer system kept returning a code that there was no response, and, as a result, Safeway had nothing to rely upon except Whight's (D) implicit representation that his ATM card was valid. Affirmed.

▸ ANALYSIS

There are two forms of theft: larceny by trick and larceny by false pretenses. Larceny by trick or device occurs, when the defendant obtains possession of (but not title to) another's property by fraud or trickery, fraud vitiates consent and takes the place of the trespass. If one, through false representations and with the intent to steal, obtains both possession and title to property, the statutory crime of theft by false pretenses has been committed.

■=■

Quicknotes

LARCENY BY TRICK The illegal taking of another's property with the intent to deprive the owner thereof and through the means of deception.

THEFT The illegal taking of another's property with the intent to deprive the owner thereof.

THEFT BY FALSE PRETENSES The illegal taking of another's property with the intent to deprive the owner thereof and through means of deception.

■=■

United States v. Czubinski

Federal government (P) v. Alleged criminal (D)

106 F.3d 1069 (1st Cir. 1997).

NATURE OF CASE: Appeal from criminal convictions for wire and computer fraud.

FACT SUMMARY: Czubinski (D), an employee of the Internal Revenue Service (IRS), was convicted of wire and computer fraud when he carried out numerous unauthorized searches of the IRS's computer systems data files.

🏛 **RULE OF LAW**
To deprive a person of his intangible property interest in confidential information under federal law, either some articulable harm must befall the holder of the information as a result of the defendant's activities, or some gainful use must be intended by the person accessing the information.

FACTS: Czubinski (D) worked for the Internal Revenue Service (IRS) and performed numerous unauthorized searches in the IRS computer database at work which were outside the scope of his employment. Czubinski (D) was found guilty under federal wire fraud statutes and appealed.

ISSUE: To deprive a person of their intangible property interest in confidential information under federal law, must some articulable harm befall the holder of the information as a result of the defendant's activities, or some gainful use be intended by the person accessing the information?

HOLDING AND DECISION: (Torruella, C.J.) Yes. To deprive a person of their intangible property interest in confidential information under federal law, either some articulable harm must befall the holder of the information as a result of the defendant's activities, or some gainful use must be intended by the person accessing the information. Nothing in the record indicates that Czubinski (D) did anything more than knowingly disregard IRS rules by observing the confidential information he accessed. There is no evidence that he used the information in any way. Neither the taking of the IRS's right to exclusive use of the confidential information, nor Czubinski's (D) gain from access to the information can be shown absent evidence of his "use" of the information. The Government (P) has not shown beyond a reasonable doubt that Czubinski (D) intended to carry out a scheme to deprive the IRS of its property interest in confidential information. Mere browsing of the records of people, about whom one might have a particular interest, although reprehensible, is not enough to sustain a wire fraud conviction on a deprivation of intangible property theory. Reversed.

▶ **ANALYSIS**

The Government (P) pursued two theories of wire fraud in this case. First, that Czubinski (D) defrauded the IRS of its property by acquiring confidential information for certain intended personal uses. Second, that he defrauded the IRS and the public of their intangible right to his honest services.

■■■

Quicknotes

FRAUD A false representation of facts with the intent that another will rely on the misrepresentation to his detriment.

INTANGIBLE RIGHT An interest in property that is not embodied in a physical object.

■■■

Common Latin Words and Phrases Encountered in the Law

A FORTIORI: Because one fact exists or has been proven, therefore a second fact that is related to the first fact must also exist.

A PRIORI: From the cause to the effect. A term of logic used to denote that when one generally accepted truth is shown to be a cause, another particular effect must necessarily follow.

AB INITIO: From the beginning; a condition which has existed throughout, as in a marriage which was void ab initio.

ACTUS REUS: The wrongful act; in criminal law, such action sufficient to trigger criminal liability.

AD VALOREM: According to value; an ad valorem tax is imposed upon an item located within the taxing jurisdiction calculated by the value of such item.

AMICUS CURIAE: Friend of the court. Its most common usage takes the form of an amicus curiae brief, filed by a person who is not a party to an action but is nonetheless allowed to offer an argument supporting his legal interests.

ARGUENDO: In arguing. A statement, possibly hypothetical, made for the purpose of argument, is one made arguendo.

BILL QUIA TIMET: A bill to quiet title (establish ownership) to real property.

BONA FIDE: True, honest, or genuine. May refer to a person's legal position based on good faith or lacking notice of fraud (such as a bona fide purchaser for value) or to the authenticity of a particular document (such as a bona fide last will and testament).

CAUSA MORTIS: With approaching death in mind. A gift causa mortis is a gift given by a party who feels certain that death is imminent.

CAVEAT EMPTOR: Let the buyer beware. This maxim is reflected in the rule of law that a buyer purchases at his own risk because it is his responsibility to examine, judge, test, and otherwise inspect what he is buying.

CERTIORARI: A writ of review. Petitions for review of a case by the United States Supreme Court are most often done by means of a writ of certiorari.

CONTRA: On the other hand. Opposite. Contrary to.

CORAM NOBIS: Before us; writs of error directed to the court that originally rendered the judgment.

CORAM VOBIS: Before you; writs of error directed by an appellate court to a lower court to correct a factual error.

CORPUS DELICTI: The body of the crime; the requisite elements of a crime amounting to objective proof that a crime has been committed.

CUM TESTAMENTO ANNEXO, ADMINISTRATOR (ADMINISTRATOR C.T.A.): With will annexed; an administrator c.t.a. settles an estate pursuant to a will in which he is not appointed.

DE BONIS NON, ADMINISTRATOR (ADMINISTRATOR D.B.N.): Of goods not administered; an administrator d.b.n. settles a partially settled estate.

DE FACTO: In fact; in reality; actually. Existing in fact but not officially approved or engendered.

DE JURE: By right; lawful. Describes a condition that is legitimate "as a matter of law," in contrast to the term "de facto," which connotes something existing in fact but not legally sanctioned or authorized. For example, de facto segregation refers to segregation brought about by housing patterns, etc., whereas de jure segregation refers to segregation created by law.

DE MINIMIS: Of minimal importance; insignificant; a trifle; not worth bothering about.

DE NOVO: Anew; a second time; afresh. A trial de novo is a new trial held at the appellate level as if the case originated there and the trial at a lower level had not taken place.

DICTA: Generally used as an abbreviated form of obiter dicta, a term describing those portions of a judicial opinion incidental or not necessary to resolution of the specific question before the court. Such nonessential statements and remarks are not considered to be binding precedent.

DUCES TECUM: Refers to a particular type of writ or subpoena requesting a party or organization to produce certain documents in their possession.

EN BANC: Full bench. Where a court sits with all justices present rather than the usual quorum.

EX PARTE: For one side or one party only. An ex parte proceeding is one undertaken for the benefit of only one party, without notice to, or an appearance by, an adverse party.

EX POST FACTO: After the fact. An ex post facto law is a law that retroactively changes the consequences of a prior act.

EX REL.: Abbreviated form of the term "ex relatione," meaning upon relation or information. When the state brings an action in which it has no interest against an individual at the instigation of one who has a private interest in the matter.

FORUM NON CONVENIENS: Inconvenient forum. Although a court may have jurisdiction over the case, the action should be tried in a more conveniently located court, one to which parties and witnesses may more easily travel, for example.

GUARDIAN AD LITEM: A guardian of an infant as to litigation, appointed to represent the infant and pursue his/her rights.

HABEAS CORPUS: You have the body. The modern writ of habeas corpus is a writ directing that a person (body) being detained (such as a prisoner) be brought before the court so that the legality of his detention can be judicially ascertained.

IN CAMERA: In private, in chambers. When a hearing is held before a judge in his chambers or when all spectators are excluded from the courtroom.

IN FORMA PAUPERIS: In the manner of a pauper. A party who proceeds in forma pauperis because of his poverty is one who is allowed to bring suit without liability for costs.

INFRA: Below, under. A word referring the reader to a later part of a book. (The opposite of supra.)

IN LOCO PARENTIS: In the place of a parent.

IN PARI DELICTO: Equally wrong; a court of equity will not grant requested relief to an applicant who is in pari delicto, or as much at fault in the transactions giving rise to the controversy as is the opponent of the applicant.

IN PARI MATERIA: On like subject matter or upon the same matter. Statutes relating to the same person or things are said to be in pari materia. It is a general rule of statutory construction that such statutes should be construed together, i.e., looked at as if they together constituted one law.

IN PERSONAM: Against the person. Jurisdiction over the person of an individual.

IN RE: In the matter of. Used to designate a proceeding involving an estate or other property.

IN REM: A term that signifies an action against the res, or thing. An action in rem is basically one that is taken directly against property, as distinguished from an action in personam, i.e., against the person.

INTER ALIA: Among other things. Used to show that the whole of a statement, pleading, list, statute, etc., has not been set forth in its entirety.

INTER PARTES: Between the parties. May refer to contracts, conveyances or other transactions having legal significance.

INTER VIVOS: Between the living. An inter vivos gift is a gift made by a living grantor, as distinguished from bequests contained in a will, which pass upon the death of the testator.

IPSO FACTO: By the mere fact itself.

JUS: Law or the entire body of law.

LEX LOCI: The law of the place; the notion that the rights of parties to a legal proceeding are governed by the law of the place where those rights arose.

MALUM IN SE: Evil or wrong in and of itself; inherently wrong. This term describes an act that is wrong by its very nature, as opposed to one which would not be wrong but for the fact that there is a specific legal prohibition against it (malum prohibitum).

MALUM PROHIBITUM: Wrong because prohibited, but not inherently evil. Used to describe something that is wrong because it is expressly forbidden by law but that is not in and of itself evil, e.g., speeding.

MANDAMUS: We command. A writ directing an official to take a certain action.

MENS REA: A guilty mind; a criminal intent. A term used to signify the mental state that accompanies a crime or other prohibited act. Some crimes require only a general mens rea (general intent to do the prohibited act), but others, like assault with intent to murder, require the existence of a specific mens rea.

MODUS OPERANDI: Method of operating; generally refers to the manner or style of a criminal in committing crimes, admissible in appropriate cases as evidence of the identity of a defendant.

NEXUS: A connection to.

NISI PRIUS: A court of first impression. A nisi prius court is one where issues of fact are tried before a judge or jury.

N.O.V. (NON OBSTANTE VEREDICTO): Notwithstanding the verdict. A judgment n.o.v. is a judgment given in favor of one party despite the fact that a verdict was returned in favor of the other party, the justification being that the verdict either had no reasonable support in fact or was contrary to law.

NUNC PRO TUNC: Now for then. This phrase refers to actions that may be taken and will then have full retroactive effect.

PENDENTE LITE: Pending the suit; pending litigation under way.

PER CAPITA: By head; beneficiaries of an estate, if they take in equal shares, take per capita.

PER CURIAM: By the court; signifies an opinion ostensibly written "by the whole court" and with no identified author.

PER SE: By itself, in itself; inherently.

PER STIRPES: By representation. Used primarily in the law of wills to describe the method of distribution where a person, generally because of death, is unable to take that which is left to him by the will of another, and therefore his heirs divide such property between them rather than take under the will individually.

PRIMA FACIE: On its face, at first sight. A prima facie case is one that is sufficient on its face, meaning that the evidence supporting it is adequate to establish the case until contradicted or overcome by other evidence.

PRO TANTO: For so much; as far as it goes. Often used in eminent domain cases when a property owner receives partial payment for his land without prejudice to his right to bring suit for the full amount he claims his land to be worth.

QUANTUM MERUIT: As much as he deserves. Refers to recovery based on the doctrine of unjust enrichment in those cases in which a party has rendered valuable services or furnished materials that were accepted and enjoyed by another under circumstances that would reasonably notify the recipient that the rendering party expected to be paid. In essence, the law implies a contract to pay the reasonable value of the services or materials furnished.

QUASI: Almost like; as if; nearly. This term is essentially used to signify that one subject or thing is almost analogous to another but that material differences between them do exist. For example, a quasi-criminal proceeding is one that is not strictly criminal but shares enough of the same characteristics to require some of the same safeguards (e.g., procedural due process must be followed in a parole hearing).

QUID PRO QUO: Something for something. In contract law, the consideration, something of value, passed between the parties to render the contract binding.

RES GESTAE: Things done; in evidence law, this principle justifies the admission of a statement that would otherwise be hearsay when it is made so closely to the event in question as to be said to be a part of it, or with such spontaneity as not to have the possibility of falsehood.

RES IPSA LOQUITUR: The thing speaks for itself. This doctrine gives rise to a rebuttable presumption of negligence when the instrumentality causing the injury was within the exclusive control of the defendant, and the injury was one that does not normally occur unless a person has been negligent.

RES JUDICATA: A matter adjudged. Doctrine which provides that once a court of competent jurisdiction has rendered a final judgment or decree on the merits, that judgment or decree is conclusive upon the parties to the case and prevents them from engaging in any other litigation on the points and issues determined therein.

RESPONDEAT SUPERIOR: Let the master reply. This doctrine holds the master liable for the wrongful acts of his servant (or the principal for his agent) in those cases in which the servant (or agent) was acting within the scope of his authority at the time of the injury.

STARE DECISIS: To stand by or adhere to that which has been decided. The common law doctrine of stare decisis attempts to give security and certainty to the law by following the policy that once a principle of law as applicable to a certain set of facts has been set forth in a decision, it forms a precedent which will subsequently be followed, even though a different decision might be made were it the first time the question had arisen. Of course, stare decisis is not an inviolable principle and is departed from in instances where there is good cause (e.g., considerations of public policy led the Supreme Court to disregard prior decisions sanctioning segregation).

SUPRA: Above. A word referring a reader to an earlier part of a book.

ULTRA VIRES: Beyond the power. This phrase is most commonly used to refer to actions taken by a corporation that are beyond the power or legal authority of the corporation.

Addendum of French Derivatives

IN PAIS: Not pursuant to legal proceedings.

CHATTEL: Tangible personal property.

CY PRES: Doctrine permitting courts to apply trust funds to purposes not expressed in the trust but necessary to carry out the settlor's intent.

PER AUTRE VIE: For another's life; during another's life. In property law, an estate may be granted that will terminate upon the death of someone other than the grantee.

PROFIT A PRENDRE: A license to remove minerals or other produce from land.

VOIR DIRE: Process of questioning jurors as to their predispositions about the case or parties to a proceeding in order to identify those jurors displaying bias or prejudice.

Casenote® Legal Briefs